"This book is a groundbreaking look into what true, sacred biblical sexuality is intended to be and the root causes and ideas that damage a couple's intimacy in marriage. Going straight to Scripture, the authors dig deep into ideologies that draw couples away from God-designed intimacy, and they seek to construct a framework for sexuality that is truly rooted in Scripture and God's beautiful design, elevating sexuality and marriage to the glory and sacredness it was intended to have. This is a must-read."

Rachael Denhollander, lawyer, victim advocate,
and author of *What Is a Girl Worth?*

"This book is so incredibly powerful! If you've ever read a Christian book on sex and marriage, you owe it to yourself to read this one. Armed with extensive survey data and equipped with compassion and common sense, the authors dismantle the devastating myths long promoted by Christian leaders that have caused untold damage to generations of Christian women. Equal parts distressing and liberating, this book is desperately needed in this moment."

Kristin Kobes Du Mez, author of *Jesus and John Wayne*

"I cannot think of a more important book (outside of the Bible) that you must read. This book is the authentic gut punch that the evangelical community needs. This exposes our historic dismal handling of sexuality and gives us a clear path forward to sexual maturity, wholeness, and health. I already want to read it again and will surely be telling my network to purchase this vital guide. Thank you for such a seminal work!"

Andrew J. Bauman, LMHC, cofounder and director of the
Christian Counseling Center for Sexual Health and Trauma

"*The Great Sex Rescue* is exactly the type of book on sex I would want my college students reading. This next generation has been personally burned by bad Christian sex advice. Both women and men will benefit from *The Great Sex Rescue*, but I think young adults may benefit most."

Dr. Heather Thompson Day, author of *Confessions of a Christian Wife* and professor of communications at Colorado Christian University

"This book should be required reading for all married Christians. Growing up in the evangelical Christian world taught me very little about what a healthy sexual dynamic should look like other than 'Don't do it until you're married. Then do it all the time!' It's time we deconstruct the destructive and harmful teachings that have gone unchallenged for so long and embrace a truly cross-centric view of sexuality, and for that I can think of no better resource than this book."

Travis Albritton, *The Practical Christian Podcast*

"With Sheila's years of experience and passionate heart for marriages and individuals struggling with sexual disconnection, her current research provides new insights that speak truthfully and directly to how the world of Christianity has not always provided the support or adequately addressed the hurts of those needing biblical love and direction. I applaud her and her team for their compassion, for their sound research, and for becoming a voice for women who are confused and hurting by what God never meant to be distorted—his design for beautiful and loving sexuality without shame or guilt."

Sheri Mueller, MA, LCPC, Growthtrac Ministries

THE GREAT SEX RESCUE

The Lies You've Been Taught and How to
Recover What God Intended

SHEILA WRAY GREGOIRE

REBECCA GREGOIRE LINDENBACH and JOANNA SAWATSKY

BakerBooks
a division of Baker Publishing Group
Grand Rapids, Michigan

© 2021 by Sheila Wray Gregoire, Rebecca Gregoire Lindenbach, and Joanna Sawatsky

Published by Baker Books
a division of Baker Publishing Group
PO Box 6287, Grand Rapids, MI 49516–6287
www.bakerbooks.com

Library of Congress Cataloging-in-Publication Data

Names: Gregoire, Sheila Wray, 1970– author. | Lindenbach, Rebecca Gregoire, 1995– author. | Sawatsky, Joanna,1990– author.

Title: The great sex rescue : the lies you've been taught and how to recover what God intended / Sheila Wray Gregoire with Rebecca Gregoire Lindenbach and Joanna Sawatsky.

Description: Grand Rapids, Michigan : Baker Books, a division of Baker Publishing Group, [2021] | Includes bibliographical references.

Identifiers: LCCN 2020038300 | ISBN 9781540900821 (paperback) | ISBN 9781540901460 (casebound)

Subjects: LCSH: Sex—Religious aspects—Christianity. | Sex—Biblical teaching. | Christian women—Sexual behavior.

Classification: LCC BT708 .G7148 2021 | DDC 241/.66—dc23

LC record available at https://lccn.loc.gov/2020038300

This publication is intended to provide helpful and informative material on the subjects addressed. It is not intended to replace the advice of trained health care professionals.

Some names and details have been changed or presented in composite form in order to protect the privacy of the individuals involved.

21 22 23 24 25 26 27   7 6 5 4 3 2 1

Contents

CHAPTER 1

What Happened to Sex?

Sex is a gift from God.

How often have we heard that? It sounds kind of like something your parents would say right after they've scarred you by telling you where babies come from.

Or it sounds like something you're told in premarital counseling, right before your red-faced counselor quickly turns the pages and says, "Now, let's talk about who wants to do the vacuuming."

It's something that your pastor says from the pulpit when he can't talk about sex too explicitly, but he really, really, really wants everyone to know how great it is. And you're trying hard not to look his wife in the face while he says it.

But for some of us who have been married for a while, the idea of sex as a gift seems more like that awful Christmas sweater your grandma knit for you in sixth grade that you had to wear for a week even though everybody knew it was lame.

Sure, it's a gift. But you really would have preferred an Xbox.

Then there are those of you who *know* it's a gift. You know sex is amazing. But it feels more like a gift that you got to open, only to be told to wrap it back up and put it on a shelf to keep it safe. It sits up there, still in sight but unused.

Your sex life is up on a shelf.

It's a gift you're not allowed to enjoy because your spouse doesn't see it as a gift. So it's out of reach, gathering dust, taunting you.

We, the authors of this book, want to tell you up front that *we get it.*

All of us—Sheila, Rebecca, and Joanna—work on Sheila's sex and marriage blog, *To Love, Honor, and Vacuum.* Rebecca (Sheila's daughter) likes to quip, "It's the weirdest job you can possibly do with your mom." When Joanna, an epidemiologist trained in statistics, moved to town, we roped her in too. None of the three of us expected to be talking about sex, orgasms, and erections professionally, but here we are.

We know that Christians, as a whole, do tend to have better sex and happier marriages than people who are not religious.[1] But here's the thing: just because something is better for the *group* does not mean you as an *individual* think it's anything to write home about (if you were the type to write home about your sex life). We get daily messages from husbands and wives who are desperate because it's just not working: he can't figure out how to make sex feel good for her, she's devastated by his hidden porn use, or they're both at the end of their rope as they fight for the forty-seventh time about libido differences. Many Christians simply aren't experiencing amazing, mind-blowing, earth-shattering, great sex.

We want to change that.

I (Sheila) am married to a pediatrician, and one thing the medical world emphasizes is the importance of evidence-based treatments. Before my husband, Keith, puts a child on a new regimen to manage asthma, he wants to know that there have been solid studies that show that this new regimen works.

We've got a lot of treatments for sex in the church. There are books, radio broadcasts, blogs, articles, and sermons galore giving advice to couples struggling with unsatisfying sex lives. But have we, as the church, taken the time to ask if any of our treatments even work?

We heard the same questions for years on end from blog readers, so we decided to investigate the sex advice offered in bestselling Christian sex and marriage books. And when we read them, alarm bells went off. We began to wonder, *What if our evangelical "treatments" for sex issues make things worse?*

We realized that giving healthy information is not enough if people are also consistently consuming bad advice from the wider Christian culture. But we didn't want to simply put forth a new set of opinions—we wanted data. We wanted an evidence-based treatment. So we surveyed over twenty thousand women in what we called "The Bare Marriage Project," asking about their sex lives, their marriages, their beliefs about sex and marriage, their upbringing, and more.[2] (Seriously, it was a looooong survey. Almost half an hour long. Over 130 questions, minimum. We are eternally grateful to the women who filled it out!) We wanted to get to the bottom of what makes sex great—but also what can make it bad. We wanted to ask the question that the Christian world has failed to ask for decades: Does our evangelical advice actually work?[3]

We uncovered some interesting answers we're excited to share with you. We want to rescue couples from teachings that have wrecked sex and put you back on the road to great sex—because that's what you should be having!

But wait—if this book is aimed at helping couples reclaim amazing, mind-blowing, toe-curling sex, then why did we survey only women?

Men certainly do matter (and we'd love to do a survey of men in the future), but we decided to start with women because of what we call the "orgasm gap." Studies have found that 95% of men orgasm every or almost every time they have sex (unless they suffer from erectile dysfunction or other sexual dysfunction disorders).[4]

Achieving orgasm is easy for the vast majority of men. In fact, a man's orgasm is such a given that if it doesn't happen, you should likely see a doctor about it.

In contrast, our survey found that only 48% of women orgasm every or almost every time they have sex. That's quite a gap! In general, women are the ones being left disappointed by sex because, frankly, it's not always that great for them. And that, in turn, leaves many men who want to rock their wives' worlds disappointed too. If we could figure out what's holding women back, we could likely make sex a whole lot better for everybody. That would be something to celebrate!

What's the Definition of Sex?

Before we get into this, though, we believe that the root of many of our sexual problems in marriage is actually a definitional one. We don't know what *sex* means.

If we were to ask you, "Did you have sex last night?" what would you think (besides that we are super creepy busybodies)? You'd probably think we meant, "Did the husband thrust his penis in his wife's vagina until he climaxed?" That's the main definition of sex—a husband penetrates his wife until he orgasms.

Let's do a thought experiment. Insert that definition of *sex* into the Bible verse about sex that we found to be the most quoted, and it's easy to see how sexual advice can go so far off-kilter.

> Do not deprive each other [of a husband penetrating his wife until he climaxes] except perhaps by mutual consent and for a time, so that you may devote yourselves to prayer. (1 Cor. 7:5)

If this is the way many of us internalize this message about sex, then many women can begin to feel that they have to invite their husbands, even *welcome* their husbands, to have very, very one-sided sex. If sex is only about a man moving around until he climaxes, then her experience and her pleasure are more of an afterthought—a bonus, for sure, but not necessary.

But that definition of sex also makes it into something that is only physical—*he reaches climax*. If we think that's what the Bible is talking about by one-flesh marriage and all the "do not deprive" talk we hear, then we may start to think that what God really cares about most is that husbands ejaculate frequently enough. Yet this has very little resemblance to the idea of intimacy that is implied in the Hebrew used in the Old Testament for *sex*, which we'll talk about in the next chapter.

Each of you were created for sex that is about so much more than just one-sided pleasure. Great sex is the fulfillment of a longing for intimacy, for connection, to be completely and utterly bare in every way before each other. Yes, baring ourselves physically is necessary for sex (though sometimes socks can help on those cold nights), but that's not the only kind of baring that real sex involves. It's also a baring of our souls, a deep hunger for connection, a longing to be completely consumed by the other—while also bringing intense pleasure to *both* of you.

In this book, then, we'd like to use correct terms for sex. When we mean a one-sided sexual encounter that's focused on his climax, we're going to say "intercourse." When we mean healthy, mutual sex, which encompasses so much more than simply his penis in her vagina, we're going to say "sex" or even "making love." Perhaps seeing the dichotomy will help us get that better picture of real intimacy in our minds.

Church, it's time for a change. We want to call Christians back to first principles about sex the way God intended. Here's what we propose, based on our survey results and biblical principles, that a healthy sex life should look like:

Sex should be *personal*: It is a chance to enter into each other's very being to truly become one; it is a knowing of each other that leads to deep intimacy.

Sex should be *pleasurable*: Sex was designed to feel good—really good—for both people.

Sex should be *pure*: Both partners can expect the other to take responsibility to keep themselves free of sexual sin.

Sex should be *prioritized*: Both partners in the relationship desire sex, even if at different levels, and both partners understand that sex is a vital part of a healthy marriage.

Sex should be *pressure-free*: Sex is a gift freely given; it's not about getting what you want through manipulation, coercion, or threat.

Sex should *put the other first*: Sex is about considering your spouse's wants and needs before you consider your own.

Sex should be *passionate*: Sex was designed to allow us to enter into a state of joyful abandon, to completely surrender ourselves to the other in an ecstasy of trust and love.

If we agree with those principles, are the teachings and messages we hear supporting them? Or are they creating an image of sex that is diametrically opposed to the sacrificial, mutually pleasurable, all-encompassing passion that God created sex to be? That's what we're going to explore together.

The Four Kinds of Research You'll Find in This Book

Our research went beyond the twenty-thousand-woman survey. To develop and craft our survey, we reviewed current academic research investigating evangelicalism and sexuality, and you'll see many of those studies cited. We also conducted focus groups and interviews to further understand our survey results and to show the people behind the statistics.

Finally, we read and reviewed bestselling Christian sex and marriage books, along with other foundational niche books that influence how women in the church see sex.[5] Books both reflect and influence what is believed in their culture. These books

What if I like one of the books or authors you discuss?

Many of the evangelical books we'll mention in *The Great Sex Rescue* contained messages that we found caused harm. But what if you feel like you benefited from any of the books found to be harmful?

That's great! These books do contain helpful information—that's why they are bestsellers! If they helped you, we're happy for you. But among the helpful bits, these books also contain teachings that we have statistically shown harm marriages and lead to worse sex for women, with some books posing higher risk than others. Our aim is to make it no longer acceptable for our Christian resources to only hurt *some* people. We should—and can—write books that help without also causing harm. Many books have succeeded in this, and we will point you to them in the appendix of this book.

in particular have largely shaped how evangelical culture has talked about sex for the last few decades. We're going to quote liberally from them. Please know, though, that we're critiquing the teachings, not the authors. We believe these authors meant well at the time they wrote the books, and many of these books were improvements on what was already out there.

However, we have also found in our data that many of these books may have inadvertently caused some of the problems they were trying so hard to fix. It's important as a culture that we confront the damage we have done—even if by accident—so we can walk forward toward the abundant life Jesus wants for us.

The beliefs that we will be addressing throughout this book, that impacted women's marital and sexual satisfaction, can be seen in figure 1.1.* You'll be seeing references to these beliefs, and how they affected both sexual and marital satisfaction, throughout this book.

---

* For more information on the figures and tables including exact wording of questions asked, see https://greatsexrescue.com/results.

Figure 1.1

Prevalence of Christian Teachings on Marriage and Sex

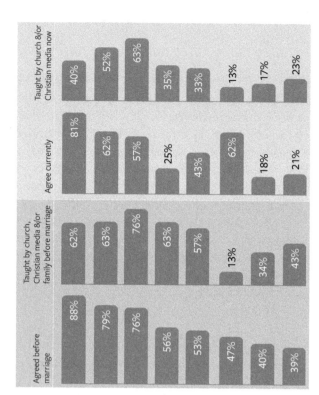

	Agreed before marriage	Taught by church, Christian media &/or family before marriage	Agree currently	Taught by church &/or Christian media now
Boys will want to push girls' sexual boundaries	88%	62%	81%	40%
All men struggle with lust, it is every man's battle	79%	63%	62%	52%
If you have sex before you are married, that means you have less of yourself to give to your future spouse because a part of you will always belong to someone else	76%	76%	57%	63%
The only biblical reason for divorce is an affair	56%	63%	25%	35%
It is a man's God-given role to provide for his family and a woman's God-given role to stay home raising her children	53%	57%	43%	33%
In a family with children, a working mom and a stay-at-home dad is as good as a stay-at-home mom and a working dad	47%	13%	62%	13%
Women should have frequent sex with their husbands to keep them from watching porn	40%	34%	18%	17%
A wife is obligated to give her husband sex when he wants it	39%	43%	21%	23%

How to Use *The Great Sex Rescue*

Maybe you've been married for ten years and you still don't know what an orgasm feels like. You know there's more—but how do you get there?

Maybe you're tired of feeling rejected and unloved by your wife. Even your most romantic gestures are followed by what you know is just "duty sex." You know you could have a fun and vibrant marriage—you just need to break through that wall.

Maybe you're angry, having found porn on your husband's phone again. You're sick and tired of feeling second place, and at this point, sex just turns you off. You know sex is supposed to be beautiful, and that's what you've always longed for. But how do you redeem something that has been so tainted?

Whether you're confused, disappointed, frustrated, or hurt, we want to help you discover what's holding back your sex life. We're so excited to share the information we have learned, but knowledge can only take you so far. That's why throughout the book you'll see check-ins, applications, and reframing exercises to help bring the message home.

Ideally, we would love it if couples read this book together. When you come to check-ins, think about the questions yourself and then share with each other. And have fun with our "Explore Together" exercises at the end of each chapter! If you're reading this alone, journal and pray through the questions and talk to your spouse about what the questions bring up. If your spouse isn't willing to read with you, you can still have these important conversations to share your experience and understand theirs better.

We also hope ministry leaders will pick up this book to learn how to talk about sex in a healthy way. At the end of each chapter, we'll have a "Rescuing and Reframing" section, which will present a better way to talk about these sensitive issues without inadvertently causing harm.

A Note for Sexual Abuse Survivors

Sexual abuse of any kind can have profound effects on your experience of sex in your marriage. We wrote this book hoping it will be a helpful resource to act as a companion to trauma treatments with a licensed counselor or psychologist, and it is not intended to replace evidence-based treatments.

As well, we know that more men are victims of sexual abuse than most people assume. So please, whether you are a man or a woman, if you have experienced any form of sexual abuse, contact a licensed mental health professional, preferably one who has experience or additional training in trauma and abuse issues.

Let's allow the harmful teachings about sex to fall away. Let's replace teachings that try to bribe, coerce, or manipulate people with ones focused on freedom, passion, and, most importantly, love. That's how we're going to rescue great sex.

So let's throw off the ropes, cut ourselves free from the moorings, and see where we end up.

Sex should be *personal*: It is a chance to enter into each other's very being to truly become one; it is a knowing of each other that leads to deep intimacy.

CHAPTER 2

Don't Sleep with Someone You Don't Know

And Adam knew Eve his wife; and she conceived, and bare Cain.

Genesis 4:1 KJV

One Sunday, when I (Sheila) was in junior high, I was sitting in the wooden pews at church flanked by my preteen friends. That day, the pastor opened his Bible to Genesis 4:1 and read from the King James Version:

> And Adam knew Eve his wife; and she conceived, and bare Cain, and said, I have gotten a man from the LORD.

We giggled so much that the pews started shaking, and my mom gave me "the look." But that was hilarious—"Adam knew his wife"! It was like God was embarrassed to use the real word or something.

As I've been blogging and writing about sex for over fifteen years now, I've learned something about that verse. It contains the same word David uses in the Psalms when he says,

> Search me, God, and know my heart;
>   test me and know my anxious thoughts. (Ps. 139:23)

Perhaps it's not that God was embarrassed about the word but instead that he wanted to point us to a greater truth. God wanted us to know that sex is not only a physical act; it's a deeply intimate one as well. Think of how much imagery there is in Scripture about God's relationship with us in terms of marriage. Heaven is described as a wedding banquet (Matt. 22:2); Christ is the bridegroom, and the church is the bride (Eph. 5:25–33). God yearns to know us deeply, and he talks about it in marriage terms because that is the closest approximation we have to the desire God has for us. He created us to long for each other as he longs for us.

That's why sex was created not only to be physically intimate but to be an emotional and spiritual "knowing" as well. When all three types of intimacy are present—spiritual, emotional, and physical—each works in tandem with the others so that they feed one another. The more you laugh and feel close, the more you desire each other and make love. The more you make love, the more connected you feel, which makes your commitment stronger.

And that's what happens! Our stats show that women are more likely to reach orgasm when the rest of their relationship is stronger. Women in our survey whose marriages scored in the top 20% for marital satisfaction were *four times*[1] more likely to orgasm reliably than women in the bottom 20% of marriages.[2]

But what if we look specifically at intimacy during sex? When we asked women, "How satisfied are you with the amount of closeness you share with your husband during sex?" women who said they were satisfied were *five times* more likely to reliably orgasm during sex.[3] That's likely also because they're *twelve times* more likely to report that their husbands make their sexual pleasure a priority and *fourteen times* more likely to say they do enough foreplay.[4] A lack of closeness during sex, then, doesn't just make sex less *meaningful*; it also makes it less *fun*.

But as important as it is to feel close during sex, you cannot simply manufacture intimacy when you're unsatisfied in your marriage. And that's why sex is not just physical; it's about your whole relationship.

A few years ago, I was invited by a large news and lifestyle website to debate about sexual ethics. I was making the point that any two bodies can have intercourse, but when we reduce sex to being merely physical, we ruin intimacy.

Another guest, who had starred in some porn films and wrote a porn blog (how do I get myself into these things?), talked about how intimate she found sex. But all she could say was, "When I have sex with a man, even if it's a man I just met, the intimacy is amazing!" Can you truly be intimate with someone when you don't even know their name?

It's not just porn stars who confuse intimacy with sex either. When I'm on Christian radio talking about *The Good Girl's Guide to Great Sex*, it's generally assumed that I won't say the word *sex* in case children are listening. We have to say *intimacy* instead. But perhaps that's part of the problem—we're treating intimacy and intercourse as if they're always synonyms. But are they?

Billions of people on this planet have had intercourse. I don't know how many have actually made love.

Does Sex Make You Feel "Known"?

For sex to feel intimate, it needs to be about saying, "I want you," not just "I want sex." It needs to be about saying, "I see you. I choose you. I want to experience something with you, and only you. I want to know you better."

You is the key word. *You* are the focus. Sex is not just about *me*; it's about *me* knowing *you* and building *us*.

But is this drive for intimacy the message that couples are getting from our evangelical culture? When we read through the bestselling Christian marriage books, this potential for sex to be about "knowing" is mysteriously absent. What we did find was that many of these books portray sex as primarily a man's need—and a physical one, at that. For instance, Focus on the Family's book *Love & Respect*, by Emerson Eggerichs, clearly states that "a husband has a need for physical release through sexual intimacy," without ever mentioning that sex should be about intimacy, not just ejaculation.[5]

Additionally, there is an absurd anecdote in Willard F. Harley Jr.'s book *His Needs, Her Needs* in which a husband's engaging in an affair actually seemed to *help* his marriage. Because he was getting his sexual needs met with Noreen, his lover, he found it easier to be kind to his wife, Mary, a full-time student who was also busy with small children. When Mary had a break from her studies and wanted to make love, he would do so eagerly, but he was able to not bug her at other times because of Noreen helping him with sexual release. Life is great—until Mary's friend Jane finds out about the affair and tells Mary.[6] While the author likely intended to show the importance of sex for men's emotional well-being, this story seems like an advertisement for *Sister Wives*.

What happens when couples are repeatedly told that sex is about men's physical release and intimacy isn't even mentioned? We are left with only the picture of sex that my porn-star fellow guest on that sexual ethics debate would have understood.

> I have been having sex with my husband for twenty years, but I do not recall that we have ever made love. He thinks groping my chest and [referring to me with pornographic terms] is showing love.

In response to her, another woman said this:

> [My husband has sex the way he has] seen modeled to him through porn. It's animalistic, it's a release during which he says stuff like,

23

"You're so hot." He feels loved during that experience because he's experiencing the highs of arousal and orgasm. . . . But making love takes vulnerability, and it's scary to be vulnerable with another person, especially if you have a rough childhood like my husband. So I get it. But it just hurts and is frustrating.

Sex without connection is empty. A survey respondent, whose husband of thirty-five years had used porn extensively and raped her repeatedly, shared with us this journal entry, written in therapy after her divorce:

> I'm angry realizing how he used me sexually. I read that some men are all about making sure the woman reaches orgasm. He sure was. But he used "things" to stimulate me even though I begged him not to.* He'd do this and manual or oral so I'd reach a peak before he'd even enter me "cause it's a lot tighter for me." It was all about him. He felt like a hero because "my wife always orgasms." But I often felt used. Now I understand I was.

Physically having intercourse, and even physically reaching orgasm, are not necessarily real "knowing." God means for us to have more than just that, and we do ourselves—and sex—a disservice when we boil it down to only the physical.

> CHECK-IN: What is the balance between the emotional and physical sides of sex in your marriage? Do you feel it is unbalanced? Do you want something to change?

Many women in our focus groups also reported that the emotional connection during sex was even more important to them than the physical connection. Even when they couldn't reach

---

* Using sexual toys on a person who has specifically requested that they not be used is a form of sexual assault. If you are being sexually assaulted, please call a sexual abuse hotline.

orgasm, they were still grateful for the gift that sex was, since it bonded them in a profound way to their spouse.

I (Joanna) have had a hectic few years. I've had enough bizarre health issues that my family calls me the "special snowflake." After eighteen months of infertility, I finally became pregnant with my first baby. But while I was in my first trimester, my mom noticed a lump in my neck. Yup, it was cancer. While we were still reeling, my husband started a new job as a lawyer, we moved across the country away from family, I defended my master's thesis, and three days later I became a mom.

I underwent surgery and was declared cancer-free, and that summer things seemed more settled, and I was happy to be expecting our second baby. But in the small hours of a Thursday morning, I found myself bleeding out during a life-threatening miscarriage, thinking about how badly I did *not* want to die while lying on a turquoise beach towel in my foyer. We called an ambulance, and thankfully it arrived in time and I was stabilized by a team of wonderful doctors.

For a few months afterward, when we did make love, I couldn't climax or even get very aroused during sex. It wasn't just the weight of the miscarriage or dealing with the effects of a near-death experience; it was the previous years of heartache that rolled over me. But during that time of healing, even though my sexual pleasure was elusive, we continued being sexually active, as we wanted to conceive and to connect emotionally. Looking back on that time, I remember the tenderness that my husband showed me throughout my grieving process. And even though the primary motivation we both had for sex was to have another baby, we also found it to be uniquely healing.

> CHECK-IN: Have there been times when sex has been meaningful and intimate even though you didn't orgasm? What made it special?

You Can't Be Intimate If You Don't Feel Valued

In healthy marriages, sex can help a couple feel closer. It is a tangible expression of the love, commitment, and tenderness that is already there. One woman in our focus groups, who has been married for twenty-eight years, explained it this way:

> Sometimes in our marriage I feel like there's some distance because he's stressed out, or I'm feeling unloved because there's not time for me, and I just take a step back and say, "You know what? Let's just have sex," and then BAM! It's like an intimacy switch is flipped on. And when I make that decision, when I take that step, I reap the benefits of feeling loved because I can just enjoy how he wants to love me. It's a beautiful give and take.

But when there isn't that foundation of feeling valued and known, we cannot expect sex on its own to create it. Indeed, sex divorced from intimacy can widen the chasm between two people. I (Sheila) think that is the root of questions like this that come in to my blog:

> We have been married just about a decade and have four kids. Yes, he's a quiet guy, but I feel like we never have a conversation, like I usually feel like I'm talking to a wall. I don't know how many times I have cried and pleaded to just talk to me and told him I am just so lonely. He just doesn't care.
>
> He's nice and attentive when he wants to have sex, and then the next day he's right back to being uncaring and rude. How can I have sex when there is zero emotional connection? I'm just so tired of doing everything by myself, taking care of everyone and everything. I've tried every love language on him. I text him that I'm proud of him and all sorts of affirmations—no text back. I've packed his lunches—no thank-you, and sometimes he even forgets them in the fridge. I've made his favorite meals and picked him little things up at the grocery store. I've used physical touch. And, of course, we've had sex. I just can't win.

In *The Act of Marriage*, the go-to sex book for Generation X couples, which sold over 2.5 million copies, Tim LaHaye tells the story of a couple named Bill and Susie. Bill had always treated Susie like a sex object, ignoring her boundaries when they were dating and doing things even when she asked him not to. Susie felt disrespected and invisible. Yet the answer? Realize that Bill needed sex. "Susie had three problems: she did not like sexual relations, she did not understand Bill's needs, and she was more interested in herself than in her husband. When she confessed her sin of selfishness and learned what loving really meant to him, it changed their bedroom life."[7]

Susie had three problems, but apparently Bill had none. The book never suggests that Bill treat Susie as a person or apologize for his treatment of her or understand *her* needs. Susie just needs to give him more nookie.

In an even worse example, LaHaye tells the story of a woman who had pulled away from sex with her stern disciplinarian husband. LaHaye reports that the wife admitted, "His awful beatings of our children made me ill."[8] Their nineteen-year-old son had cut off contact and went to live in a commune to get away from his father. But the solution LaHaye suggested? That the wife repent and give herself sexually to her physically abusive husband who had stolen her relationship with her children from her.

Again and again, in these books and others, when women have legitimate emotional, and even physical, safety needs in their marriages that aren't being met, they are told that having sex will fix things.

In healthy marriages, sometimes the solution really is that you both need to have some sex. But sex cannot fix selfishness or laziness. It cannot fix an abusive relationship. It cannot cure an affair or porn use or lust. It is dangerous to tell a reader to have sex with an abusive spouse. If you are in an abusive relationship, where you feel as if you have to walk on eggshells to avoid setting off your spouse, and you feel unsafe, please call an abuse hotline.[†] Having sex cannot fix serious issues in your relationship.

It is not only women who suffer from this message that sex alone can bring you close. What many of these books fail to mention is that husbands need emotional connection too. Physical release without real intimacy feels empty and unsatisfying. One man told us,

> The worst thing is to have sex with my wife when it's obvious she's not that interested. As a man, to be sexually satisfied, I want my wife to long for my touch and the pleasure I give her. Having sex just to ejaculate is miserable. I know most women think sex is purely physical for a man, but it's not. I would argue it's the most emotional thing a man can experience. Nothing says I love you, need you, accept you, and want you like having great sex with my wife where we are both equally pleasured. One-sided sex, where all I do is ejaculate, feels like deep rejection.

This man does not just need physical release; he has a need for more. Physical release alone is not enough for him to feel physically satisfied. It's not about orgasm as much as it is about connection. Whether intentionally or not, by describing sexual need in terms of physical release instead of intimacy, many women "let" men have intercourse and feel proud of themselves for doing their wifely duty, while their lonely husbands are left desperate for connection. After all, *Love & Respect* doesn't even mention that intimacy is a benefit of sex for men; only physical release and feelings of respect. That kind of talk makes men feel empty and women feel used. Many women, when they hear advice like these books are giving, hear loudly and clearly, *I don't matter.*

[†] To find an abuse hotline near you, search "domestic violence hotline," followed by your country, city, and province or state.

Sex can't be intimate if you feel like you don't matter. In fact, that's not even sex as we've defined it. That's only intercourse, and that's a pale imitation of what God intended. Sex, after all, is so highly personal. You're naked in a way that you wouldn't be with anyone else; you show a side of yourself to each other that you would never show to anyone else; you experience passion in a way in which you are most yourself, in which you let go of control and surrender to the moment. Because of that surrender and vulnerability, sex becomes the culmination of you as a couple, not just you as bodies. It is physical, yes, but it's so much more than that.

This intense vulnerability may be what holds the key to why emotional closeness makes such a difference to women's sexual satisfaction: emotional closeness brings trust. When you feel close to your spouse and can trust them, it's easier to speak up: "Hey, you know what I'd like to try?" or "I don't actually like that, can we try something else?" That's what's likely behind our finding that women who experience closeness during sex are far more likely to have husbands who excel at foreplay. Emotional connection simply cannot be divorced from sexual connection. They are meant to feed each other.

Sex as "Knowing" Requires True Mutuality

When you start dating someone, you date them because you like them. You want to be around them. You value what they have to say. You fall in love.

But as soon as you get married, the dynamic often shifts. It's no longer about this person, with their particular quirks and strengths and weaknesses and personality; it becomes about what you're "supposed" to do. Dating is about what you want to do, what's natural, who fits you like a puzzle piece. When you're married, it's about deciding what puzzle piece you're supposed to look like.

Here's an interesting finding from our research: Women who do not believe traditional gender roles are moral imperatives feel more heard and seen in their marriages. In fact, women who act out the typical breadwinner-homemaker dynamic also feel more seen if they see it as a choice and not a God-given role.[9]

Does this mean it's wrong to have a breadwinner and a stay-at-home spouse? Nope. All three of us writing this book specifically chose careers that would allow us to be home with our kids. But when we unquestioningly buy into traditional gender roles, we create a strange dynamic in marriage in which we view each other as categories rather than as people. We are all made with unique strengths, giftings, and callings, and these do not always fit with traditional gender roles. When a couple makes decisions based on who God created them to be versus who gender roles say they *should* be, it allows them to live in God's plan for their lives while feeling known and valued. Trying to live up to gender roles can mean that we're not fully ourselves; we're wearing a mask, and sometimes that mask doesn't fit.

Intimate sex requires that you feel as if your spouse values you not just for what you can give them but for *who you are.* Sex can't be about saying, "I want you," if *who you are* is being covered up by an expectation of who you should be. In our focus groups, women consistently reported that granting themselves and their husbands permission to live outside of traditional gender roles revitalized their marriages—and their sex lives. Michelle explained, "Letting go of gender roles has improved our marriage in so many ways—he doesn't feel he has to be this leader anymore that he was never meant to be, and he is so much happier. . . . We always loved each other, but we like each other now because we're free to be who we are as individuals. And things just keep getting better."

Kay echoed, "I tried so hard to be the things that I was supposed to be as a good Christian woman, and I just wasn't good at it. I'm a big, opinionated personality, and my husband is more laid back. I was always trying to get him to take the lead. When we learned about personality types and allowed ourselves the freedom to be who we are, our marriage clicked."

When couples allow each other to flourish as God made them, they feel emotionally closer, and that leads to better sex. As we'll see throughout this book, many gender stereotypes can do more harm than good, whether they are about who should make the decisions or libido differences or lust or porn use. Women feel far freer sexually, and have far better marriages, when they feel they matter and are accepted just as they are.

> CHECK-IN: How do you decide who does what in your marriage? Do you default to gender roles reflexively, or have you thought through how to use your God-given strengths?

But there's one other gender stereotype that had an even bigger effect on marriages and sexual satisfaction: gender-based hierarchies. Most Christian books we reviewed promoted a hierarchical view of marriage, in which the husband decides and the wife follows, not only as the template for a healthy marriage but also as a requirement for a satisfying sex life.[10]

- "The submissive role of the wife implies that whether the husband acts like it or not, he is responsible for the important decisions in the home. . . . A responsive and receptive wife willingly demonstrates that she surrenders her freedom for his love, adoration, protection, and provision."—*Intended for Pleasure*[11]
- "A man may have many bosses outside the home, but inside the home, he has the opportunity to kindly provide authority and to receive his rightful respect."—*Sheet Music*[12]

- "God designed man to be the aggressor, provider, and leader of his family. Somehow that is tied to his sex drive. The woman who resents her husband's sex drive while enjoying his aggressive leadership had better face the fact that she cannot have one without the other."—*The Act of Marriage*[13]

Some books take this even further. *Love & Respect*, for instance, claims that "to set up a marriage with two equals at the head is to set it up for failure. That is one of the big reasons that people are divorcing right and left today."[14] A common thread among all these books is that marriages without a tiebreaker are doomed to fail because relationships need someone to be in charge.

And 62.2% of our survey respondents were on board with these books—they agreed that a Christian wife submitting to her husband's leadership is one of the best ways she can love him. Additionally, 39.4% of our respondents believed that the husband should have decision-making power in the marriage. However, despite so many believing this, we found that only 17.3% of couples actually act out men having the final say. In contrast, 78.9% of marriages function without a tiebreaker. (The remaining respondents were in marriages in which the wife made the final decisions.) In these marriages, couples either make decisions together or forgo making a decision if they don't agree. Many couples may say they believe the husband has the final say, but their actions speak more to mutuality.

What happens to couples when one spouse makes the decisions, though, even if they talk their decisions over with their spouse first and seek their input? They are 7.4 times *more* likely to be divorced than couples who share decision-making power.[15] We're not the only ones who have found this, either. Our figures mirror closely what The Gottman Institute also found about decision-making:

"Statistically speaking, when a man is not willing to share power with his partner there is an 81 percent chance that his marriage will self-destruct."[16]

The key is sharing power—and we have to be careful about this, because imbalanced power can *seem* shared if the husband is a kind man. In *Love & Respect*, Eggerichs notes that a good husband will take into account his wife's opinions and even decide to go with her preference. This all sounds very idyllic—a good husband's sacrificial leading should result in such a great marriage that his wife forgets her opinions don't have as much weight.

However, feeling heard and feeling like your opinions matter are both key to marital satisfaction. In marriages with collaborative decision-making, women are almost three times more likely to feel heard during arguments.[17] But when women don't feel heard, and instead feel as if their opinions are not as important as their husbands', their marriages are twenty-six times more likely to end in divorce.[18] *Twenty-six times.* That may be why we found that the risk of divorce skyrockets in marriages in which the husband is the one who ultimately makes the decisions, even if he consults his wife on them. When we set up marriages where a husband has decision-making power, we create marriages in which his opinions, by definition, matter more than hers. And when women feel their opinions are not given the same weight as their husbands', sex suffers and marriages crumble.

> CHECK-IN: How do you tend to make decisions in your marriage? Are you both happy with that arrangement? Do you both feel heard?

But here's some good news: treating each other as equals doesn't just give you a better marriage—it gives you better sex! When couples share power (make decisions together), wives are four times (4.36) more likely to rate themselves among the happiest 20% of marriages than among the least happy 20%[19] and are 67% more likely to frequently orgasm during sex.[20]

CHECK-IN: Do you feel as if you value your spouse's opinions as much as your own? Do you feel as if your spouse values your opinions?

Figure 2.1

Women Who Feel Their Voice Matters in Marriage Report Better Sex

How believing "In our marriage, my opinions are just as important as my husband's" affects the likelihood of the following sexual satisfaction outcomes (times more or less likely):

I am very satisfied with the amount of closeness I share with my husband during sex	9.20
My husband makes my sexual pleasure a priority when we have sex	6.74
My husband spends enough attention on foreplay that I feel excited and aroused when we begin intercourse	4.72
I am comfortable talking to my husband about what feels good sexually and what I need sexually	4.31
I am frequently aroused during sexual activity	3.24
I am confident about my ability to become sexually aroused	2.43
I frequently orgasm during sexual activity with my husband	2.26
I have experienced vaginismus	-1.38
When it comes to sex, I could take it or leave it	-1.90
I engage in sex with my husband only because I feel I have to	-3.61

Is Deeply Intimate and Passionate Sex Possible?

One of my favorite and most memorable blog commenters was an older gentleman I only ever knew as "P." He would encourage others in their marriage and tell us that his marriage was his greatest source of happiness. He'd write things like, "We don't 'do' Valentine's Day because we are each other's Valentine EVERY day!" or "I can assure you that marriage gets better and better as time goes by. We are more in love than ever. An extra bonus is that lovemaking gets more exciting too!"

One day he told us, "Every night when we go to bed we cuddle before we go to sleep. Often we wear nothing in bed. The cuddle does not lead to lovemaking but it is so friendly and relaxing and something we can do with no one else in the world. It is wonderful and I feel so blessed to have my wonderful wife in my arms. We break off and pray for our family and our marriage, then go to sleep." A few minutes later he chimed back in: "Oh, by the way, we usually make love in the mornings!"

He told us how they tended to only use one position now because for health reasons it was easier, but sex meant so much to them, even if he had to take a little blue pill first! They just loved feeling close to each other.

The last comment we ever received from P was this one:

We have been married over 40 years. My wife has chronic pain and eye problems, I have a new problem which causes me to have "good" and "bad" days. We cannot engage in sex. Despite all these problems it is wonderful to know that we love each other so much that we are simply "there" for each other as and when needed. Some days she looks after me, some days I look after her. We thank God daily for our marriage. We are both so blessed.

A few months later I received an email from P's wife. P had passed away from cancer. But he loved her to the very end and had dropped in to encourage all of us younger folks to have that same gratitude for our spouses.

Sex is not about only the physical—sex is about the emotional and spiritual too. When we understand the depth of the passionate love we have for one another, bolstered by years of trust and shared experience, as P explained, it transcends. It becomes something different—it switches from intercourse and turns into making love. That's what so many Christian couples have experienced, despite some of the teaching they've received. And we'd like to invite you on our journey as we deconstruct harmful ideas and find this mutual, passionate knowing that God meant for us to share.

EXPLORE TOGETHER:
How to Feel Emotionally Close during Sex

Make love, don't just have intercourse!

1. Start with Emotional Connection
   Choose one (or more) of the following before you start anything sexual:
   - Share your "high" and "low" of the day. When did you feel most "in the groove"? When did you feel most discouraged and defeated?
   - Pray for help and strength for your spouse's concerns about the coming day.
   - Speak a blessing over your spouse: Affirm their giftings and character, and then pray that God will breathe into your spouse and grow them in these unique areas.
2. Move on to Affection
   - Massage each other's shoulders, neck, and temples (or any other part of the body!).

- Kiss and touch each other for a few minutes before moving on to any erogenous zones.
3. Keep It Personal
   - Say your spouse's name, tell your spouse you love them, and look in your spouse's eyes—even if it means you keep the lights on!
   - Pay attention to what your spouse is feeling, and try to increase their pleasure.
   - If one of you reaches climax before the other, help the other reach climax too (unless this has been difficult and stressful for you—in which case, wait until the next exercise).
4. Rest in the Afterglow
   - After cleaning up, lie naked in each other's arms for a few minutes. Kiss some more before drifting off to sleep.

RESCUING AND REFRAMING

- Instead of saying, "A husband has a need for physical release through sexual intimacy," say, "God made sex to be intimate, physically and emotionally, for both partners. Both of you have a need for intimacy through sex, even if you feel it differently."
- Instead of saying, "He can't feel close to you unless you have sex with him," say, "Sex can help a couple feel closer, but it cannot sustain intimacy on its own."
- Instead of saying, "You have predetermined roles in your marriage because of your gender," say, "God created you and your spouse to reflect his image in a unique way. Follow God's unique calling for your life individually and as a couple."

Sex should be *pleasurable*:
Sex was designed to
feel good–really good!–
for both people.

CHAPTER 3

Bridging the Orgasm Gap

Daughters of Jerusalem, I charge you—
if you find my beloved,
what will you tell him?
Tell him I am faint with love.

Song of Songs 5:8

Which message have you heard more often in church, studies, or Christian books?

- Do not deprive your husband.
- Women's sexual pleasure matters.

I ran that simple poll on Twitter and Facebook. The results? 95% versus 5%. More than 1,500 respondents over both platforms overwhelmingly confirmed our suspicion—the message about sex in the evangelical church is focused on a husband's fulfillment, while ignoring a wife's.

That distorted message came up again and again in our surveys and focus groups too. Kay told us her marriage started out great in the bedroom. But after her third child, while battling

39

postpartum depression and the physical ramifications of pushing out three kids, sex just stopped feeling pleasurable. Over the next few years, Kay made sure she and her husband still had sex on schedule because, as she said, "I knew he needed it." It wasn't until she realized she needed it, too, that things started to improve.

For Natalie, orgasm has been an elusive goal. For six years of marriage, she dutifully ensured her husband's satisfaction. But two years ago she woke up and said to herself, *I'm sick of this; this is stupid. We need to figure out how this can be for me too.*

God Designed Sex to Be Pleasurable for Both People

Why did Kay and Natalie, and so many evangelical women like them, assume that sex is mostly for their husbands? After all, in the very creation of our bodies, God showed that both genders are made for sexual pleasure. Certainly the man's orgasm is needed for procreation (although we think his climax is meant for much more than that), but God didn't leave women out! The clitoris, that small knob of flesh at the top of the labia minora (the inner lips), and between the labia majora (the outer folds of female genitalia), was created with as many nerve endings as the penis. Unlike the penis, though, it only has one function: pleasure.

The clitoris is also designed with internal "roots" that travel up the front wall of the vagina, which can provide additional pleasure when a particular area is stimulated. (This is commonly called the "G-spot," after Ernst Gräfenberg, who first wrote about it. We're pretty sure women discovered it first; he was just the one to name it.)

We also know that women, unlike men, are capable of multiple orgasms at a time. While men have a refractory period after orgasm, when they are not physically capable of growing erect or reaching orgasm, women's refractory period is quite different. Direct stimulation may be too intense following orgasm, but many women are able to "ride the wave" of orgasm and turn it into several in a row. And many women find that sex after orgasm is still very pleasurable and helps them reach orgasm all over again.

So God made women to feel good during sex—and, on the whole, women do.

In our survey, 70.0% of currently married women report being frequently aroused during sexual encounters with their husbands. Most married women are regularly reaching orgasm (48.7% reach orgasm all the time or almost all the time, and an additional 18.7% reach orgasm slightly more than half of the time). We still have lots of room for improvement, though, because 12.0% of women in our survey rarely or never reach orgasm, and 11.0% reach orgasm less than half of the time. And that's what we'd like to help fix, starting with this chapter but also throughout the rest of the book.

Figure 3.1

Sex Frequency among Married Christian Women

Note: In first marriages only.

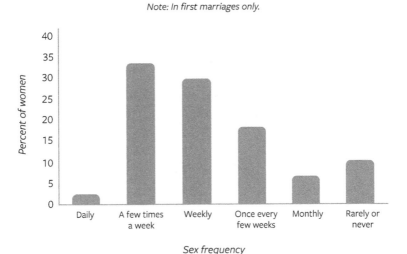

Sex frequency

CHECK-IN: Where would you put yourself on figure 3.2 below? Where would your spouse be? If you don't go into sex expecting to orgasm, is this a temporary issue or a longer-term issue?

What Message Have We Been Given about Women's Pleasure?

Christian books written specifically about sex tend to do an excellent job at emphasizing women's orgasm and telling men that it's their responsibility to ensure their wives feel pleasure.[1] They all echo *Intended for Pleasure*'s message, "Every physical union should be an exciting contest to see which partner can out-please the other."[2]

Figure 3.2

Orgasm Rates among Married Christian Women

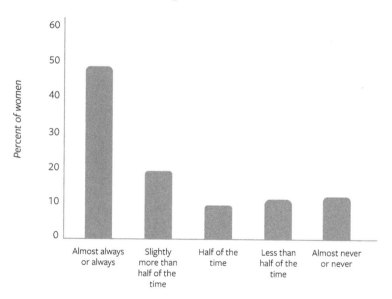

Orgasm frequency

42

So how do women, like Kay and Natalie, get married not knowing sex is for them too? Well, when it comes to evangelical online resources and books dedicated to marriage in general rather than solely focused on sex, we see something quite different. Here are just a few examples (of many):

- After talking about how sex for women is really about affection (rather than her need for pleasure), *The Power of a Praying Wife* says, "But for a husband, sex is pure need. His eyes, ears, brain and emotions get clouded if he doesn't have that release."[3]
- *His Needs, Her Needs* talks about men's and women's sexual experiences this way: "He trusts her to be sexually available to him whenever he needs to make love and to meet all his sexual needs, just as she trusts him to meet her emotional needs."[4]
- *Love & Respect* claims, "If your husband is typical, he has a need you don't have."[5]

When evangelical culture frames sexual fulfillment again and again as something he needs and she might get as a bonus, what message are couples going to internalize? *Women won't expect to enjoy sex, and men won't think anything's particularly wrong if she doesn't.*

One commenter told us,

I'm completely perplexed about why my husband isn't interested in figuring out how to make sex good for me. I asked him to help me figure out how I like to be touched, but he said he was too tired. I was really hopeful that we could talk through more and make sex more than a two-minute drill. When we talk about sex, he seems uncomfortable and reminded me that he's a farm boy and understands how sex works because he has raised hogs. But I'm NOT a hog!

Charlotte from one of our focus groups told us something similar. When she started wondering if sex could feel good for her, too, she began to read some sex books about different techniques to try. When she talked to her husband about it, though, he shut down. He already knew how to have sex, he said. She just needed to catch up.

> CHECK-IN: Think back to the messages you heard about sex in your teen and young adult years. Was sex portrayed as something that was for both of you, or was it mostly talked about as a man's need? When did you learn that female orgasms existed?

Men know that intercourse feels good; what's wrong with women that it doesn't feel good for them? Too often, Christian resources reinforce the idea that men know how to have sex and women don't. Women's lack of sexual pleasure then becomes their own fault. Despite explaining that women need clitoral stimulation, *The Act of Marriage*, the bestselling marriage book read by Generation X, also said this: "Men have a higher rate of orgasm largely because they are more active in lovemaking."[6] Actually, men have a higher rate of orgasm primarily because they get more direct stimulation during intercourse. It shouldn't be a groundbreaking revelation that a woman's genitalia doesn't reach orgasm the same way a penis does.

Most (51.3%) of the women in our sample do not have a "guaranteed orgasm" every time they have sex (that is, they do not orgasm in every or almost every sexual encounter), and it's not necessarily because they're not more active during intercourse. Grief, relationship problems, and hormonal issues can all impact her ability to orgasm. Yet, while many things contribute to women's orgasm rates, one stands out more than any other: *women need foreplay*. The reason for women's lack of orgasm is not that they're not active enough during lovemaking; more likely, it's that he is not active *in the right way*. Often that's because he was never

44

taught that he should be, and that leaves many women feeling disappointed, frustrated, or even used when sex is over.

> CHECK-IN: How do you feel after sex? How do your emotions after sex affect how you feel about sex?

Lack of Foreplay Is the Main Reason for the Orgasm Gap

Let's talk about what researchers call the "orgasm gap." Research has repeatedly found that over 90% of men almost always or always orgasm.[7] Compare that to the rate of orgasm for women from our survey (48%), and we find ourselves with at least a 42% orgasm gap.

Is this gap simply because women don't orgasm easily? Nope! Research shows that when masturbating, women can reach orgasm in under ten minutes.[8] Women's physical ability to orgasm, then,

Figure 3.3
How Married Christian Women Feel after Sex

Note: Respondents could choose multiple categories.

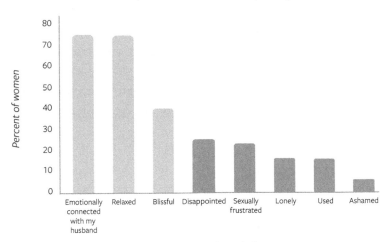

Emotions experienced after sex

isn't the problem. What if the real issue is that we have failed to teach couples how to have sex that's good for her?

Men and women reach orgasm differently. While men easily reach orgasm with intercourse (and, indeed, their orgasm often signals the end of the encounter), for women the relationship between intercourse and orgasm is not as straightforward. Of the women in our survey who are able to orgasm, only 39% are able to orgasm through penetrative intercourse alone. The rest needed some other kind of stimulation.

The women who reach orgasm regularly during sexual encounters, then, do not usually reach it just through intercourse. *And this is the norm.* Unfortunately, many of the Christian classics written about sex, even though they were so adamant that women's sexual experience was important, still downplayed women's best routes to orgasm.[9] *Intended for Pleasure* frames oral sex as an imitation of the real thing: "As a solution they turn to oral-genital sex to bring her to orgasm, and this becomes in a sense a shortcut, avoiding the development of the discipline and skillful control that are demanded in learning how to consistently provide a maximum of physical pleasure for both through regular intercourse."[10] *The Act of Marriage*, the main sex book for couples marrying in the 1980s and 1990s, set the goal as simultaneous orgasm during intercourse,[11] while other forms of orgasm were frowned upon: "Oral sex is on the increase today, thanks to amoral sex education, pornography, modern sex literature, and the moral breakdown of our times."[12]

Couples should not feel they are failing if they don't achieve simultaneous orgasm; in fact, while researchers recognize that simultaneous orgasm can be lovely, they also note that it is rare, even in the most sexually active and fulfilled relationships. They even question whether or not it is worth aiming for.[13] It's much more important to focus on the most consistent means of orgasm in lovemaking than to try to squeeze women into a sexual box into which most will not fit.

Besides, what if women's challenge reaching orgasm through intercourse, and thus requiring other stimulation, is actually a feature and not a bug? Could it be that God intended for men to have to spend some time helping their wives achieve pleasure in a way that does not directly stimulate the husband at all?

Here's how I (Sheila) explained it in my book *31 Days to Great Sex* (a thirty-one-day challenge for couples):

> God could have made women's bodies so that we get maximum pleasure from intercourse. But he didn't. That doesn't mean women can't feel pleasure from intercourse, but in general, most women report that they reach orgasm easier from clitoral stimulation. They tend to need a lot of manual or oral stimulation first if they're going to reach orgasm through intercourse. Why did God make the clitoris this way? Here's my theory: while men often reach climax quite quickly through intercourse alone, women don't. That means that for women to feel pleasure, men have to slow down and think about their wives. Sex is best when it isn't just "animal" style, where you simply have intercourse with no foreplay, because that won't feel good for her. Men have to learn to be unselfish if sex is going to work well for both partners. So often the woman can feel she is doing most of the caretaking of and serving her family, but God deliberately made our bodies so that if we're going to feel good during sex, men have to take time to serve women.[14]

Foreplay is not just the price of admission to the main event; for many women, foreplay *is* the main event, just as much as intercourse. In fact, we found that adequate foreplay makes a woman 6.43 times more likely to frequently orgasm.[15] And yet, so many women have told us that their husbands aren't interested in it at all:

- "My husband doesn't really get that sex itself doesn't do much for me. I need a lot of warming up. He seems to think there's something wrong with me; like, why should we have to spend so much time on this 'other stuff' instead of sex?"

- "I have explained to my husband about how men and women are different. He does understand. But he says sex is all we're required to do, and if sex doesn't cut it for me, then I should just take care of things myself. If I ask him to help me get aroused, he tells me that's my business and my responsibility."
- "My husband hates spending time on foreplay, so I feel rushed and move on to sex, even if I'm not completely ready."
- "I've been married for 1½ years. My husband wouldn't know foreplay if it bit him. It is straight to sex, and if I have an orgasm is not important as long as he does. . . . I have come to dislike sex."

This emphasis on intercourse over foreplay doesn't only leave women feeling frustrated if their husbands are in a rush to get to the deed; it also leaves many women hesitant to ask for what they want, even with husbands who are more than willing to give it. Another woman echoes a sentiment we hear frequently:

I've never faked an orgasm, but I guess I have lied by telling my husband I wasn't interested in finishing on occasion. That is never the truth for me, but I can only get there through manual stimulation, and if it starts taking long, I begin to feel sorry for my husband and start thinking he must be getting tired or his hand is getting sore. That makes me feel stressed and I lose the enjoyment. He's sweet and tells me he doesn't care how long it takes, but somehow I can't believe him. I don't want to get enjoyment when I think it makes him secretly miserable, praying that I'd hurry up and orgasm!

CHECK-IN: When did you first hear about the clitoris? Do you feel you know how the clitoris works?

Husbands Need to Take the Time to Make Sure Their Wives Feel Pleasure

We need to encourage couples, then, to work with God's design for her body and take the time she needs to ensure she feels good, not simply expect wives to "catch up" to their husbands and be able to enjoy intercourse the "right" way.

So often, though, the opposite happens in our marriage resources. Take this bizarre anecdote in *Love & Respect*, for instance, where Eggerichs tells the story of a mother convincing her daughter to give her husband more sex. The big selling point? "Why would you deprive him of something that takes such a short amount of time and makes him sooooo happy!?"[16] Frankly, we can't imagine why anyone expecting sex to feel good for a woman would emphasize its brevity above all else.

After I (Sheila) gave a sex talk at a marriage conference, a diminutive woman waited in the wings to talk to me after the crowds dispersed. She'd been married for twenty-three years, but she just had no desire for sex and didn't understand how it was supposed to feel good. After peppering her with my usual questions about arousal and technique, the problem was revealed: foreplay was nonexistent, and intercourse lasted about three minutes. And the two of them had no idea this wasn't normal.

Instead of expecting that sex shouldn't take very long, we'd like to offer a new expectation: *no man should be satisfied unless his wife is also regularly satisfied.* That doesn't mean a wife has to reach orgasm every single time, but the expectation should be that he does everything within his power to help her get there. Ephesians 5:28 says that husbands "ought to love their wives as their own bodies," meaning that her experience should matter to him as much as his own does. We'd like to see that orgasm gap close, but that will only happen when we start to believe that she doesn't just need to "catch up"; he may need to slow down.

CHECK-IN: Do you feel satisfied with the amount of foreplay in your sex life? Does your spouse? If one of you wants more, what is holding you back?

Kathleen was married for thirty-one years to her first husband, a marriage that was characterized by emotional distance and anger. Not surprisingly, this made her sexual response much more difficult. But that was not the only problem. Kathleen explains,

> I had a husband who didn't care if I had an orgasm. His nails were not cut down, and he really didn't know what to do with his hands. I was young and inexperienced and had no clue what to ask for. I needed a man who wouldn't get upset when things weren't working but who would patiently keep trying and help me feel at ease. When I told him, he never chose to take up the challenge. He dismissed it and figured it was my problem. I went more than 33 years without an orgasm. I thought I was broken, and he allowed me to feel this way.
>
> I eventually divorced him. I am now 58 and married to a wonderful man. I can have a G-spot orgasm, clitoral orgasm, and more. I can even have multiple orgasms! I'm not broken. I just needed someone to take the time to help me figure myself out.

Women's Pleasure Matters *for Her Own Sake*

No married woman should have to wait thirty-three years for an orgasm. In fact, the Bible tells us that women should not be deprived. "*The husband should fulfill his marital duty to his wife, and likewise the wife to her husband*" (1 Cor. 7:3, emphasis ours).

Too often, though, books portray that verse and the surrounding ones as applying only to men. Fred and Brenda Stoeker's *Every Heart Restored* even says this: "Sure, men are promised regular sexual release by Scripture. But by the same token, women are promised that their husbands will treat them with honor and tenderness (1 Pet. 3:7)."[17] Let's look more closely though. Notice something interesting about that passage they referred to about men's needs? They forgot to mention that it's directed at *both* spouses. If they use that verse to show women they need to give their husbands "sexual release" (i.e., orgasm), then by their own logic, they should have charged men with the same responsibility to bring their wives release too.

The Bible does not assume that one spouse will be perpetually sexually deprived by the other. No, the Bible tells us that both genders need to look out for the other, and it's expected that women will experience pleasure too. Even "It is better to marry than to burn with passion" is addressed to "the unmarried and to widows" (1 Cor. 7:8–9). Paul assumed that women would have passions! Sex is about *both* of you. Both of you should give and receive; both of you should feel loved and cherished.

Most Christian sex and marriage books (even the ones that emphasize women's sexual pleasure) spend an inordinate amount of time warning women not to deprive their husbands. To be fair, I (Sheila) have even done this in the past, before I started listening to sexually deprived women. What we'd like to submit now is that the spouse most likely to be deprived is not actually the *husband* but the *wife*. If deprivation is about not receiving sexual release (orgasm), then many more women are struggling than men. One woman commented with this sad story:

> I know it takes 15–20 minutes of foreplay for most women to get aroused, but there's no way my husband would be okay with devoting that much time to foreplay (he calls it lovey dovey stuff). If I initiate sex, he's like, "Ok, but I don't feel like doing any of the lovey dovey stuff." That means painful, dry sex and no fun for me. I try to show him what I like, but he gets frustrated and tells me, "I got this," then after a couple of minutes stops, says "It's not going to work anyway," and then goes on with his favorite part. Maybe I should be thankful it doesn't hurt as much anymore. He's frustrated

nearly every time that I don't climax, but how can I? Sex has either hurt to the point of bringing me to tears, felt like nothing, or I'm so stressed about the whole event I barely remember it. I feel like that broken toy that winds up halfway but only takes three steps. If I knew sex was going to be this way, I would have stayed single.

Our Christian resources should make it clear that this is unacceptable. Unfortunately, they haven't, leaving many women feeling the same way our commenter feels and leaving many men frustrated, too, that their wives don't want or know how to give themselves over to passion.

> CHECK-IN: Do you struggle to reach orgasm? How do you feel about that? How does your spouse feel about that? Are you laying the responsibility for this at one spouse's feet in particular? Why or why not?

Whose Responsibility Is It to Make Sex Feel Good for Women?

When books do discuss women's pleasure, unfortunately this unbalanced teaching can become even more unbalanced. Instead of saying "no man should be satisfied unless his wife is also regularly satisfied," too many books have said, "men feel more satisfied if their wives are satisfied, so wives—*make sure you're satisfied*," without any charge to him to care for her needs. The responsibility for her satisfaction is put solely on *her*—and not even for her own sake, but for *his*. Instead of telling men to satisfy their wives for their wives' benefit, women are told to make sure they're satisfied for their husbands' benefit. This is really backward.

In the book *For Women Only*, Shaunti Feldhahn warns wives that just having sex is not enough—men need to feel wanted. "Having a regular, mutually enjoyed sex life was critical to the man's feeling of being loved and desired."[18] But then, in that same chapter, Feldhahn says, "If responding physically is out of the question, let your words be heart words—reassuring, affirming, adoring."[19] The wife has to affirm her husband, even if he is not tending to her needs in bed. Feldhahn does acknowledge that some women will have a hard time responding physically, but then she frames this as being a personal issue that may need counseling rather than the far greater likelihood that he has never learned to prioritize foreplay or her pleasure.[20] We find it problematic to tell a woman she must enjoy something without also telling her that she can expect him to make it enjoyable.[21]

Then *The Act of Marriage* chimes in, "A wise and considerate woman goes out of her way to let her man know that he is a good lover and that she enjoys their relations together."[22] Yet it says this without saying the husband should actually *be* a good lover. And if she can't feel satisfied? Then she might "consider herself unsuccessful in bed."[23] This language incentivizes women to fake orgasm (something 60% of women report having done[24]) to avoid bruising their husbands' egos instead of pushing for open and honest communication about sex. A husband's ego is not more important than a wife's sexual pleasure.

As Natalie explained in her interview, "I did not believe that my sexuality was for me; it was all for him. Once when we were having sex I moaned and it got him really excited. So I asked him, 'Did you like that?' and he told me he did. So I started moaning a lot more after that. But I was moaning even if I wasn't really feeling anything."

So let's add one more expectation to the mix: We've already said no man should be satisfied if his wife isn't regularly satisfied. Now we'd also like to add this: *Women's sexual pleasure matters for her own sake, not just for his.*

In conducting our survey we were encouraged that more women are regularly reaching orgasm than we thought (yay, women!). But if Christian women are orgasming at relatively high rates even when the majority of our resources ignore their pleasure, how many of the women who struggle to find pleasure have simply never been taught that pleasure is a thing? What if the women who don't orgasm simply don't have the resources to help them realize that this is not normal? Just like that diminutive woman at the marriage conference, many women don't know what foreplay is. So many of us put up with mediocre sex for so long because we don't realize there's anything better.

In fact, mediocre sex is often presented as the norm. In Tim Keller's book *The Meaning of Marriage*, he tells that, early in his marriage to Kathy, sex wasn't working very well. He recounts that, after they were finished, he would check in to see how Kathy had felt. "If I asked her, 'How was that?' and she said, 'It just hurt,' I felt devastated, and she did, too."[25] Like many couples we interviewed, they weren't communicating during intercourse, and so he was in the dark about her experience as it was happening.

He goes on to explain that they decided that trying to work toward her orgasm led to too much stress. "We stopped worrying about what we were getting and started to say, 'Well, what can we do just to give something to the other?'"[26] The problem for the Kellers may very well have been the pressure to orgasm, but when women like Kay, Natalie, and others we interviewed hear stories like this, what they often internalize is that if intercourse is going badly—if she is in pain, or if her orgasm is too difficult—she might as well just let him finish, enjoying what she can give to him.

For many women, a better solution would be to encourage her to ask for what she wants *during* sex rather than only telling him *afterward* that it wasn't good for her (let alone that she was in pain). Almost all of the women we talked to who struggled with orgasm explained that their breakthrough began when they realized they could speak up and change what was happening— even if that meant stopping in the middle of intercourse. As Kay

Rules about Speaking Up during Intercourse

How to speak up:

1. If it hurts, say something—even if you're just "a little uncomfortable." You deserve pain-free sex.

2. If something is keeping you from getting aroused (more on how to "get there" in the next chapter), say, "Let's stop for a moment and try something else."

3. Want more of something—or less of something? Tell your spouse when something is feeling good (even if it's just by moaning). If something isn't feeling good, take your spouse's hand and put it where you'd like it to be.

4. Don't fake it—orgasm, arousal, anything.

How to help your spouse speak up:

1. When you're not sure if your spouse is ready for penetrative sex yet, ask!

2. If you sense your spouse is not enjoying things, stop and go back to kissing and touching for a while.

3. Watch your spouse's cues. If it's obviously not enjoyable, be the one to pull back and say, "Let's take a rain check." Show your spouse sex can stop without you getting angry.

explained it, "I felt there was a point of no return. Once we got going, I thought it wasn't fair for me to ask him to stop."

At first, stopping can feel very selfish. Kay was so used to unbalanced sex in his favor that she "needed to learn that even though it feels like I want selfish sex, it's actually not selfish. If I'm not experiencing pleasure, I need to say stop. That's okay. In fact, my husband wants me to speak up—he wants it to be good for me."

When you're used to unbalanced sex, and then you try to make it balanced, it can feel like you've tipped the scales in the other direction. You're so used to it being lopsided one way that equality feels like you're taking something from the other. And that lack of equality in the conversation around sex has led to sex being not only disappointing for many women but actively bad.

> CHECK-IN: Do each of you speak up when something doesn't feel good during sex? What rules can you put in place so you feel freer to speak up?

What about When Sex Hurts?

It's sad if a woman never experiences sexual pleasure, but it's tragic if sex is actually painful and she feels like she has to endure that pain to avoid depriving him. And female sexual pain is very prevalent, whether due to childbirth complications or primary sexual dysfunction.[27] We found that a full 32.3% of women have experienced some form of sexual pain in their marriages (26.7% of women reported pain due to childbirth, and 22.6% reported pain from vaginismus or another form of dyspareunia. Some women

---

Female Sexual Dysfunction

Vaginismus: Pain during vaginal penetration, sometimes so severe that tampons cannot be inserted, caused by involuntary spasming of the muscles in the vaginal wall.

Dyspareunia: Painful sex with any cause—childbirth, excessive dryness, hormonal changes, inflammatory conditions, and more.

Vulvodynia: Burning pain during sex, located in any area of the vagina or vulva.

Pain during sex is always something that is worth bringing up with your medical provider. It is often very treatable, and you're worth it!

---

reported both).[28] For 6.8% of women the pain is so intense that penetration is impossible. Yet very few people are talking about this.

We did some digging. While PubMed (the National Institutes of Health online database for scientific journal articles) has 41,473 articles for the keywords "erectile dysfunction," it only has 4,809 for "dyspareunia" (aka painful sex).[29] Similarly, there were 1,796 studies on "premature ejaculation" but only 401 for "vaginismus." We don't want to downplay the importance or severity of male sexual health issues. However, if you've watched *Wheel of Fortune* in the last decade, you've likely seen a myriad of advertisements for erectile dysfunction treatments. Before reading this book, had you even heard of vaginismus?

It's long been known in medical circles that conservative religious women experience more pain with sex than the general population.[30] Yet if scholars are doing poorly on this topic, the church is doing worse. Both The Gospel Coalition and Focus on the Family have online articles on erectile dysfunction while failing

Male Sexual Dysfunction

Erectile dysfunction: A persistent inability to create or maintain an erection long enough to have sex.

Premature ejaculation: A condition in which the period between when sex starts and when he ejaculates is very short (typically around two minutes or less).

Delayed ejaculation: A condition in which it takes an extended period of time to reach ejaculation, if it can be reached at all.

If you are suffering from any of these conditions, please see a doctor. Medical treatments and sexual techniques can be used to make sex great for both of you again.

to provide any information on vaginismus, sexual pain, or post-partum pain.[31]

Additionally, we couldn't find a single marriage book (other than my own[32]) that even mentioned vaginismus, though some of the books dedicated solely to sex touched on it.[33] Even in these cases, though, the way it is framed is often harmful (*The Gift of Sex* and *Sheet Music* are exceptions). *The Act of Marriage* never mentions vaginismus but does say that women can be irrationally afraid they will be too tight to experience penetration comfortably.[34] *Intended for Pleasure* acknowledges the problem, but then totally bungs things up with this claim: "Vaginismus can usually be eliminated in about one week with the following procedure."[35] The book then describes the use of dilators. I (Sheila) had severe vaginismus, and I tried that. Did it by the book; got the T-shirt. Recovery still took years. And that's not unusual, because research shows that vaginismus can be very resistant to treatment.[36]

And pain matters. Having someone derive pleasure from something that causes you pain compounds the hurt. That's why we're going to be looking at the problem of sexual pain throughout the book and the different beliefs that lead to higher rates of vaginismus.

Sex is meant to be a mutual experience. That means his pleasure matters, yes. But so does her pleasure, and so does her pain.

Sexual Dysfunction That Can Affect Either Men or Women

Hypoactive sexual desire disorder: A clinically low libido.

Anorgasmia: The inability to achieve orgasm. May be complete lack of orgasm or may be characterized by very infrequent climax.

Postorgasmic illness syndrome (for men) or postcoital dysphoria (for women): conditions in which a wide variety of symptoms from migraines to anxiety occur after orgasm.

When we get this right, then sex becomes what God intended it to be. As one commenter told us,

> When we make love, I am able to be so connected to my husband and feel so loved by him. It's exciting to see the passion in his eyes as he looks deep into mine. It hasn't always been this way, and we have had some challenges in our marriage. We have had to learn what feels good. But the pleasure we feel with each other is so worth any effort that we have had to put in. Sex is an amazing privilege that we have to be able to come together. I really wish all marriages could experience this amazingly powerful thing that God gave us.

That's beautiful—and that's what we wish for all of you too.

EXPLORE TOGETHER

Learn how to make each other feel great in ways other than intercourse—especially because that's often the key to her pleasure! First, we're going to ask you to do something rather graphic: Make the hand motion used to manually stimulate a man. Now make the hand motion used for women. Which one is more like intercourse? What does that tell you about the importance of other stimulation for women?

Below you'll find three different suggestions to help you apply this concept to bring each other pleasure. Try all if you can, working through one per night. Have one spouse go first, and then switch roles.

1. *Don't Move!* Set a timer for fifteen minutes, and have your spouse lie on their back on the bed. Touch your spouse, exploring their body. Study your spouse's reactions. What makes your spouse show the most arousal? Try to hold off orgasm until the end of the fifteen minutes.

2. *A or B?* When you get your eyes checked at the optometrist, they ask, "What's better: 1 or 2?" Play a game like that tonight! Touch your spouse in two ways or in two places. Do they like it with less pressure or more pressure? Is pressure better than movement? Is licking better than touching? Try as many combos as you can think of and learn what makes your spouse tick! And for the spouse being touched—be honest. The goal is not to stoke your spouse's ego but to uncover what feels good.

3. *Teacher.* Here's the challenging one: Play teacher! If you're confident, take ten minutes and be very directive toward your spouse. Tell him or her exactly what to do, and don't be afraid to order them around. "Faster, not so hard, a little to the left." Give clear directions—and then clear praise.

RESCUING AND REFRAMING

- Instead of saying, "She has emotional needs, and he has sexual needs," say, "Both spouses have sexual and emotional needs, even if they feel one to a greater degree."

- Instead of saying, "Women need to meet men's sexual needs," say, "Each spouse should make the other's sexual pleasure their first priority."

- Instead of implying that foreplay is something to get through so they can get to the main event, teach couples that sex encompasses the whole experience of bringing each other pleasure.

- Instead of telling women, "Assure your husband that you enjoy sex," tell men, "Become a great lover for your wife."

CHAPTER 4

Let Me Hear Your Body Talk

Promise me, O women of Jerusalem,
not to awaken love until the time is right.
Song of Songs 8:4 NLT

Two of us live in Belleville, a small city between two large ones—
Toronto and Ottawa. If you want to catch a train to one of those
big cities, you have limited options, because not all trains stop in
Belleville. But they all stop in Kingston, a larger city near us. You
can go from Toronto to Ottawa without stopping in Belleville, but
you can't get there without stopping in Kingston. All trains must
go through Kingston.

We've just finished talking about how sex is supposed to be
pleasurable and women are supposed to experience orgasm, too,
but we'd like to take that one step further and talk about what
that journey actually looks like. Sex can't be pleasurable—she
can't experience an orgasm—until couples figure out that arousal
piece. Arousal is like that train stop in Kingston. You can't get to
orgasm unless you go through arousal on the way.

When Piper (one of our survey respondents) and her now husband were dating, they enjoyed a few steamy make-out sessions.

But both Piper and her husband were dedicated to waiting until marriage for sex, and whenever Piper felt like they had let things go a little too far, she'd declare a fast from kissing for forty days, when they would shift gears and focus on Jesus. She liked kissing, but she also felt very convicted about it.

After their wedding, they awkwardly tried to have intercourse—with *tried* being the operative word. They quickly discovered that Piper suffered from vaginismus, and penetration was too painful. For the six years it took for them to finally achieve penetration, they did other forms of stimulation that helped him reach orgasm. But the disappointment and frustration grew.

I asked Piper if she had felt aroused before she tried intercourse for the first time. "Nope," she admitted. They had tried to make it straight from Toronto to Ottawa without going through Kingston—and they had stalled out. Piper said she often wondered what would have happened if they had just tried intercourse one of the times she felt "steamy" before they were married. It's not that she wishes they'd had sex when they were dating; it's just that she wishes the first time they tried to have sex, she had actually been aroused. Maybe if that had been the case, her story would not have been what it was. But she'll never know.

Piper wasn't the only one to say that. So did Charlotte. Charlotte and her husband had spent their dating days making out without going any further, but Charlotte had been on high alert to make sure things didn't go too far. As the "gatekeeper," she was hypervigilant, making sure they stopped in time. It took Charlotte twenty-six years of marriage before she finally figured out what arousal was and how to reach orgasm. Would it have taken twenty-six years if they had given in when she was aroused?

Shannon wonders that too. Like Piper, Shannon suffered from vaginismus that they discovered on her wedding night. She told us, "I remember two specific instances when we were dating, we had to stop ourselves because we almost went too far, and we were so proud of stopping ourselves, but now I can't help but wonder what our marriage would look like if the first time I had sex I was aroused. Would it have been less traumatic and less painful if my body actually wanted it that first time?" All three women still say they don't believe in sex before marriage. They just wonder, and they wish sex had started differently.

But even if a couple has sex before the wedding night, there's no guarantee they figured out the arousal piece either. Natalie, one of the women we interviewed, told us that she and her husband started their sex life before they were married, but even now, six years into marriage, she's still struggling. When they were dating he wasn't a Christian yet. Even though he never pressured her, Natalie assumed he would expect sex, and so, in trying to make him feel loved and wanted, she decided to give it to him. She was happy to feel close to him, but she felt no physical pleasure at all. She decided to start having sex before her body was ready. And now her body doesn't know what to do.

> CHECK-IN: What was your first consensual sexual experience like? Were you aroused and ready to go, or did you ask your body to do something it wasn't ready for?

We are told in church that the key to great sex is waiting until the wedding night. But if that's the case, why do so many of the women in our survey who waited until their wedding night have the same story as Natalie, who didn't? Here's an uncomfortable truth: your marital status is not what makes sex orgasmic or not—your arousal level is. Many single women have no problem orgasming, and that fact shouldn't threaten our traditional Christian view of sex. Saving sex for marriage is not about making it more orgasmic but about making it more meaningful—a deep knowing—while protecting ourselves from heartache, diseases, and single parenthood. The key to sexual pleasure is not a wedding ring.

That's why, if you want an orgasmic marriage, having sex within twenty-four hours of saying "I do" does not guarantee anything. Our catchphrase should not just be "Wait for sex until you're married"; our catchphrase should be "Wait for sex until you're married and turned on!" Save sex for when you're married, and then once you're married, *don't have sex until your body is begging for it.*

Each of these women, whether they waited for marriage or not, missed the natural progression of sexual arousal. And that progression looks something like this:

- low-key physical contact that makes you feel close, such as holding hands, having your arms around each other, or short kisses
- kissing and touching that is drawn out when you start to feel aroused
- removing some clothing and learning to touch each other without awkwardness
- exploring each other's bodies to see what arouses you and what arouses the other
- learning to bring each other to orgasm without intercourse
- having intercourse

When you allow your body to tell you when it's time to move forward, these steps naturally follow, one after the other. That's why when a dating couple has sex "by accident," he doesn't just slip into her vagina by surprise. It's often that they've been cuddling and kissing while they talk, and that kissing turns to making out. They start to get turned on, so their hands start wandering, making them even more aroused. And eventually they get to the point where their bodies are screaming out to them, *We know what the next step is. Can we just do the next step already?!* They've been kissing and making out and touching for so long that their bodies

Kissing before Marriage

While many Christian celebrities have advocated for not kissing before the wedding, we had no idea how often couples had their first kiss at the altar. So we asked. An overwhelming number of Christian women married to their first husband had kissed before the wedding—95.1%!

We wondered how much this had changed over time, especially compared to the heyday of purity culture. Here's what we found: this whole "Don't kiss until the altar" thing is a really newfangled idea. More than 99% of Christian women over sixty who are married to their first husbands had kissed their husbands before the wedding. Among women with the same characteristics under forty, 93.2% kissed their husbands before the altar.

What does this mean? Even at the height of the purity culture craze, the vast majority of Christian women were kissing before marriage.

are saying, *We NEED the sex!* And it truly feels like they are out of control—they just can't contain all this passion and desire, and they end up having sex. "Accidental" sex isn't so accidental at all. It's often hours in the making. But for many women, sex initially moves at too fast a pace and steps are skipped. Their bodies never had a chance to say, "I need this!"

This is one of those chapters we weren't planning on writing. We didn't realize how many women struggled with arousal until we saw our survey results and conducted some focus groups. So we took an informal poll on Twitter and Facebook and asked, "If you were a virgin on your wedding night, were you aroused the first time you had sex?" Only 52% were.[1] That means approximately half of the women who waited until their wedding night were not aroused the first time they had sex. And many for whom the wedding night was not "the first time" commented that they did not necessarily feel arousal beforehand, either, and still had trouble with it. For many women, messages they heard growing up became a roadblock to arousal—even once in a safe marriage. Let's look at why.

How Being the "Gatekeeper" Can Hamper Women's Arousal

Girls are frequently warned as soon as they hit puberty: boys are going to push your sexual boundaries. As one commenter explained on my blog, "I was told he pushes the accelerator, and I push the brakes."

In our study, 81.2% of women currently believe that boys will want to push girls' sexual boundaries. That gatekeeper idea that women must be the ones to hit the brake pedal, though, was one of the most damaging for women's marital and sexual satisfaction. In large part, women adopt gatekeeping to protect their purity,

Figure 4.1

High School Girls Who Believe They Must Be Sexual Gatekeepers Grow Up to Be Less Sexually Satisfied in Marriage

What happens to women's sex lives if they agreed in high school that boys will want to push girls' sexual boundaries?

which tends to be defined in the evangelical world as virginity. And is it any surprise when our teenagers are growing up reading these kinds of messages in Christian books:

- In *When God Writes Your Love Story*, Eric and Leslie Ludy tell the story of Karly and Todd, who succumbed to temptation and had sex when they were dating. Karly was distraught: "She had made the mistake of giving him her most precious gift—her virginity—but now he was distant and cold toward her."[2] Todd, however, had been a virgin too. But he is not described as having lost anything or having given up *his* most precious gift. Instead, he becomes distant and cold, angry at her for having sex with him.
- The same book tells another story of a young woman weeping in similar despair: "I have given away the most

Figure 4.2

High School Girls Who Believe They Must Be Sexual Gatekeepers Grow Up to Be Less Happy in Their Marriages

What happens to women's marital satisfaction if they agreed in high school that boys will want to push girls' sexual boundaries?

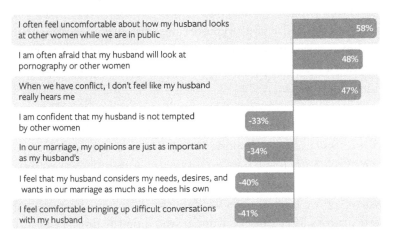

I often feel uncomfortable about how my husband looks at other women while we are in public	58%
I am often afraid that my husband will look at pornography or other women	48%
When we have conflict, I don't feel like my husband really hears me	47%
I am confident that my husband is not tempted by other women	-33%
In our marriage, my opinions are just as important as my husband's	-34%
I feel that my husband considers my needs, desires, and wants in our marriage as much as he does his own	-40%
I feel comfortable bringing up difficult conversations with my husband	-41%

precious thing I had—my purity. There's nothing left of my treasure. . . . I've ruined my whole life."[3] Even though the resolution to this was that she was forgiven by Jesus, the authors don't tell her that she *hasn't* ruined her whole life.

- In *For Young Women Only*, Shaunti Feldhahn reports, "Many guys feel neither the ability nor the responsibility to stop the sexual progression with you. And those who *do* feel the responsibility don't want to have to stop it alone."[4] After revealing the results of her survey, she concludes, "That adds up to 82 percent of guys reporting serious difficulty in bringing things to a halt in a make-out situation—or no desire to halt things at all!"[5]

If you grow up as an evangelical girl, then, you may be taught that losing your virginity is the worst thing that can happen to you and that your boyfriend will not be able to resist having sex, and so you have to become the gatekeeper to protect purity for both of you. All the responsibility, risk, and repercussions of sex are on your shoulders. One of the big reasons we think this message is so damaging is that it's so one-sided. If the message were simply "Both of you need to practice self-control," we may not have seen the stark results we did, because self-control is, after all, a fruit of the Spirit.[6] But when the message given instead is that the boy is incapable of practicing self-control and won't want to practice self-control so you must do it on his behalf? That's when things go haywire.

When we tell girls that all boys will want to pressure them, we set a very low standard for boys and a very high one for girls. If all guys will push your boundaries, and you need to fight off every one of them, then will girls even know that they deserve to date and marry someone who will respect their boundaries? Or even worse, are we priming girls for date rape? We were heartbroken to hear story after story of women who didn't realize until years later that they had been raped or assaulted when they thought the issue was that they let a boy go too far—even if they had said no.

Too often men are portrayed as helpless to control themselves. *The Act of Marriage* includes a story about Susie, as she complains about her husband: "Ever since I met him it seems I've been fighting him off!"[7] She thinks of Bill as a beast, and even when they were dating, she was always trying to get his hands off of her. But let's think more about what's going on in Susie's head. She's dating Bill, and they're making out on the couch. It feels good, but rather than concentrating on what she's feeling, she's paying attention to what Bill is doing. *Where are his hands? Is he breathing too hard?* If his hands start to wander, she swats them away. If he puts them back, she sits up and says they have to stop. She's learned that she can never truly relax, even when they are just kissing.

Bill, on the other hand, has been given carte blanche to relax and enjoy it all because he knows Susie will stop when it's time. So Bill is able to become sexually aroused and enjoy exploring—to a point— while Susie is frantically trying to prevent herself from becoming aroused or else she won't be able to stop him. For many women, this learned behavior does not evaporate when marriage vows are recited.

> CHECK-IN: How do you feel when your spouse gropes you? Is it okay in some contexts but not others?

In looking back over why she could never respond sexually to her husband, Charlotte believes this gatekeeper role was one of the main reasons. She never allowed herself to feel anything while they were making out. She was constantly asking herself, *When do I put on the brakes? Is it now? Is it now? Is it now?*

When she married, she was so used to that observer role that she couldn't just drop it. She didn't know how to be in the moment or how to relax and just feel what her body was feeling. She reverted to *judging* what was going on rather than *experiencing* what was going on, and that made the arousal piece very difficult. Natalie used the word "spectator-ing" to describe the same phenomenon: *Did I look good? Did I do that right?* And that's exactly what we found in our study: women who believed in high school that they had to be gatekeepers for boys are less likely to be comfortable talking to their husbands about what feels good sexually and what they want sexually today.[8] And being able to talk about what feels good sexually is crucial in discovering and experiencing sexual pleasure.

> CHECK-IN: Did you feel like a gatekeeper during the dating or engagement phase of your relationship?

Sex is better when you can tell each other what you want. That's a no-brainer. But how do you tell your spouse what you want when you've been systematically trained to not listen to your body?

Throw Out the Paint-by-Number Approach to Sex

The Christian sex books we reviewed understand that women reaching orgasm is a challenge, and their solution is often to give detailed instructions, in very graphic terms, of how to help her reach climax. *The Act of Marriage* lays out what you should do on your wedding night, step by step, moment by moment.[9] *Sheet Music* gives instructions on how to give a wife oral sex that ends with her "biting the pillow for fear she'll wake up the kids."[10]

In the focus groups we conducted, the women all appreciated explicit, detailed advice about how anatomy and arousal work. But they were very negative toward the prescriptive "paint-by-numbers" approach. They felt like these instructions made sex into a pass/fail endeavor. One woman asked, "What if I'm not biting the pillow?" And another woman laughed, saying she felt like she'd have to have the book beside her, checking every few minutes to make sure she was holding her pelvis at the right angle.

Is Christian Sex Advice Condescending to Women?

We ran a series of focus groups asking women how they felt about passages in sex books, including the following:*

- "Their maidenly inhibitions and misconceptions compel them to lie on their backs and allow the vigorous young husbands to satisfy themselves."—*The Act of Marriage*[11]
- "Whether you're on top or she's on top, whether you're behind with her on her knees, or the two of you are spooning, you can reach around and oh, so carefully, find that tender little friend."—*Sheet Music*[12]
- "For those women who want to serve up a special treat for their husbands, let's talk about making 'Mr. Happy' smile" and a longer passage that included the phrase "Mr. Happy likes to be kissed."—*Sheet Music*[13]

Across the board, women were unimpressed when they felt they were being talked down to. And some of the greatest offenders were the cutesy euphemisms such as "Mr. Happy" for "penis" and "tender little friend" for "clitoris." These words made women feel infantilized, which is hardly sexy. When we read the "Mr. Happy" passages, women's eyebrows darted up, they started shaking their heads, and in one group we even heard a chorus of "Eeeeeewwwww." One woman said of Mr. Happy, "If it wasn't about sex, this could be a puppet show for kids."[†] Another said, "It sounds like Mister Rogers's Neighborhood, where everything is a friend. That's very disturbing!"

Universally, women did not shy away from explicit instruction, but they preferred passages using proper terminology. We believe these authors wanted to make sex less shameful by talking openly, perhaps even by adding some humor. However, talking to women as if they're children does not end shame; rather, it treats them like they're inadequate and not up to the task.

Takeaway: Because men tend to reach orgasm more easily and want sex more, books portray them as sexual, while women need to be coaxed along. Unfortunately, this often leads to assuming men are good at sex and women aren't, reinforcing the very problem they are trying to fix.

---

* Feedback from our focus groups included statements like "Victorian," "outdated," "a generalization," and "It's condescending to assume that she has misconceptions." Some emotions women associated with this passage from *The Act of Marriage* were "frustration," feeling "used," "disgusted," and "vulnerable," and other reactions to the passages were that they were "toxic," "disturbing," and "sexist."

† After hearing all the euphemistic passages, one woman said, "Too much glib nature can make it icky, icky, icky!"

What if these authors only partially diagnosed the problem—and because of that, they're giving the wrong solution? What if the reason women aren't reaching orgasm isn't that couples don't know how to follow these steps but that women don't know how to listen to their bodies and experience arousal in the first place?

Telling couples, "Do A, then B, then C," just doesn't work for women who are missing the arousal piece. The ability to listen to your body is a more important skill than knowing exactly where to put your fingers. That's what Natalie is still struggling with. She's very self-aware, but she hasn't zeroed in on a solution that has opened up arousal. One thing she does know is that it's not about learning how to touch places better; it's about unlocking whatever residual shame messages are still in her brain. "I feel like I've learned how to push on the accelerator," she explained. "But I still can't stop pushing on the brakes at the same time. So I can get 75% of the way there and then I stall out."

Women don't only need to know how sex works; they need to know how *they* work. And that includes getting to the root of why they repressed their sexuality in the first place. Evangelical culture primes women to repress their sexuality but then turns around and chastises them when they are married for doing that very thing. Is it any wonder many women feel like they just can't win?

> CHECK-IN: Do you feel like a sexual person? What does sexual confidence look like to you?

Why Stimulation Doesn't Always Arouse Her

Recently, when discussing this missing arousal piece on the blog, many commenters expressed their frustration. "He's touching all the right places, but I don't feel anything!" They had read that the clitoris is the key to arousal, and he was flicking the clitoris, twirling the clitoris, rubbing the clitoris, but nothing was happening.

And many were begging for more and detailed instructions. Just tell them exactly how to flick, twirl, rub, poke, bop, whatever!

As the comment section grew and women shared their stories, the penny dropped for one woman. She and her husband had been going straight to clitoral stimulation before her body was asking for it. They had never learned the middle steps. And jumping into clitoral stimulation or intercourse without arousal can actually set a couple backward.

Men, imagine trying to have sex or masturbate right after you've orgasmed. It's not enjoyable at all. Women similarly can find having the clitoris rubbed or fingers inserted into the vagina prior to arousal uncomfortable and unpleasant. It can feel an awful lot like a pap smear. If you follow detailed instructions on how you're supposed to stimulate her nipples or clitoris or other erogenous zones before she's the least bit aroused, it usually doesn't lead to arousal. Instead, it often feels awkward and invasive and can even turn her *off*.

Go Back to No Pressure

Anyone who grew up watching *Happy Days* reruns will remember Richie Cunningham singing, "*I found my thrill . . . on Blueberry Hill . . .*" every time he took a girlfriend up to the make-out spot. The show steered clear of sex in the early years (before Joanie and Chachi became a thing) but portrayed making out as very enjoyable, even if it wasn't leading anywhere else.

Or was it *because* it wasn't leading anywhere else?

Women in our focus groups reported feeling much more freedom to explore and experience when there was not simultaneous pressure to perform. When women feel pressured to have intercourse, or even to reach orgasm, they can short-circuit the arousal process if they become self-conscious that they're taking too long or their husbands are getting bored—even if their husbands really want to help them discover arousal. For many women, the freedom to *feel* without it going anywhere was one of the keys to unlocking arousal, and ultimately orgasm.

Maybe what couples need more than detailed instructions on nipple play or clitoral stimulation is a trip back up to Blueberry Hill. After all, why was making out so much more arousing before you were married than it is now? Often it's because you watched a movie together, and then you started kissing for an hour, and your hands were stroking each other's hair, and you wanted to rip the clothes off of each other—but you couldn't yet. You took enough time on those preliminary steps because that was as far as you could go, and so you gave arousal time to awaken.

If you've been having sex for years, and she's never felt aroused, it may be time to go back some steps. It may mean that he has to put his own orgasm on hold temporarily to help her figure out that arousal piece with no pressure. That "no pressure" piece, for many women, is the only route to learning to listen to her own body, and that's why step-by-step foreplay instructions won't work if she knows they always end in intercourse.

Another commenter told us this:

> My husband and I were clueless virgins when we got married. When my husband asked or I asked myself mentally if it felt good, as long as it didn't hurt I said yes. My "A-HA" moment came when we were making out one time and I started having a feeling that I had gotten a few times before when I was younger and reading Christian romance novels. Embarrassing but true—I got aroused from that stuff but didn't have the language or awareness to identify what was happening. It felt like a warm heartbeat in my clitoris that spread outward. So when I began to feel that with my husband, I wondered if that was what "good" meant. I focused on what was causing me to feel that way and what would intensify that feeling, and that's how I figured out how to orgasm. Once I knew what "good" felt like, I was able to listen to my body and learn what different things made me feel that way, and it got easier with practice.

74

She had no clue what arousal was, and for several years she just had sex, feeling nothing. But when she and her husband simply made out again, she realized what arousal was supposed to be. She learned to ride it, and things finally worked!

> CHECK-IN: When was the first time you remember feeling aroused (if you have)? What were you doing?

What If She Still Can't Relax?

For many couples, giving her permission to explore and feel without being obligated to go any further is all it takes to fill in that arousal piece. Other couples still reach roadblocks because, even if they want her not to feel pressure, she still does. She wants to get off the train at Kingston and just explore, but she can't let herself. Often that's due to messages she's internalized about sex: she's obligated to give him sex when he wants it or she's a bad wife; if she doesn't have sex, he'll be tempted to watch porn or have an affair; he won't feel loved if she doesn't have sex with him, so she can't expect him to talk to her if she isn't also giving him sex.

For some women, and for some men, these messages are very loud. For them, the journey to fulfilling sex doesn't start with her learning the arousal piece. It actually starts with both of them ditching the messages that are keeping them from seeing sex in a healthy way. And it's to those messages that we now turn.

EXPLORE TOGETHER: A Trip to Blueberry Hill

If orgasm has been elusive and arousal is difficult, remove the pressure to perform. Here are some ways to do that:

- Decide on a time period when sex will be totally off the table (two to four weeks). Use this time as a chance to emphasize physical affection—even if it means parking and making out on a back road!

- Prioritize touching each other without sex afterward. Set the kitchen timer and kiss for at least fifteen seconds a day. If you're watching a movie, snuggle up.

Tips for reintroducing sex:

- Have him lie still and let her kiss him and explore his body to build her sexual confidence as she discovers how to make him feel good.
- Until she is aroused, do not pass Go, do not collect $200. Do not touch her clitoris or her nipples until she wants it.

RESCUING AND REFRAMING

- Instead of saying, "Boys will push girls' boundaries," say the following to both genders:
  1. "It's natural and healthy to want sex."
  2. "You are capable of resisting temptation, and you are responsible to not violate anyone else's boundaries."
  3. "If you are pressured to do something you do not want to do, that is not a safe relationship."
- Instead of saying, "Don't have sex until marriage," say, "Don't have sex until you're married and turned on!"
- Instead of saying, "The wedding night will be the best night of your life," say, "Sex is a journey of discovery and joy, so don't expect to be experts on the first day."

Sex should be *pure*:
Both partners can expect
the other to take
responsibility to keep
themselves free of sexual sin.

CHAPTER 5

Do You Only Have Eyes for Me?

> But I tell you that anyone who looks at a woman lustfully has already committed adultery with her in his heart.
>
> Matthew 5:28

We (Sheila and Rebecca) once attended a wedding where the sweet couple wrote their own vows. It was a lovely ceremony, punctuated with handmade arches and decorations and original music.

But at the end of the vows, we turned to each other with surprise. They forgot something important—"forsaking all others." It was just an oversight but, nevertheless, that is a rather crucial promise. We're supposed to expect that our spouse will be able to say, in the words of the 1950s jazz group The Flamingos, "I only have eyes for you." Despite the stretch marks and the baby weight, despite the expanding middle and the receding hair, despite the years and the wrinkles and the fading health, we want to know "I am yours, and you are mine, exclusively and forever." That's safety. That's acceptance. That's love.

That's what we all dream of.

But is that all it can ever be—just a dream?

The Battle Starts

One of the bestselling Christian books in the 2000s was *Every Man's Battle* by Stephen Arterburn and Fred Stoeker.[1] And what was this battle that every man was fighting? Lust. Every man struggles with it, every man is tempted by it, every man must fight really, really hard to overcome it. Thus the term *bouncing your eyes* was born. "When your eyes bounce toward a woman, they must bounce away immediately."[2] Girls were called to modesty as a sign of love for their brothers in Christ. It didn't take long for the "Modest is Hottest" slogan to catch on.

The way we talk about the struggle—like it's every man's battle and men are naturally visually stimulated—makes it sounds like if a guy doesn't struggle with lust, he's not a real man. Just listen to these excerpts from various books:

- "Women must cultivate the problem of visual lust, whereas men almost universally must cope with the problem just because they are men."—*The Act of Marriage*[3]
- "Because men and women are wired so differently, women often don't realize how the opposite sex sees the world. Most women simply aren't aware of what men's visual nature means, or how much it impacts literally every area of most men's lives and relationships."—*Through a Man's Eyes*[4]
- "We find another reason for the prevalence of sexual sin among men. We got there naturally—simply by being male."—*Every Man's Battle*[5]
- "A man can't not want to look."—*For Women Only*[6]

Can We Call Men to More?

When I (Rebecca) was a fourteen-year-old homeschooler, my mom assigned *To Kill a Mockingbird* to me. I lay on our yellow couch devouring that book for thirteen hours straight, skipping meals and bathroom breaks until I finally discovered how Jem broke his arm. I curled up into a ball, sobbing when the masterpiece was finished. To me, Atticus Finch epitomized what it meant to be a good man. Of course he wasn't perfect; he certainly was plagued by his own uncertainty. Yet he stood up for what was right and fought against injustice, all while keeping a belief in the ultimate good of humanity.

Fast-forward two years, and I was introduced to *Jersey Shore*. The men on the show knew what they wanted, and they wanted it now. They were entitled and vain, and there was no expectation that they would ever be more.

What bothers all of us writing this book is that the Christian world has tended to describe all men as having an inner "Jersey Shore" party boy. Instead of yearning for men to be like Atticus Finch, girls and women are taught that Atticus Finch is a figment of our imagination. We need to resign ourselves to being married to a Pauly D.

We can even hear this when listening to those highest up in evangelical circles. Paige Patterson, before he was fired from his presidency of Southwestern Baptist Theological Seminary, defended two teen boys for objectifying a girl in a now-infamous sermon.[7] The girl walked by the boys and one turned to the other and said, "Man, is she built." The then-seventy-two-year-old pastor apparently agreed, describing the girl in a way that made women's skin crawl: "She wasn't more than about sixteen but [clears throat] let me just say [pauses with a smirk] she was nice." The mother of one of the boys whipped around and chastised her son for his disrespect of the girl. But Patterson steps in with a swift rebuke: "Ma'am, leave him alone. He is just being biblical." According to Patterson, it's not right to tell boys to not objectify women; disrespecting women is biblical. No Atticus Finch here.

CHECK-IN: What messages did you hear as a teenager about boys and men and lust? How did that make you feel about the opposite sex? How did it make you feel about your own?

Noticing Is Not Lusting

Perhaps the reason this "every man's battle" phenomenon became so dominant is actually a definitional problem. Too often, it seems to us, books that talk about lust equate noticing a woman is beautiful with lusting after her. But is noticing actually lusting?

When commenting on lust, we often pull out this Bible passage: "You have heard that it was said, 'YOU SHALL NOT COMMIT ADULTERY'; but I say to you that everyone who looks at a woman with lust for her has already committed adultery with her in his heart" (Matt. 5:27–28 AMP).

Let's dissect this passage for a moment. It does not say that everyone who *sees* a woman has committed adultery. It says that a man who *looks* at a woman *with lust* has committed adultery. Seeing is not wrong. You can't help but see if your eyes are open. Looking, on the other hand, is a deliberate action. But looking, in and of itself, is *also* not wrong. It's looking at her for your sexual gratification that crosses the line.

It is not that he *sees.*

It is not even that he *looks.*

It is that he looks *with a specific purpose*—to ogle her and fantasize about her.

That means that sexual attraction is not lust. It is possible to notice that someone is very good looking and then do absolutely nothing else with that information. We believe that the temptation to lust can feel insurmountable because we conflate it with attraction. This makes men and boys hypervigilant, trying not to

Figure 5.1
Fear-Based Model of Arousal and Lust

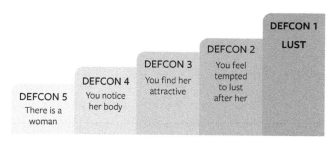

even see. It's like the pink elephant phenomenon. As soon as you tell someone, "Don't think of pink elephants!" what's the first thing they do? They think of pink elephants.

On average, men respond more to visual sexual stimuli than women do, yes (although we'll soon look at how women are very visually sensitive as well!). But too many people have misrepresented what the psychological research says. It is one thing to say, for most men, sexual arousal results primarily from visual stimulation, and quite another to say, for all men, lustful thoughts will happen unless he avoids any visual stimulation. Psychological research definitely says the former. Yet whole doctrines (and books!) have been written on lust and modesty assuming the latter.

Reading these books, we are given a picture of how seeing a woman leads to lust that looks like figure 5.1. Seeing a woman, noticing her body, being attracted to her, lusting after her—they're presented as steps that inevitably follow after one another. Like a moving sidewalk at an airport, it's difficult to get off that sidewalk once you're on it. And you really, really don't want to get to the end. The only way to exit the moving sidewalk is to avoid her completely by bouncing your eyes, neutralizing the threat.

We propose that it looks more like figure 5.2. The route to lust is not straightforward, and there are many, many chances to avoid lust that don't need to lead to stress. It is possible to notice a woman is beautiful, and even to feel a flash of attraction, and then to think nothing more of it and go on about your day.

Frankly, this hypervigilance is stressing out a lot of men who are simply trying to be good guys. The first chapter of *Through a Man's Eyes* explains the battle that men face on a daily basis with sexual stimuli all around them: trying not to look at billboards on the drive to work, trying to bounce their eyes from the barista's chest, worrying that a female coworker in a tight blouse might sit directly across from them. In the book, we read that "Jack breathes a sigh of relief" when a coworker's skirt doesn't ride up too high, and "the next few hours are tough" because another attractive coworker is in his line of sight.[8]

My (Sheila's) husband works in an almost all-female setting (he's a pediatrician; his colleagues are female, the nurses tend to be female, and the parents bringing in the kids tend to be female). Did he experience this level of stress all day? After reading that

Figure 5.2

Our Alternative Model of Arousal and Lust

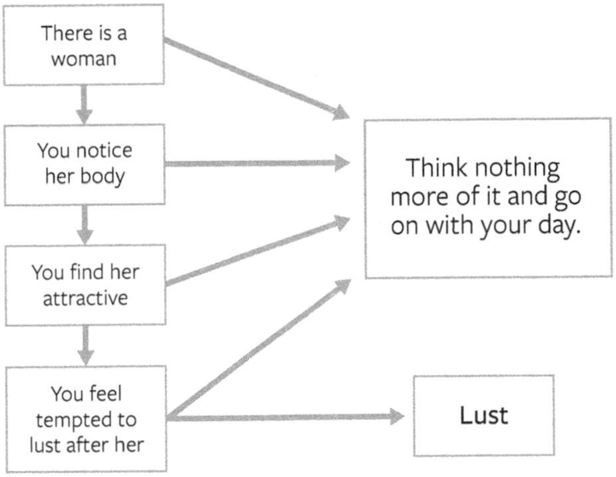

83

chapter, I asked him. He laughed. I asked again. He made another joke. I got rather perturbed that he wasn't taking me seriously.

"Wait," he said, "you're saying that there are guys who are stressed to go to work because they might lust? That's crazy." But could I believe my husband? The book told me all men struggle with this, but they don't know how to explain it or are afraid to confess their struggle to their wives.[9]

What if the way we're talking about lust makes these problems seem bigger than they otherwise would be? That's what Chris, a male commenter on my blog, found.

> As someone who grew up in the Every Man's Battle / purity movement era, I've been working on resetting my brain for a few years now. So many years of struggling daily to just avoid looking. The Bible says His burden is easy and His yoke is light, but spending every part of every day spending energy to make sure I didn't look at an attractive woman is the opposite of easy and light.
>
> I was forced to confront my wrong thinking while on a vacation in Europe. The first day on a topless beach in Spain was excruciating. I was giving myself a migraine constantly bouncing my eyes but having nowhere to bounce them to. I was definitely not enjoying the beautiful beach nor enjoying time with my beautiful wife.
>
> Near the end of the first day I realized this was no way to live. I remembered your writing about focusing on the whole person without making them into a sexual object.
>
> I talked to my wife and explained all this to her. . . . With some fear and apprehension, I looked up at a beach full of [breasts] and started to talk through the process of not making them there for my sexual gratification. The rest of the trip was so relaxing and enjoyable, and I had such a good time with my wife on the beach. Since then, I can see an attractive woman and not become aroused.

CHECK-IN: Has the overly broad definition of *lust* made your life difficult? Would it make a difference in your life to see noticing and lusting as two different things? How?

Chris experienced freedom from a lifelong struggle simply by rejecting the lie that he could not help but lust. But what if it's not only men who are hurt by this teaching?

Does Hearing about Men's "Struggles" Help Women?

The authors of books about lust state that they write these books to help women understand the struggles men go through.[10] But our research shows that reading these books doesn't help marriages or women's sex lives; it actually harms them. We found that women who agree that all men lust have lower marital and

Figure 5.3

Women Report Worse Sex If They Believe Lust Is a Universal, Constant Battle for Men

What happens to women's sex lives when they agree that "all men struggle with lust; it is every man's battle"?

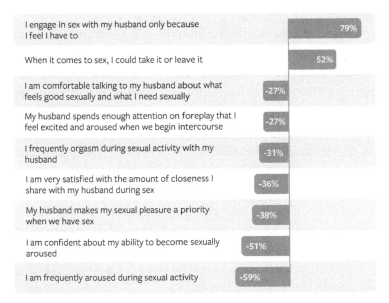

I engage in sex with my husband only because I feel I have to	79%
When it comes to sex, I could take it or leave it	52%
I am comfortable talking to my husband about what feels good sexually and what I need sexually	-27%
My husband spends enough attention on foreplay that I feel excited and aroused when we begin intercourse	-27%
I frequently orgasm during sexual activity with my husband	-31%
I am very satisfied with the amount of closeness I share with my husband during sex	-36%
My husband makes my sexual pleasure a priority when we have sex	-38%
I am confident about my ability to become sexually aroused	-51%
I am frequently aroused during sexual activity	-59%

Figure 5.4

Women Are Less Happy in Marriage If They Believe Lust Is a Universal, Constant Battle for Men

What happens to women's marital satisfaction when they agree that "all men struggle with lust; it is every man's battle"?

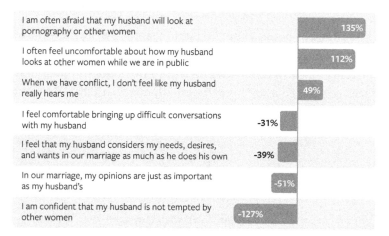

sexual satisfaction than those who do not. They are 79% more likely to have sex out of a sense of obligation and 59% less likely to be frequently aroused during sex.[11] In fact, believing this message as a high school student means that when a woman gets married, she is 43% more likely to be mistrusting of her husband, afraid that he will look at pornography or other women.[12]

Let that sink in: *girls are told this in high school.* If a girl met her man at college, he never stood a chance! She had been taught that no man is able to be faithful in his thought life *before she even met the man she would marry.* She was told that the Atticus Finch she dreamed of was a mirage. And then what happens when a woman who has been taught from her teenage years that men cannot be trusted marries a man who truly *can* be trusted? Here's how one male commenter describes it:

I had great relationships with girls all through my teen years that didn't involve lust. The problem started once I got married. My wife thought that seeing was lusting and she couldn't be convinced otherwise. Eventually I just gave in and tried not to see. Looking back I can see the incredible damage this did not just to me but to our family. I can't tell you the number of couples that we weren't allowed to be friends with because she thought the woman was attractive (didn't matter if I did or not). Our family did not go to the beach or swimming or to waterparks because of the possibility of there being a woman there that might be immodestly dressed. I remember one time at church after singing a song, she was glaring at me, and I was like, "What?" She later told me that I had looked at one of the worship team members who was attractive. I couldn't even figure out which one I was supposedly looking at. I lived in constant fear of her deciding that I might be lusting after someone.

So now imagine a marriage in which a woman has nothing to worry about because her husband is a noble man, like the couple above, *and* she doesn't believe the "all men lust" message. Surely that marriage must be safe from the negative effects of this teaching, right?

Nope. Turns out that even if a woman says she disagrees with the message that all men lust, if she is being taught that message, *it still has an effect.* When a woman believes the every man's battle message, she is 127% less likely to be confident that her husband is not tempted by other women. What if she doesn't believe it but is still being taught it? She's still 64% less likely. Could this be because the husband actually *isn't* a noble man? Again, nope. The trends stayed stable even for marriages in which she did not believe he struggled with porn. When we are repeatedly told by our churches and the Christian media we consume that we can't trust our husbands, even if our husbands are trustworthy, that plants seeds of doubt.

CHECK-IN: Women, when you were in high school, what messages did you hear about whether every man lusts? How did this affect your view of men? How did this affect your view of your husband?

We Haven't Just Normalized Lust; We've Normalized Predation

Not only have the books we've talked about normalized lust; some have also confused lusting with true predation, horrifying their female readers.[13] Read this excerpt that *Every Man's Battle* portrays as something normal men deal with:

> Maybe it's true that when you and a woman reach a door simultaneously, you wait to let her go first, but not out of honor. You want to follow her up the stairs and look her over. Maybe you've driven your rental car to the parking lot of a local gym between appointments, watching scantily clad women bouncing in and out, fantasizing and lusting—even masturbating—in the car.[14]

Reading this causes a strange flashback to *Sesame Street* days: "One of these things is not like the other." Staring at a woman's behind and masturbating in a car in a gym parking lot are very different. The latter is not just abnormal; it is illegal in many jurisdictions. And so is masturbating in the open to the sight of your sister-in-law sleeping mere feet away from you—another anecdote given in *Every Man's Battle*.[15] To treat these things like common male behavior, as if public masturbation is widespread, does such a disservice to men.

That's what hurt Erik, who commented on my *Every Man's Battle* thread on Twitter: "I can't say loud enough how much this book specifically made me believe that I was going to grow up to be a monster. Like it was fate, rooted in my biology. Because even at their best, these authors still think men are muzzled monsters. It took a long time to see the lie."[16]

CHECK-IN: Men, do you believe that you are inherently marred in terms of sexual purity simply by being male? If so, how has that affected you?

It's not hard to understand why Erik thought he was going to be a monster or why our survey takers named *Every Man's Battle* as one of the most harmful resources for their marriage.[17] And the weird thing is that the authors of books about male lust admitted *in their very books* that women were hurt by their message!

- "Men seem like untrustworthy pigs whose minds and thoughts just go wherever they want," [Brenda] commented. "Is nothing sacred to them? As women, do we trust men after reading this? . . . I feel that if anything ever happened to Fred, I'd never remarry because I would have very little trust in men."—the wife of an author responds after reading her husband's words in *Every Man's Battle*[18]
- "Several [women] told us, 'I'm never going to be able to trust my husband again, now that I know how visual he is,' and more than a few devastated husbands have told us that their wives stopped being intimate with them altogether once they learned the truth about how men are wired."—*Through a Man's Eyes*[19]

Yet how do these authors respond? *Women just need to understand men.* In the lust discussion in *Love & Respect*, Emerson Eggerichs says that part of respecting your husband is accepting this struggle as part of his manhood. "If your husband feels you do not respect his struggle, his desire for you, *and his maleness,* he'll pull back from you."[20] Sounds threatening, doesn't it?

Maybe the fact that women feel so upset by this "every man struggles with lust" message isn't because women simply need to understand men better; maybe it's because women are being asked to accept something that reflects the kingdom of darkness rather than Christ. Maybe women can't accept being seen as objects and do not feel safe in a society that does not treat them as human beings—*and maybe women are right to feel that way.*

Does Scripture Present Lust as Every Man's Battle?

Let's take a step back and ask, Does Scripture talk about lust the way these books do? According to the Bible, once we are indwelled with the Holy Spirit, we should expect that lust will be defeated. Paul tells us in Colossians 3:5, "Put to death, therefore, whatever belongs to your earthly nature: sexual immorality, impurity, lust, evil desires and greed, which is idolatry." We're not to fight a perpetual battle; *we're to win the battle.* Sexual sin can feel like a thick chain that ties us down, but we are called to put lust to death and live in freedom—and we can!

It is perfectly reasonable for a woman to expect her husband to live out his wedding vows. She isn't being selfish. She isn't failing to understand what it is to be a guy. She is standing on biblical principles! And we are so, so sorry that the Christian community has made women think men are animals who can't help themselves and made men think they are sinning simply for seeing.[21]

The "all men struggle with lust" message has taught us to trade trust for fear in our marriages, so it shouldn't be surprising when sex doesn't work. Jesus told us to look at the fruit to judge the tree, and the fruit of this tree is nasty. Wives are made paranoid because they are told they can't trust the man they married, the good man who loves them. These books unjustly paint husbands as sex addicts and pathological liars, while normalizing ogling women. If this is the fruit, why have we kept the tree?

Respect: The Missing Piece of the Lust Puzzle

What these books emphasize is the protection of men's purity. But what if the real problem with lust is not that it taints the man but that it objectifies and dehumanizes those whom Christ values and calls precious?

Much of the solution to the lust problem as advocated in *Every Man's Battle* views women through the lust lens rather than through a kingdom lens. Women are the threat to men's purity. "Bouncing your eyes" tells men to ask the question, *Is this woman dangerous to me?* A more biblical question to ask is, *Am I being respectful to this person as an image bearer of Christ?*

But what does being respectful mean? In *Through a Man's Eyes*, Jack is portrayed as being respectful by "wrenching his head away" and turning his chair away from Abbie, his attractive coworker who is so distracting to him.[22] If he can avoid looking at her, then he can stop lusting after her, and thus he will honor his wife and Abbie. But if I were in Abbie's shoes, I would not feel honored and respected if someone turned their chair away from me. I would feel objectified and erased.

One woman told us this story:

> When I was almost college age, I had been working out with a coach to prepare for college sports. I was not dressed immodestly for the activity. I was wearing regular shorts, a sleeveless shirt, and a sports bra. Some kids I went to school with and a father walked into the gym, and the coach introduced me. The father wanted to know if I would work with his daughter to improve her skills. When I introduced myself, he shook my hand very briefly and wouldn't look at me. He talked to everyone around me but wouldn't look at me even though I was the reason that he was there. I was embarrassed and confused. I excused myself and apparently the father made a comment trying to laugh off his behavior that he was a devout Christian with a lust problem. I was so embarrassed. It made me feel horrible. I hadn't done anything wrong. His response made me feel dirty.

Another told us this one:

> I was on a Christian-based tour, and my sister and I got into the elevator with two other couples from the group. We said hi and smiled; we didn't know the couples, but we did know one thing. The men were both pastors. So it was a bit more pointed when each of them offered up a short, formal "hello" before physically turning their heads and refusing to look at me.
>
> No eye contact. Barely an acknowledgment.
>
> I was wearing a floor length sleeveless jumpsuit with a square neckline. Not tight, not low-cut. But I don't think it would have mattered either way. I wasn't a person, a human, a woman, a sister in that elevator. I was a potential stumbling block, an object. I was a walking, talking collection of tempting body parts.
>
> I was the enemy.
>
> It was dehumanization at its finest.

Not being able to look at a woman treats women like threats rather than people. And what do you do with threats? You neutralize them. When dealing with alcoholism, you dump the booze down the sink and stay away from places with booze. Well, many people treat lust like it's alcoholism—just get rid of the women! Or at least tell them to cover up. But even if every single woman in church dresses like the Amish, the rest of society won't.[23] Besides, you can't live your life avoiding women, nor should you. A woman who runs an anti-sex-trafficking organization summed it up to us this way: "The irony is that by equating attraction with lust, we've boiled women down to their bodies, whether a man is avoiding her completely or lusting about her."

Defeating lust is not about limiting a man's encounters with women; it's about empowering men to treat the women around them as whole people, daughters of Christ. The key to defeating lust is not to avoid looking at women; it's to *actually see them*. That's what this commenter's husband instinctively understood—perhaps because he didn't grow up in the church:

My husband became a Christian in his 20s. His exposure to church prior to this was extremely limited. I get a special kick out of explaining Christian-ese to him sometimes! ("Every man's battle" was one of the phrases that needed explaining. I asked him if he knew what it meant, and he said, "Sin? Everyone struggles against sin.") He has only recently become aware of the lust issue within the church, and he has been appalled. Most of his friends have generally been women—he even had a best woman instead of a best man at our wedding—and most of them are quite attractive. But even as a non-Christian he told me he didn't lust after them. It was far too disrespectful.

It is crazy to him—and me—that even as a non-Christian he could control himself, but the church treats this as an insurmountable obstacle for men who are indwelled with the Holy Spirit! He has told me that the easiest way not to disrespect women is to view them as people. If a non-Christian could figure that out, what is giving the church so much trouble?

But there's still more baggage from the lust conversation to unpack.

How Men Can Fight Lust

The key to fighting lust is to see women as whole people rather than potential threats.

1. When you are passing by a woman, instead of bouncing your eyes, look her in the eye, give a quick, friendly nod, and turn away.

2. When you are with a woman, look her in the eye, and engage her in conversation. Ask her opinion about different topics.

3. Don't live a sex-segregated life. Join groups where women are in leadership roles or where women's opinions are considered.

4. Identify women in your life from whom you can learn, whether it's advice about work, parenting, finances, etc. Make it a practice to consult women as well as men when you are making a decision.

How We Gave Women Body Image Issues

My (Sheila's) youngest daughter, Katie, hit puberty rather early. One Sunday morning, when she was barely eleven, her Sunday school teacher took her aside and told her that she'd have to start watching what she wore and avoid V-necks, because she didn't want the men in the church to lust after her. Katie was afraid to go to church for weeks, completely grossed out that adult men would be staring at her chest.

I (Rebecca) grew up reading Focus on the Family's *Brio* magazine, where I first remember hearing that pants were only modest if I could pinch an inch of fabric over my thighs. But I had big thighs and a bubble butt with a small waist, so I simply could not find pants that fit me that were not tight around my thighs or hips. My curves made it impossible to dress according to some people's modesty standards without going back a few centuries. My *body* became the problem. And *Brio* reinforced this idea that my body was dangerous with messages like these: "If a guy sees a girl walking around in tight clothes, a miniskirt or short shorts, you might as well hang a noose around the neck of his spiritual life."[24] If a guy so much as *sees* a girl in tight clothes—not *looks* with lust, but merely *sees*—his spiritual life will be dead. Twelve- and thirteen-year-old me, along with millions of other millennials, got the message loud and clear: *My body is so dangerous that it can kill boys' spiritual lives.*

But it's not just boys that we endanger. In her article "A Letter to Our Teenage Daughters about How They Dress," Shaunti Feldhahn warns girls about their effect on men: "When that guy sees you—this attractive girl who is drawing attention to her figure (even though you may not think of it that way)—a part of his brain called the *nucleus accumbens* is automatically stimulated. Instantly, even the most honorable guy is instinctively tempted to want to visually take in. . . . EVEN the dads who are there."[25]

Rethinking the Rebelution's Modesty Survey

In 2007, the Rebelution website conducted a survey of guys, asking what they thought about modesty—a survey that was widely publicized and reported in Focus on the Family's *Brio* magazine. And yet today, Shaney Irene, a moderator of the Rebelution, says, "If you ask me what I think of the Survey, I'll tell you I regret having been a part of it." She explains,

> Perhaps the biggest and most disturbing problem is that we gave a platform to guys just because, well, they were guys. We had no way of knowing whether the respondents had a healthy understanding of their own sexuality, knew the difference between attraction and lust, truly respected women, etc. . . . Many guys admitted to losing respect for girls who didn't live up to their ideas of modesty, feeling "disgusted" or "angered" by these same girls. . . . The word "cause" in relation to guys' lust also made a frequent appearance. This is the same attitude that says victims of sexual assault and harassment who wear "immodest" clothing are "asking for it."[26]

Let that sink in: teenagers are told that their friends' fathers will struggle to not lust after them. We put the responsibility for adult men's sins on the shoulders of *children*. Perhaps instead of telling eleven-year-olds to cover up, pastors should be giving messages on the evils of pedophilia and ephebophilia (sexual attraction to pubescent children). In following what Jesus taught us when discussing lust, let's put the responsibility back on whom it belongs: the one who has the eye causing him to stumble.

I (Sheila) was once debating women's modesty on a popular Christian radio show. I was arguing that we should stop framing modesty around modesty rules, and we should simply teach women to respect themselves in the way they dress.[27] While I was on that program, a caller relayed a disturbing story. She admitted that she had always been a large woman, and one day at church, a beautiful woman walked by. Discouraged, she prayed, "God, why couldn't you have made me that beautiful?" And then she said that God told her, "Be grateful that you don't look like her, because she causes many men to sin."

I firmly believe that was not God's voice. God does not blame women for causing men to sin simply *by existing*. Is it any wonder that so many women grow up with body image issues that make sex so difficult?

CHECK-IN: Wives, did the lust message affect how you felt about your body growing up? Does it affect you now?

Equating Lust with Maleness Makes Women Who Are Visually Stimulated Feel Like Freaks

But this gets even more complicated when it's a woman who struggles with lust. Because this is every *man's* battle, she can feel like a freak—and feel ashamed of her sexuality.

The evangelical world tends to assume that men's and women's sexual responses are polar opposites. Women just don't get turned on the way dudes do. But while men and women may, *on average*, respond differently to visual stimuli,[28] that doesn't mean that *every* man responds more than *every* woman.

Here's an example: we all know that men are, on average, taller than women. But my (Sheila's) great-grandmother was 5'11", and her husband was only 5'6", and scientists didn't knock at their door trying to understand how this could possibly be. No, we understand that the average height for each gender does not dictate how tall an individual will be. We know this so intrinsically that we don't say "all men are tall and all women are short," or "tallness is a biblically masculine trait because that's how God designed it." No, we understand that some men are short and some women are tall—even if on the whole men tend to be taller than women.

Pretty much every gender difference that exists on a spectrum shows a similar pattern: it's not that men are one way and women are the other; there tends to be a lot of overlap.

This is how we need to talk about visual stimulation too. The average man may be more stimulated than the average woman, but that says nothing about the individual.[29] When we talk about men being *this* way sexually and women being *that* way sexually, then we're generalizing and often missing the bigger picture. As one of my blog commenters explained,

> I'm definitely a woman, and I definitely notice men. All the time. Everywhere. 100% physical attraction, total strangers, know nothing about them and never will. Trust me, we women absolutely look—I mean, I fight not to look twice, so to speak, but we look. I am hardly the only woman I know to be wired this way. It really frustrates me when people perpetuate the misconception of "Women aren't visual," because it's utterly false, widens the understanding gulf between the sexes, and then, to add insult to injury, shames and silences women for perfectly normal impulses.

Men and women, if you're battling lust, remember that we all battle something. And the fact that you're actually battling instead of giving in is admirable! But men, please know that this is not every man's battle, and women, please know you are not a freak if you struggle. This is a battle that can be defeated—that you can win. And noticing is not lusting! The more you're able to see each other as whole people and the less you try to avoid the opposite sex because you view them as dangerous, the more victory you will have.

And for the rest of the women reading, please hear us: you were never meant to feel as if you're in competition for your husband's eyes with every woman out there. You were never meant to feel as if your body itself is dangerous and evil. You were meant to be valued for who you are. You are precious, you were made by our Creator, and you deserve to be respected. Let's expect no less from each other.

EXPLORE TOGETHER: "I Only Have Eyes for You!"

Show your spouse that they are the only object of your affection. Take turns doing the following exercise:

1. Pick five things that you find sexy about your spouse (it's okay if one or two aren't physical—maybe you get turned on by your spouse's voice or by their job), but at least three must be physical.

2. Share the five things with your spouse. As you share each one, spend a few minutes paying special attention to that body part or telling your spouse what is so sexy about what you like.

Build your spouse's confidence so they never have to wonder, "Am I enough for you?"

RESCUING AND REFRAMING

- Instead of saying, "All men struggle with lust; it is every man's battle," say, "Lust is a battle many people struggle with. In Christ, we are no longer slaves to sin but to the Spirit. When the Son sets you free, you will be free indeed."

- Instead of saying, "Don't dress in a way that could be a stumbling block for your brothers in Christ," say, "You have a responsibility to treat others with respect regardless of what they wear. Take every thought captive to Christ— you cannot be forced to sin by another's clothing. Sin is a choice."

- Instead of saying, "Men are visually stimulated," say, "People are visually stimulated, some more than others, and often but not always, men to a greater degree. But being visually stimulated does not mean you are doomed to lust."

- Instead of saying, "Bounce your eyes to ensure you never become tempted by women around you," say, "Treat and respect women as whole people made in the image of God."

CHAPTER 6

Your Spouse Is Not Your Methadone

It is God's will that you should be sanctified: that you should avoid sexual immorality; that each of you should learn to control your own body in a way that is holy and honorable, not in passionate lust like the pagans, who do not know God; and that in this matter no one should wrong or take advantage of a brother or sister.

1 Thessalonians 4:3-6

Rick can't remember a time before he had seen porn. As a young boy he'd been mesmerized by the magazines hidden around his uncle's house. When he was first married, he only used porn a few times a month, whenever he needed to relieve some stress. But once his wife was pregnant, he found that porn helped him to not pester her. Lately he's found it easier to turn to porn than it is to try to have sex with his always exhausted wife. Every few months she catches him, and he promises to change, but the truth is that life is easier this way. He doesn't find sex with his wife exciting anymore, and it's becoming more difficult to keep an erection going.

It wasn't until leaving for college, and feeling alone and over-whelmed, that Sam first stumbled onto porn. Living in that secret world while going to a Christian university was guilt-inducing but also somewhat exhilarating. Sam yearned for sex to be exciting like that one day. When Sam married, though, sex didn't cut it. Without pulling up the images from porn, climax was elusive. Often Sam climbs out of bed at night to turn to porn to relieve the day's frustration, but also to make it easier to sleep.

One thing may surprise you about Sam. Sam is not short for Samuel. It's short for Samantha.[1]

Pornography is changing our world and the nature of our relationships. Instead of saying "I love you," the message of porn is "I want to use you." Porn trains your mind and body to get aroused and have an orgasm through pairing masturbation with sexually graphic, and often violent, images. And, of course, the porn industry is the biggest driver of sex trafficking.[2] Porn has devastating effects on the user and their marriage, but it also hurts the people in porn itself.[3] The sin is not only against your marriage.

> CHECK-IN: How old were you when you first saw porn (if you have)? Did it affect how you saw sex? Did it affect how you saw yourself?

How Big a Problem Is Porn?

While the rate of porn use has been increasing for men in the general population over the last thirty years, for Christian men under forty who ascribe to biblical literalism, the rate has been remarkably steady. Approximately 40% of these men report having viewed porn in the last year, compared with 60% of the general population.[4] Our study found that 29% of Christian women believe their husbands use porn, which is understandably an underestimation because we couldn't ask the men themselves.

101

And what about women porn users? In our survey, 13% of women who are married or have been married report ever using pornography, and 3.7% report using it regularly or in intermittent binges.

Porn in and of itself certainly steals great sex from couples. But what if the way we're handling porn use is actually making things worse? Wives of male porn addicts have been told, "Give him sex so he won't be tempted!" And women porn users? They've been overlooked entirely. Both of these responses have hurt our sex lives. Let's look at them one by one.

Women Porn Users Are Not Unicorns

In all the Christian books we studied, we didn't find one that mentioned porn use by women.[5] The only resource we read that discussed female porn use was *The Seven Principles for Making Marriage Work* by John Gottman, whose work is not specific to a particular religious group. What happens when women porn users are left out of the Christian conversation?

Audrey Assad—whose hymn collection, *Inheritance*, got me (Joanna) through both my infertility journey and my miscarriage—has been open about her experience with pornography and the deep sense of shame she felt as a female evangelical porn user:

The first time I heard about [porn] in a church setting, it was a Sunday school that focused mainly on men, their biology and potential weaknesses. It warned that all serial killers interviewed on the subject were addicted to hardcore porn. You can imagine how that made me feel as a 15-year-old female pornography addict, and I can tell you with certainty how it did not make me feel. It did not make me feel safe or welcome to speak out loud what I was struggling with in private. I only felt shame and a deep, growing reticence to ever inform anyone of my addiction because I felt certain that I was a freak and not "feminine" enough.[6]

102

Considering this lack of information when it comes to female porn use, it's no wonder conservative Protestant women are less likely than their male counterparts to turn to pastors or counselors for help with their porn struggle.[7] Jessica Harris, the founder of Beggar's Daughter, an online ministry for women struggling with porn addiction, recounts this experience she had as a young adult:

> When I was a freshman in college, a female Christian speaker came to our campus. She talked about pornography, obviously addressing the guys. . . . When I got back to my dorm room, I wrote her a letter, telling her my struggle and asking for help. I handed that to her that night at a special "girls night."
>
> On one hand, it felt good for somebody to "know" but at the same time that didn't feel like enough. I wanted her to not only know but also know how to fix me.
>
> A few days later, I got a letter in the mail. It was from her—typed—and said, "Sorry, there's nothing out there for girls like you. Here's this book for guys. Only read chapter 10; the rest probably won't help." And that was it.
>
> I felt so . . . deflated. Sure, somebody knew, and while it might have felt good to "confess" it, in the end, I was left feeling more ashamed than when she didn't know.[8]

But women are not only bearing the shame and responsibility of their own porn use—apparently, they're also to blame for men's.

How Should We Talk about Men and Porn?

On the November 5, 2019, *Focus on the Family* broadcast, one of the hosts said of pornography, "I think one of the reasons men are getting into trouble in this area is that that need [for sex] is not being met."[9] We found this attitude one of the most prevalent throughout the many books and articles we analyzed. The blame for men's porn use is laid at the women's feet. The victim in this scenario—the wife whose husband has been using porn—has now become the perpetrator. How did that happen?

In Focus on the Family's article "Sex Is a Spiritual Need," wives are told, "If you're married, your husband depends on you to be his partner in his battle against sexual temptation."[10] Using logic quite typical of many Christian books and articles about porn and marriage, the author explains how sex is a man's main defense against tremendous temptation. If he doesn't get enough, he will eventually succumb to porn, even though he doesn't want to and even though he'd prefer sex with his wife. And then, in the conclusion, the author gives the caveat that while you're not responsible for his sin, you need to realize he's going to sin unless you give him sex. "Don't be motivated out of fear that he will act out if you don't meet his needs; rather be motivated out of love and a desire to share his spiritual journey with him."[11]

This is similar to the way Kevin Leman, in *Sheet Music*, portrays a porn-affected marriage:

> The most difficult time for this man was during his wife's period, because she was unavailable to him sexually. After about ten years, she finally realized that pleasing her husband with oral sex or a simple "hand job" did wonders to help her husband through that difficult time. She realized that faithfulness is a two-person job. That doesn't mean a husband can escape the blame for using pornography by pointing to an uncooperative wife—we all make our own choices—but a wife can make it much easier for her husband to maintain a pure mind.[12]

Though he gives the caveat that the husband is ultimately to blame, what is the main message a wife hears? If she doesn't service him, even while on her period, he will watch porn. Authors can couch it however they want, but women hear the underlying threat.[13]

How is this supposed to make women excited about sex? Spoiler alert: it doesn't. Women who believe *before* they are married that frequent sex prevents porn use are 37% more likely when they *are* married to have sex only because they feel they must and 38% less likely to be happy with the amount of emotional closeness they share with their husbands during sex.[14]

> CHECK-IN: Were you taught before you were married that sex in marriage will prevent porn use? Do any of the findings in figure 6.1 or 6.2 resonate particularly with you?

And yet books and articles keep repeating this message as if they're using the same playbook. *Love & Respect* explicitly says, "The cold, hard truth is that men are often lured into affairs because they are sexually deprived at home,"[15] and then shares a cheating husband's insight: "I don't blame her for [my] immorality, but she doesn't own up to anything. I'm not blaming her, but she is not blameless."[16] Men are portrayed like sex zombies who need to be kept sedated by giving them enough sex so they don't find themselves unable to say no to temptation.

Figure 6.1

Women Report Worse Sex If They Believe They Must Have Sex with Their Husbands to Keep Them from Watching Pornography

What happens to women's sex lives when they agree that "women should have frequent sex with their husbands to keep them from watching porn"?

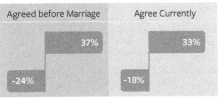

	Agreed before Marriage	Agree Currently
I engage in sex with my husband only because I feel I have to	37%	33%
I am frequently aroused during sexual activity	-24%	-18%

In the opening of *Sheet Music*, Kevin Leman shares Brenda and Mark's story. They're growing apart because Brenda is busy with the kids and ignores her husband's attempts at romance, and so Mark starts masturbating two or three times a week to porn because he is "tired of being reluctantly accommodated and never pursued."[17] How does Leman frame this problem? "What Brenda didn't realize was how much this sexual winter was costing them as a couple, and how, if they didn't turn things around, they'd probably be divorced within another five years."[18] Leman doesn't include anything about what Mark has failed to realize. It is all about Brenda's responsibility for fixing her husband's porn use and the sexual distance between them.

In a similar vein, *Every Man's Battle* tells wives, "When men aren't getting regular sexual release, their eyes are more difficult to control. Help him out in this battle. *Give him release.*"[19] Instead of seeing sex as a holistic experience that is passionate, pure, and personal, sex becomes about meeting his quota for climaxes.

Figure 6.2

Women Are Less Happy in Marriage If They Believe They Must Have Sex in Order to Keep Their Husbands from Watching Pornography

What happens to women's marital satisfaction when they agree that "women should have frequent sex with their husbands to keep them from watching porn"?

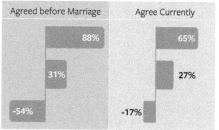

	Agreed before Marriage	Agree Currently
I am often afraid that my husband will look at pornography or other women	88%	65%
I often feel uncomfortable about how my husband looks at other women while we are in public	31%	27%
I am confident that my husband is not tempted by other women	-54%	-17%

When we originally wrote about this on our blog, we were trying to convey, with as much shock value as possible, how wrong this message was. So I (Rebecca) came up with the best analogy I could: "Women cannot be the methadone treatment to a husband's porn addiction." We thought that was so in your face, so terrible, that people may see how degrading the idea was.

And then we read the Every Man series and learned that Rebecca was not the first to come up with the methadone analogy. The authors actually say, "Your wife can be a methadone-like fix when your temperature is rising."[20] And to women, they advise, "Once he tells you he's going cold turkey, be like a merciful vial of methadone for him."[21]

Instead of realizing this explanation would destroy a woman's spirit, the authors promote it as a selling feature of sex! There is no depiction of God's design for sex as an ultimate, personal knowing of each other rather than just intercourse during which she feels like a receptacle. It is just accepted that men can't experience sex the way God intended.[22] Do we honestly believe that men are somehow less able to understand God's design for sex simply because they're male? That is such a low view of men. Yet this is how it's portrayed: men's use of porn and temptation by porn is accepted, a given. And because of that, the solution can't lie at his feet. It must lie at hers.

> CHECK-IN: Have you heard the message that men's porn use is her fault? How does that make you feel about sex? About yourself? About your spouse?

Porn Can Wreck a Man's Libido—and His Sexual Performance

Telling women "Just have sex so he won't watch porn" is doubly hurtful to women married to porn-addicted husbands who are turning to masturbation and porn *instead* of to their wives.

Many women live in sexless marriages because the husband prefers pornography. Or he's used porn so much for so long that he suffers from erectile dysfunction, premature ejaculation, or delayed ejaculation, all of which increase with porn use. Without the stimulation of pornography and masturbation, many men are unable to maintain an erection or reach climax.[23] Other men have so trained their bodies to react to sexual stimulation quickly that they have no ability to last very long.

And yet the Christian resources we reviewed rarely mention this in conjunction with porn. Perhaps it is because they were written before the research on this was conducted—large-scale studies on porn use and erectile dysfunction did not appear until after 2006, when porn sites and high-speed internet became more widespread.[24] Many bestselling evangelical books, then, have passed their best-before date because they were written too long ago. Listen to these letters from women for whom the "simply have more sex" solution feels like a slap in the face:

- "I lie here beside my husband, who yet again tonight has turned me down. Tonight it was that 'his back hurt.' We are both in our late 30s and have been married for four years. In the beginning sex was wonderful. We couldn't get enough of each other! And then almost overnight, he stopped wanting to have sex and started making every excuse under the sun. He has had many issues with porn. He promises me now that he isn't looking at it anymore, but with the past issues we've had, I don't believe him."

- "We got married four months ago. He's been watching porn since we were dating, but I didn't know. We sometimes go more than a week without sex, and sometimes he can't get hard enough to keep going. It hurts me to know he watches porn. He says that he enjoys seeing naked bodies and he gets turned on and masturbating is easier than having sex."

- "When we first got together five years ago we had amazing sex . . . all the time. About seven months ago he started traveling a lot with work. I've noticed that more and more he is having difficulty keeping his erection and getting aroused. I know he has watched porn while he's been gone. He has not been to the doctor yet but repeatedly said just being with me makes him happy . . . like he's already given up on sex."

We need to have a better response to porn addiction than simply "Do more in the sack."

> CHECK-IN: Has porn use affected your sex life together? If you use porn or erotica, does your spouse know the extent of it?

How the Church's Teaching on Porn Can Affect a Couple

Let's follow the marriage of Jared and Melissa, a composite of so many couples we've heard from. As is the case for many millennials, the prevalence of internet porn when Jared was growing up meant that by the time he got married, he had already been using porn for twelve years.[25]

When he's getting married, Jared believes, "Finally, I'll be able to get over this because surely sex is going to make it so much easier to quit." And during the honeymoon stage, his struggle indeed subsides. But all too soon what was new and exciting starts to become routine. They stop having sex as frequently. She gets pregnant. He starts taking on more responsibilities at work. They spend less time together.

He finds himself alone late at night while his wife sleeps. In his boredom and the stress of everyday life, he reverts back to what has been his habit for most of his life. He immediately feels ashamed,

109

but that quickly turns to defensive anger. Jared finds that on days when he has sex, he doesn't feel the need to look at porn as much, and soon the days when they don't have sex begin to feel like Melissa is personally attacking him. She has the key to his struggle and refuses to give it to him. She doesn't even need to have sex—a simple hand job will do.[26] But Melissa doesn't seem to care.

At the same time, Jared's men's group starts going through *Every Man's Battle*. He hears that wives need to have sex with their husbands so their husbands don't succumb to temptation. Jared feels seen and understood. "See?" he says to Melissa. "We need to have more sex because I want to be faithful to you. You can't possibly understand my struggle because you're a woman. Why can't you just do this for me?"

Melissa feels like she's been punched in the gut. She's pregnant, working full-time, keeping house, and she's still not enough for him? Now, every time they have sex, all she can picture is her husband watching porn. Sex is fast, quick, and to the point. Even when he wants to try something for her, she can't stomach it because she wonders if he learned it from porn.

Eventually Melissa's had enough. She hates sex, and she is in despair. Her dream of a loving, faithful marriage has been destroyed. She realizes the only people who will ever really love her are her kids, and she now turns to them with her attention. Hurt and fed up, she tells Jared, "Just take care of yourself, then," since she feels he's simply been masturbating into her for the last decade anyway.[27]

Jared doesn't want that, so he brings it up to his pastor that his wife told him to masturbate instead of having sex. The pastor berates her. "Don't you know sex is a gift from God in your marriage?"

Melissa hears the words, but they don't penetrate. She has been reduced to a physical receptacle for Jared to orgasm into in order to keep him from temptation. If that's what sex is, she's not having any of it. Jared has systematically destroyed his wife's libido by allowing his porn addiction to infiltrate his marriage, all in the attempt to keep it out of it.

We doubt that Jared and Melissa's experience is what those writing the books and articles intended. But this is what we have heard over and over from both men and women. This is what we saw in our surveys. This is the result of telling women, "Without sex, he'll watch porn," and telling men, "You need her to be your methadone." How would Jared and Melissa's story have been different if, instead of expecting Melissa to cure his problem, Jared took responsibility himself? You don't build a great sex life by telling a woman that unless she becomes wholly available to her husband in such a vulnerable way, he will betray her by turning to pornography.

Women who get married believing they need to have sex with their husbands to help prevent their porn use are 19% more likely to experience significant sexual pain unrelated to childbirth.[28] Women who believe now that frequent sex will prevent porn use are 18% more likely to report being disinterested in sex, 37% more likely to have sex out of a sense of obligation, 24% less likely to orgasm reliably during sex, and 24% less likely to be confident they will be aroused during sex.[29] They are, however, 42% more likely to have sex at least twice a week.[30] If sex is worse for her, then why is she doing it more often? Because we have threatened her if she doesn't.

Does the Bible Say We Cure Porn with an Active Sex Life?

Is the biblical solution to porn use an active sex life? After all, that's what 1 Corinthians 7:3–5 seems to imply. But just three chapters later, Paul writes, "No temptation has overtaken you except what is common to mankind. And God is faithful; he will not let you be tempted beyond what you can bear. But when you are tempted,

WIVES WHOSE HUSBANDS USE PORN FREQUENTLY are more likely to feel personally responsible for his porn use.

Women who are often afraid their husbands will look at porn or other women are 88% more likely to agree that women should have frequent sex with their husbands to keep them from watching porn than other Christian women.[31]

And what about women who know their husbands are using porn? They are 37% more likely to agree that women should have frequent sex to prevent porn use than women who don't believe their husbands are using porn.[32]

he will also provide a way out so that you can endure it" (1 Cor. 10:13). We posit that 1 Corinthians 7 is more about sharing in one another's burdens to help each other deal with *normal* temptations of life, not placate each other's addiction. You cannot free someone from their sin—that was Jesus's job on the cross, not yours in the bedroom.

Additionally, Paul is adamant in 1 Thessalonians 4:3–5 that a basic Christian responsibility is for each person to deal with their own sexual sin. "It is God's will that you should be sanctified: that you should avoid sexual immorality; that each of you should learn to control your own body in a way that is holy and honorable, not in passionate lust like the pagans, who do not know God."

Let us repeat that: "*that each of you should learn to control your own body in a way that is holy and honorable.*" Not because your wife takes away the temptation but because you are living in the power of the Spirit! The idea that men need sex or they will watch porn is in direct opposition to how the Bible portrays sexual immorality and temptation. We are called to be holy and renewed—not to remain addicted but placated by having enough intercourse.

The Wrong Route to Porn Recovery

So how do we defeat sexual immorality? Most of the books we surveyed follow the *Every Man's Battle* approach: pray more and get right with God. But when it comes to practical action steps in the bedroom, their solution is to transfer all your sexual energy onto your wife. By doing this, men's libidos for their wives will apparently skyrocket. Fred, one of the authors of *Every Man's Battle*, explains it like this:

> This newfound hunger will shock her. She has been accustomed to providing you five bowls a week, primarily through physical foreplay and sexual intercourse. . . . Suddenly you need an extra five bowls from her. For no apparent reason, you come calling for intercourse twice as often.[33]

Then, in an astonishing lack of insight into women, the book tells husbands, "This is vaguely pleasant to her."[34] Nothing in the book, though, talks about seeing sex as something intimate that is done for her benefit and pleasure as well as his. In fact, in the entire book, *her pleasure is never mentioned*. The only reason given for having sex is to relieve his sexual temptation.

What was his wife's perspective after Fred started wanting sex more often? We hear about it in *Every Heart Restored* when Brenda explains: "Practically overnight he couldn't keep his hands off me, forever squeezing me or patting my behind. It didn't matter if I was frying burgers, sorting clothes, or drying my hair after a shower."[35] (We should note that many women report that a major pet peeve is their husbands' "pawing" at them at inopportune times.)

What these books fail to express is that a wife cannot placate her husband's sexual desires if those desires have been distorted by pornography. In 2014, actress Jennifer Lawrence's cloud accounts were hacked, and nude pictures of her were released online. Explaining why she had these pictures, Lawrence said, "Either your boyfriend is going to look at porn or he's going to look at you."[36]

In response, Gabe Deem, a former porn user, wrote in *Cosmopolitan* that Lawrence had it all wrong. "If you try to compete with porn, you will lose every time."[37] The allure of porn is that it's always new and different; no real-life woman can be perpetually new and different.

Marcy, one of our respondents, felt responsible for keeping her husband from using porn, and it turned out disastrously. She explains,

> I thought the only way to "help" him was to give him sex however he wanted, as often as he wanted. He works away weeks at a time, and sending him photos and videos became something he wanted constantly. Whenever I did, he would always want more. Finally I realized (after much heartbreak) that no matter what I did, I couldn't be the reason why he did or did not choose to use porn. I was still feeding his unhealthy addiction. He was essentially using me the same as porn, but we both felt a bit better about it since it was "legal"—aka between just us.
>
> After realizing this, I went through a deep depression. He pulled away from me since I was no longer providing him the pictures that he wanted. I never refused sex just to refuse, but if it wasn't working for me, I would ask him for help to get going. He would get mad and just stop and pout for weeks on end. Even though he hasn't used porn for 6 months, we are still really struggling to find a healthy normal.

Marcy was allowing her husband to redirect his sexual cravings on to her (and was even acting out whatever fantasies he asked), yet this did not result in a healthy marriage or a healthy sex life. He became increasingly selfish and dismissive of her legitimate needs, and she became an object to him to the point that asking for her own pleasure turned him off.

You can't defeat porn by simply having a husband transfer his lust and objectification to a "safe" source—his wife. You defeat porn by rejecting the kingdom of darkness view of sex, that it is only about taking and using someone to meet your needs, and adopting a kingdom of heaven view of sex: that it's about a mutual, passionate knowing and sacrificial serving. God never meant for women to be men's sexual methadone. Gary Thomas agrees. "Addressing this spiritual element of sex is crucial in helping men experience deliverance from sexual addiction. When sex is reduced to pleasure alone, no wife can possibly meet a husband's expectations."[38]

Emotional damage can be done if you constantly feel betrayed and used without any hope that it can be better. This makes passages like this one from *Every Heart Restored* gut-wrenching: "On the battlefield of broken sexual trust, your husband must become trustworthy and you must eventually choose to trust again. . . . *It's self-defeating to worry about which should come first.*"[39] He has broken trust—but she is "self-defeating" if she requires him to be trustworthy before she actually trusts him again. She must have sex with him, even if he is making no move toward building a healthy sex life.

Just as you can't cure an alcoholic by giving him so many sedatives that he won't want to go to a bar, you can't cure a porn addict by giving him so much sex that he won't want to log on to the computer. Even if it does lead to less porn use, the issue is not healed—it's only been numbed.

God doesn't want to *numb* us. God wants to *free* us.

What Should Recovery Look Like?

Thankfully, despite this teaching, huge numbers of marriages have been freed from porn addictions. But this has happened mainly when the responsibility for the porn use is put squarely back where it belongs: at the feet of the porn user. Karen shared her story:

> A friend showed my husband online porn when he was 14. He was hooked, and struggled secretly for years.

On our wedding night, I was prepared for the typical virgin male problem—finishing way too soon. It was the opposite. He could not orgasm. For almost 16 years of marriage, sex lasted foreeeeever. This is not actually a good thing. I dreaded sex more and more every time. I had no idea what was actually wrong, and he was in denial.

Not that long ago, one of our elders mentioned porn during his sermon. It was like lightning had struck my husband. He'd always known it was wrong, but he was convicted that he needed to come clean with me, with our pastor, and take concrete steps to stop. The fact that he confessed voluntarily without excuses went a long way toward healing. He did everything I asked of him. He meets with the elder every week. We have become much more intentional about talking to each other. I ask difficult questions I'm not sure I want answered, and he answers them, and it gets a little easier every time. Even now, when I become suspicious, he doesn't become angry. He accepts that this is the consequence of lying for so long. He has not gone back to it since.

I believe 100% that his repentance is real. My heart breaks for that 14-year-old boy who never had a chance to learn about sex and sexuality in a healthy way, for how miserably his parents failed him. Yes, he chose to sin and continue sinning, but it is, in my opinion, much different from men who embrace porn as a great thing that wives need to get over, or who only confess when they're caught. His entire personality has changed for the better as well. He's become less intensely introverted; he does hard things without being nagged; he spends time with the kids, and not just because he knows he has to. Our sex life is much, much different now. I'm still getting over the knee-jerk dread reaction, and he is still somewhat plagued by anxiety, but we have a lot more fun now. I'm sad for all the wasted time, but I'm so grateful that God convicted him of his sin and has worked such a change in him.

The messages women hear about men and porn, though, can make it difficult to accept repentant husbands. Anne told us in an interview that early in her marriage, she read *For Women Only*'s take on men's lust and was appalled. She couldn't get the anecdotes out of her mind. He might fantasize later about the hot waitress who served them on their date night? How could she even go out of the house with him ever again? She thought, "If I had known that men were that weak, I never would have gotten married—the risk of being hurt was too high."

Anne was relieved when the author of that book conceded that a small number of men didn't find this an issue. Anne thought, "Well, that's my guy—I got one of the good ones."

After medical issues led to the couple not being able to have sex for a year, Anne's husband confessed to her that he had watched porn a few isolated times. Everything came crashing down. When he made a mistake, Anne jumped to the conclusion that he *wasn't* one of the good ones after all. And if he wasn't good, then he must be as bad as the rest.

The books she read made men sound so insatiable that she believed men were either perfect or perverted—there was no room for a nuanced conversation about sexual sin and temptation. But Anne's breakthrough came when she was simultaneously able to name the sinfulness of her husband's actions while putting them in perspective. He completely owned up to his actions, and they did not need to define his entire character. Even though he was not perfect, he was repentant, and he was still a good man.

After working on our blog for over a decade and hearing thousands of stories of marriages impacted by porn, we have found that two things are needed for recovery: owning your sexual sin without justifying it and taking practical steps to make withstanding the temptation easier. If someone is not justifying their sin, and they're not being controlled by it, then healing is not only possible but probable, as Anne and her husband found, and as many others have found too.

If, however, porn users are continuing to excuse their behavior, either by downplaying its importance or placing the blame on someone else, or if they are being controlled by the sin and are taking no measurable steps to purge it from their life, then the couple needs outside intervention and help. More sex won't cut it.

The problem with porn is not just that it is sinful but that when it sucks us in, it changes how we see sex. Porn is not relational, mutual, or loving—it is degrading, violent, and purely carnal. Our concern is that many Christian books, in their efforts to free couples of sexual sin, reinforce pornography's view of sex by encouraging men to use their wives' bodies without consideration for their hearts. When people fully reject pornography and all it stands for, like Karen's and Anne's husbands did, they can defeat it. But when they try to defeat it just by having more sex, they're fighting the losing "every man's battle."

EXPLORE TOGETHER:
Kick Intruders out of Your Marriage Bed

One of the problems with porn or erotica use is that it pairs sexual arousal and response with external stimuli rather than with your spouse. People often then dissociate by fantasizing or pulling up images in their minds to become aroused when they're with their spouse. If this is an issue in your marriage, here are some tips:

1. Spend time touching and engaging in foreplay while naked to reinforce the erotic feeling of being naked together.
2. Talk during sex. Keep the focus on your spouse.
3. Use your spouse's name. Keep it personal.
4. If you find yourself pulling up images in your mind, stop and ask yourself, *What feels good right now? What do I want my spouse to touch?* Bring your mind back to what is happening.

5. Give the struggling spouse permission to stop in the middle of sex if they are unable to stop fantasizing or dissociating. Go back to kissing and touching before starting again, or simply take a rain check and do something non-sexual together.

RESCUING AND REFRAMING

- Instead of saying, "The reason men watch porn is because they're not getting enough sex at home," say, "It is not your spouse's responsibility to keep you away from pornography."
- Instead of saying, "The cold, hard truth is that men are often lured into affairs because they are sexually deprived at home,"[40] say, "You have a responsibility to stay faithful to your spouse regardless of what is happening in the marriage. If there are big problems in your marriage, seek help. Stay faithful."
- Instead of saying, "Watching porn is a sin," say, "Watching porn is a sin because it contributes to the abuse of others and reduces them to objects to be used."
- Instead of saying to teenage boys, "You are going to be tempted by pornography," say to both genders, "Many people struggle with pornography temptations, but many do not. If you do struggle, know that it is a struggle you can overcome."

Sex should be *prioritized*: Both partners in the relationship desire sex, even if at different levels, and both partners understand that sex is a vital part of a healthy marriage.

CHAPTER 7

I Want You to Want Me

Strengthen me with raisins,
refresh me with apples,
for I am faint with love.
His left arm is under my head,
and his right arm embraces me.
Song of Songs 2:5-6

In the parenting world, French parents reign when it comes to raising adventurous eaters. French children, on the whole, are simply not the picky eaters that American children are.[1] Out of a desperation to ditch the hot dogs, North American parents have been trying to figure out what magic elixir French parents use to convince kids that vegetables are appetizing.

The key seems to be that French parents do not consider some foods children's foods that kids will like and some foods adult foods that kids won't like. French parents just see food as food. They don't expect that kids won't like broccoli; they expect that kids will like broccoli! And lo and behold, French kids like broccoli a lot more than American kids do.

If you want your children to like broccoli, and you expect that they will like broccoli, then you tell your kids that broccoli is yummy. You don't feed it to them saying, "You probably won't like this, but try just three bites. Then Mommy will let you have a yummy hot dog."

Self-fulfilling prophecy is a thing.

What if the Christian world portrays sex for women like American parents portray broccoli to their kids? Take this example from *Love & Respect*, for instance, when the author is counseling a woman to have sex for her husband's sake. He asks her, "Who is supposed to be the mature one here? He is a new believer and you've been in Christ for many years," and the book concludes the story by saying, "She decided to minister to her husband sexually, not because she particularly wanted to, but because she wanted to do it as unto Jesus Christ. She just didn't have that need for sex."[2] *Every Heart Restored* summarizes it this way: "Wives don't experience sexuality like men do."[3]

What happens when women keep hearing the message *"Your sexuality isn't like his, and you just don't have that need for sex"*? Maybe we shouldn't be surprised when some women see sex like American kids see broccoli—hardly very appealing.

What's the Truth about Libido?

Let's look at what the data actually says about libido. At first glance, it does seem that men have a higher felt need for sex than women do. In our survey, 25.4% of women report they only have intercourse because they feel they have to. Most women (58.5%) have lower libidos than their husbands,[4] and 40.8% report that they could take or leave sex. This leaves many husbands high and dry, lonely, and wondering, *Does she even want me at all?*

That's why I (Sheila) feel that most of my job on my blog is being a cheerleader—"Come on, ladies! You can do it! If God made sex to be this amazing, you don't want to miss out on it!" Rebecca and I even created our Boost Your Libido course because it was such a common problem. Women want to want sex, but their libido doesn't seem to get with the program.

Could part of the problem be that we don't actually understand what libido is? Watch any TV show or movie, and the plot when it comes to sex is always the same: The couple is together, and they're panting. So they start to kiss, they take off their clothes, and they end up in bed. That's basically it, right? They pant, and then they kiss, and then the clothes come off, and then they're in bed.

Pant. Kiss. Clothes. Bed.

That's what we think libido looks like.

But what if that's not the way libido works for many people?

Some people have a felt need for sex that leaves them feeling physically frustrated if they don't have sex. That's what we call *spontaneous* libido. But some people have more of a *responsive* libido. Once they begin making love, arousal kicks in. In our follow-up survey, we found that among women who are reliably aroused by the time sex is over, 29.1% were aroused when they started, but 70.9% weren't yet aroused but knew they would get there. If libido is simply the ability to desire and enjoy sex, then just because you're not aroused first does not mean you don't have a libido; it just means yours may work differently from your spouse's.[5]

Having a responsive libido is not the same thing as not being a sexual person. People with responsive libidos still have libidos! If you get to the point where you are panting, whether it's before you start or after, then your body likes sex. In fact, when we ran the numbers, women who said they are already sexually aroused before sex starts and those who said they aren't aroused before sex but know they'll get there answered similarly when we asked them how they felt *after* sex.[6]

Figure 7.1

How Does Arousal Level during Sex Affect How Married Christian Women Feel after Sex?

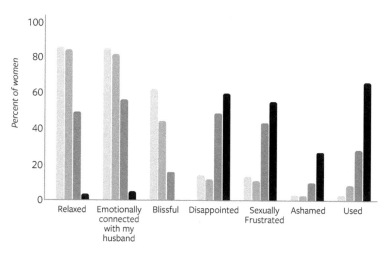

Women were asked, "Before sex, I feel . . ."

- already sexually aroused
- not yet sexually aroused but I know I will get there when we're having sex
- not yet sexually aroused and I am unsure as to whether or not I will get aroused during sex
- not aroused and I know I will not become aroused during sex

Arousal makes sex better, whether women start out aroused or become aroused later.

The contrast between spontaneous and responsive libidos shows that there are many different "normals" when it comes to sexual desire. You aren't made wrong if your libido manifests differently than your spouse's. But what often happens is that those with responsive libidos say to themselves, *I'll initiate sex when I begin to pant.* So they wait to pant. And nothing really happens, so they figure, "not tonight" and go stream a few more episodes of *Law & Order.* But if they had just jumped in, they likely would have started panting. We don't have to operate like the pant-kiss-clothes-bed scenario. It's okay if one of you is like that and the other is more kiss-clothes-bed-pant, or even bed-kiss-clothes-pant. As long as you're both panting at some point, and you're both enjoying yourselves, that's perfectly healthy sex.

> CHECK-IN: Do you think you have a responsive libido, or a spontaneous libido? What about your spouse?

We Think Too Much about Libido in Gendered Terms

Have you ever heard it said that men are like microwaves, and women are like slow cookers? I think it's supposed to mean that men heat up fast (I sure hope it doesn't mean they're done fast), while women take longer to heat up, but once they do, they're nice and tender or something.

What it's really implying is that men have spontaneous libidos, and women have responsive libidos. But again, these are all *trends*. They're not hard-and-fast rules. In few areas of Christian sexuality-teaching is gender essentialism as obvious as it is when it comes to libido. But it simply isn't true that all men want sex and all women don't. Some men act more like slow cookers, and some women act more like microwaves. Our survey found that 41.5% of marriages do not have wives with lower libidos than their husbands, with 19.2% of women reporting higher libidos than their husbands and 22.3% reporting equal libidos. Yes, it's a minority, but it's not a small one.[7] Maybe we'd do better to cut the microwave–slow cooker stereotypes and understand that there's a wide variation.[8]

> CHECK-IN: Right now, who has the higher libido in your marriage? Have there been times when it's been switched? Or the same?

Do Only Women Crave Emotional Connection?

This "men are one way and women are the other" mentality goes beyond how we talk about libido to shape how we talk about relationships in general. *Love & Respect* says, "He needs sexual release just as you need emotional release."[9] *The Act of Marriage* says, "His need for romantic love is either nonexistent or minimal. But he is married to a creature with an extraordinary need for romance."[10] Apparently women want romance and emotional connection, while men want sex.

The truth, however, is far murkier.

Two of us, Sheila and Rebecca, are married to men who are far more romantic than we are. Rebecca may rewatch *Sense and Sensibility* every year for her birthday, but it's her rock-climbing, black-belt husband who puts on music and invites her to waltz in the kitchen.

To assume that men aren't romantic does a disservice to men. And to assume men don't need emotional connection does a disservice to everyone. If one person prefers to drink a glass of water before they have dinner, and the other prefers water after they eat a few bites, we wouldn't say that one has a need for water and one has a need for food. The Christian marriage classic *His Needs, Her Needs* says that the "first thing she can't do without" is affection, and the "first thing he can't do without" is sex.[11] But the author then goes on to talk about sex as if it's only for men, and affection as if it's only for women, reinforcing the libido gap and convincing women with responsive libidos that they're not sexual. Further, it frames men as not needing relationship but only sex. If men don't need relationship, then we must ask if they want a wife at all.

It is not healthy to downplay women's libidos and men's need for relationship if we want marriages to thrive. Sure, many women may report that they have low libidos, and many men report that they have high ones. But if libido for women is largely determined by how we think about sex, then how does reinforcing this "men want sex but women don't" message help marriages?

CHECK-IN: Do you crave romance and emotional connection? Is this need being fulfilled? How can you increase this in your marriage?

What Happens When We Assume She Doesn't Really Want Sex?

On his *Desiring God* podcast, John Piper answered a question about a marriage in which the wife didn't seem to want sex:

> I am married to a gracious woman who will gladly oblige me if I ask her, but I find that though I do need sex, I do not desire it when I know she obliges without any sexual desire for me. If I sense she is getting no enjoyment out of the act, it makes it feel utterly disgusting to me. What advice do you have for me?

We read that question and think, *Way to go! The husband wants a mutual, passionate sex life—hopefully he can help his wife want this too!* But in his response, Piper doesn't even present mutual passion as an option. He quotes 1 Corinthians 7:3–5, noting that both should be acceding to the spouse's desires. How does he say this plays out in a marriage in which one spouse wants sex and one doesn't?

> She will want to honor him by giving him what he desires. And he will want to honor her by giving her what she desires, which may be less of his desire. To the wife: Don't say "yes" to your husband's desire tonight by complying, and then in a half a dozen ways communicating: "I wish I weren't here." You don't have to have the same kind of pleasure to make him feel loved. If you are not enjoying the actual physical realities of touch and sexual union . . . take joy in the fact that you can give him pleasure. . . . To [the husband]: Don't assume the worst about her. Assume that, even without sexual desires, she has other good desires to please you, and that is a kind of love that you can receive and enjoy.[12]

Piper's response is very typical within the evangelical world when addressing libido differences. It's assumed that she won't enjoy sex, so increasing her pleasure isn't even presented as an option. His solution is the husband gets less of what he wants, and the wife gets to do less of what she doesn't want, which, quite frankly, sounds kind of depressing.

Libido exists on a spectrum, and a couple will occupy two points of that spectrum. One will be higher, one will be lower, or the two will overlap. On the extreme ends of that spectrum, we cross over into dysfunction: at some point libido becomes so high that we have sex addiction issues, or so low that it disappears into hypoactive sexual desire disorder, often combined with anorgasmia (see fig. 7.2).

Unfortunately, much Christian teaching treats women who are lower on the spectrum than their husbands as if they are already past that cutoff point, even if they're not.

This mentality toward lower-drive wives can also make men feel incredibly guilty for desiring sex. One man left this comment on our blog:

> As a husband, I have never initiated because I felt that the way to be the most polite and caring for my wife is to never bother her with sex. I now intellectually believe this idea to be wrong, and I believe her when she tells me that it is wrong. But after more than a

Figure 7.2

The Libido Spectrum

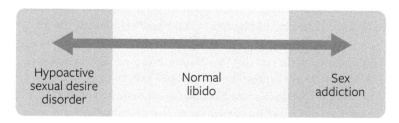

128

year of working on it, I still can't remove the hardwired emotional gut feeling that as an understanding, caring, loving husband, the best thing I can do for my wife is to never want sex.

CHECK-IN: In your marriage, have you felt that your spouse has an abnormal libido—like there's something wrong with them? Do you think that's actually true, or is it just a normal difference in felt need?

What If Your Libidos Aren't Stereotypical?

Treating libido differences in such stereotypically stark ways can kill women's libidos and make men feel guilty. But it can also hurt those whose libidos don't fit the stereotypes, as this high-drive wife explains in a comment on my blog:

> I recently got married, and have been dealing with a lot of unexpected anger. As I emotionally and mentally prepared myself for marriage, I was worried that I wouldn't want sex as much (since I'm the woman), and I'd have to prepare myself to have sex at times when I didn't feel like it. That's what I heard in most of Christian marriage advice. Both my husband and I assumed he would want sex more. We were wrong. I could easily have sex 4–5 times per week. He is interested in sex maybe 1–2 times per week. My husband doesn't watch porn or masturbate. He enjoys having sex when we have it, but doesn't seem to miss it too much when we don't. I don't feel satisfied at all. I feel lonely, isolated, and angry. I don't know if it's my imagination, but I feel like a chasm is growing between us. He's the man, so I feel like he should be initiating and wanting sex more. I know this isn't necessarily true, but I just don't know how to not feel angry and trapped in a constant feeling of dissatisfaction and hunger for sexual connection with my husband.

This isn't abnormal and there is nothing wrong. He's not channeling sexual energy elsewhere; she doesn't have some sex addiction problem. This is a simple communication challenge, but it feels so much bigger because failed expectations loom over the conversation. Could this woman handle her feelings of frustration more easily if she didn't expect his desire to overwhelm her? Would she feel as disappointed and helpless if she had grown up hearing "You may have differing libidos, and that's okay"? Perhaps if that had been the message, she'd see libido differences as an opportunity to grow in love and kindness to one another rather than as something unfairly stolen from her.[13]

But of course, many higher-drive men and women are not married to spouses who want a reasonable but lower amount of sex. Many are married to spouses with almost no sex drive at all, and we will be discussing that further in the next chapter.

Libido for the Masses

The evangelical culture has defined the problem of libido differences as "He wants sex and she doesn't." We know that this both oversimplifies and reinforces the problem, but then what is evangelicalism's prescribed solution to libido differences? *Simply honor the seventy-two-hour cycle.* By ensuring couples are having sex every seventy-two hours, we can all rest easy knowing that everyone is doing their duty and receiving their dues.

When we were reviewing Christian sex and marriage books, we found this seventy-two-hour rule peppered throughout almost all of them, like this: "A normal and healthy man has a semen build-up every 48 to 72 hours that produces a pressure that needs to be released."[14] And there was this advice from *Every Man's Battle*:

> In relation to your own husband, understanding the seventy-two-hour cycle can help you keep him satisfied. Ellen said, "His purity is extremely important to me, so I try to meet his needs so that he goes out each day with his cup full. During the earlier years, with much energy going into childcare and with my monthly cycle, it

was a lot more difficult for me to do that. There weren't too many "ideal times" when everything was just right. But that's life, and I did it anyway.[15]

We've heard the seventy-two-hour rule in marriage conferences, in blogs—everywhere! And many couples try to follow this. When Janet married Chris, she went into her honeymoon confident that she knew how to keep him happy. Every three days, on the dot, she'd get naked and get busy because that was how she was supposed to satisfy her unquenchable man. But after a few months, she realized she was the only one initiating and started to feel miffed: "What, am I not attractive enough or something?" So she confronted Chris and asked, "Why don't you ever initiate?" Perplexed, he said, "Well, I've just been trying to keep up with you."

As they discussed it, they each realized they had incorrectly assumed the other had the higher libido. In fact, both were quite happy with sex once or twice a week (and for them, less-frequent sex actually led to better quality because it allowed desire to build). Chris originally thought this was funny until he realized that part of his wife's motivation to initiate was out of a fear that if she didn't, he would be vulnerable to sexual sin. He assured his wife that he was fine, and they could just go with what felt right.

Charlotte recounted an almost identical story. After initiating every seventy-two hours for almost twenty years, her husband was horrified to learn that the reason for this frequency was so that Charlotte could help keep him from sin.

What is the source of this seventy-two-hour rule? We spent some time searching and finally located it in *Every Man's Battle*, which sent us back to a book that James Dobson wrote in 1977—*What Wives Wish Their Husbands Knew About Women*.

> For most men, this buildup to heightened sexual desire takes only about seventy-two hours. "Many women," Dr. Dobson notes,

"stand in amazement at how regularly their husbands desire sexual intercourse."[16]

But on what was Dobson basing this statement? We scoured medical and scientific journals but couldn't find anything that proved men got sexually frustrated at hour seventy-three. The closest we could find were studies on how men's sperm replenishes usually within seventy-two hours, but none of them mentioned male discomfort. Though some men's testes may get a little testy after seventy-two hours, we have no proof that this is the case for all or even most men.[17] In fact, studies on masturbation habits show that preferred length of time between emissions may be more of a cultural difference than a biological one.[18] So how did this seventy-two-hour rule become gospel? It seems like Dobson set a timeline, and then everyone followed suit.

Obviously some men experience sexual frustration, as do some women. No one is arguing against that. But what matters is not what *some* men or *some* women may feel; what matters is what *you* and *your spouse* feel. Couples have different life situations, libidos, levels of emotional connection, and more. All of that should be factored into what your sex life should look like, rather than an arbitrary rule set in 1977.

Kay's story starts out just like Janet's and Charlotte's stories. Had sex every seventy-two hours, told husband why, husband was appalled, they decided to go with what felt right instead. But what Kay and her husband laugh about now is that as Kay has spent the last two years trying to get in touch with her own sexuality and rediscover sexual pleasure, they've ended up settling into the seventy-two-hour routine naturally. The difference, however, is that now it doesn't feel like a duty or a burden. Rather, it has become a part of the rhythm of their marriage where a missed encounter here or there is not a reason for fear. That distinction makes all the difference.

CHECK-IN: In an ideal world, how often would you have sex? How often do you think your spouse would have sex? What do you think would be a healthy frequency for your marriage?

Evangelical culture has used frequency as the measure of marital and sexual satisfaction even though research has found that frequency is not an accurate predictor at all—even for men.[19] Sexual satisfaction and interpersonal dynamics are far superior measures, as our survey also revealed. We found that how often a couple has sex is not directly related to their marital quality. However, women who are more sexually satisfied (who consistently orgasm and feel close during sex) reliably have better marriages.[20] How happy your marriage is reflects the *quality* of your emotional and sexual relationship far more than it does the frequency of intercourse.

Are Libido Differences the Real Problem?

So, what characterizes couples who have figured out the libido piece? *They are mutually satisfied during sex and treat each other well outside the bedroom too.* That's why it's not a surprise that couples who have the same level of libido are overrepresented in the happiest marriage group—not because having the same libido makes people happier, but because the way happy couples negotiate frequency of sex minimizes the issues found in libido-difference conflicts.

After all, what does it actually mean if you have the same libido? Is it that both of you need sex every 87 hours, and you just managed to find your perfect sexual match? We think a better explanation is that for these couples, sex isn't a source of contention, so any libido differences that exist just don't register. If the Netflix movie ends and the couple starts kissing and that leads to

Are We Lowering Women's Libidos with Our Teachings about Sex?

Our survey found that women's libidos could be dampened by exposure to certain teachings. One such teaching was the "every man's battle" mentality discussed in chapters 5 and 6.

Let's make sure we aren't making libido conflicts worse by offering faulty solutions.

Figure 7.3

Who has the higher libido when she believes that lust is every man's battle?

Note: Due to rounding, totals may add to more than 100%.

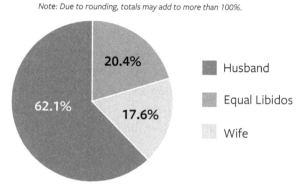

- 20.4%
- 62.1%
- 17.6%
- Husband
- Equal Libidos
- Wife

Figure 7.4

Who has the higher libido when she does not believe that lust is every man's battle?

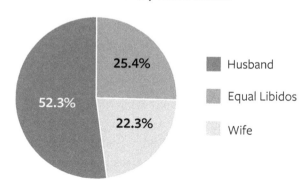

- 25.4%
- 52.3%
- 22.3%
- Husband
- Equal Libidos
- Wife

Women who believe lust is every man's battle are more likely to report having a lower libido than their husbands.

sex, who initiated it? In marriages in which sex is a natural result of the closeness they share, it can be hard to quantify who asks for it more when both of you are eager and willing.

This dynamic explains successful marriages with significant libido differences as well. If mutual serving is the norm, then libido differences do not pose the same threat they do in marriages with less sacrificial giving. In marriages marked by mutual serving, each spouse can delight in meeting the other's needs knowing that their needs will also be met because they can trust each other's goodwill. The lower-drive spouse doesn't feel that more sex is an inconvenience because caring for your spouse is not seen as a hassle. Likewise, the higher-drive spouse doesn't feel resentment when practicing self-control because it's a way to serve and honor the other.

Libido differences become a source of marital strain when there is something else going on below the surface besides one person wanting sex more than the other. In other words, libido differences aren't always about libido. For instance, as our survey shows, women who are not getting anything out of sex are more likely to want it less. Women who infrequently orgasm were 57% more likely to report having the lower libido, and women who infrequently get aroused were 205% more likely to report having the lower libido. The root problem for many women, then, is not that they don't want sex enough; it is that they simply don't have a reason to want it.

But what about the women who can orgasm but still have a low libido? Psychology conceptualizes needs as being in a hierarchy of sorts: physiological needs like food and water are foundational, and love and connection needs come after. In general, if your base needs are not met the others don't register as strongly. That's why a woman in labor doesn't care that her vagina is on full display. If, however, that same woman were to trip in a grocery store and accidentally flash the lady in aisle 9—even if it was her delivery nurse—she would be mortified. If your libido is in hibernation because of an unmet need, merely having more sex is not going to suddenly awaken passion and desire. Dealing with financial strain, teaching the nine-month-old to sleep, getting out of toxic Facebook groups, booking an appointment with a therapist, or becoming more physically active are often more effective at reawakening sexuality than making low-libido spouses feel like they're broken.

Failing to recognize when low libido is a symptom of a larger problem can exacerbate libido conflicts because what the higher-drive spouse needs is not only physical release but also to feel desired. But if sex does nothing for the lower-drive spouse or if life is overwhelming, the lower-drive spouse's desire wanes. The higher-drive spouse becomes more and more desperate to reassure themselves they are desired and so initiates even more frequently, creating a vicious cycle where the higher-drive spouse feels rejected and the lower-drive spouse feels perpetually put upon. Instead of seeing this as a libido problem with a frequency solution—one asks less and the other gives more—we need to see it as a sexual and marital satisfaction problem.

This is why the evangelical church has been focusing on the wrong thing. Perhaps frequency has been used as the main measure of sexual satisfaction because it's easier to tell couples to have more sex than it is to help her reach orgasm or solve underlying marital problems or deal with the stresses of life. But what we've found is that when you work on marital satisfaction, reducing stress, and making sex feel pleasurable and passionate, libido differences usually take care of themselves.

But *usually* doesn't mean *always*. And we turn there next.

EXPLORE TOGETHER: Turn-Ons and Turn-Offs

(for couples not experiencing sexual dysfunction or abuse)

Discovering Turn-Ons

1. Think back to the last two times you can remember really wanting and enjoying sex.

136

- What happened in the hours leading up to that?
- What happened in the day leading up to that?
- Who initiated sex?
- Who took the lead during sex?
- Were there any commonalities? Think about things like
  - How was I physically feeling (sleep, health)?
  - How busy was I, or how much was on my plate?
  - How stressed was I about work, kids, friendships, housework, etc.?
  - What did we do leading up to sex—did we spend time together? Apart? Did I have time to myself over the course of the day?
  - Did we head to bed earlier than usual? Did we initiate out of the blue, or did sex start once we were in bed?
  - Did we have screens on or off that evening leading up to sex?
  - During sex, did we do anything differently? Did we spice things up? Did we concentrate on one person's pleasure more? Did we do more foreplay?

2. Before sharing your answers with your spouse, see if they can answer for you. Then compare. What elements go into a great sexual encounter for you? What about for your spouse? Be as specific as possible.

Understanding Turn-Offs

3. Repeat this exercise for the last two times you had sex without really desiring or enjoying it, when it was a disappointing experience.

4. What elements go into a disappointing sexual encounter for you? Be as specific as possible.

Working with Your Spouse's Libido

5. What can you do to make great sexual encounters more common and disappointing ones less common? What activities leading up to sex get your spouse more in the mood? What kills the mood? What are five concrete action steps you will take to make sex better?

RESCUING AND REFRAMING

- Instead of saying, "Wives don't experience sexuality like men do," say, "Each spouse has sexual needs, even if they look different from their spouse's."
- Instead of saying, "Men want sex," say, "People want sex."
- Instead of saying, "Men have the higher libido," say, "In marriage, one spouse may have the higher libido, and who that is may change throughout the marriage."
- Instead of saying, "Women just don't have that need for sex," say, "If your wife has no libido, let's figure out why."
- Instead of saying, "Have sex every seventy-two hours," say, "You have been entrusted with your spouse's sexuality. Don't take that lightly, and be kind to them."

CHAPTER 8

Becoming More than Roommates

A time to embrace and a time to refrain from embracing.

Ecclesiastes 3:5

To borrow from Tolstoy's *Anna Karenina*, healthy sex lives are all alike; every unhealthy sex life is unhealthy in its own way.[1] Sex can go wrong in so many different ways. That's why we shouldn't think of sex like a thermostat that you crank higher if you want your marriage to be better. Instead, sex is more like a thermometer that measures the state of your marriage.

What if sex just isn't happening? Or what if it's happening, but so rarely it may as well be off the table entirely? Our survey found that 6.9% of marriages are completely sexless, with no sexual contact in the last year. Those marriages are 1.5 times as likely as sexually active marriages to have a husband with a higher libido, so we suspect that these marriages are usually sexless due to her choice, not his.[2] Of the sexually active married couples, 7% have sex rarely or never, and 4.7% only have sex monthly.[3]

Sometimes marriages that are otherwise largely healthy become sexless or sex-starved. In that case, we need to challenge people to put more priority on sex. Sometimes, though, sexless marriages happen because the marriage itself is not healthy—and you can't solve sex without solving the marriage issues first. And then sometimes one spouse is being deprived of sexual satisfaction even though intercourse is happening with regularity. Let's see how these three different scenarios play out.

Scenario 1: The Sexless Marriage Due to Selfishness or Brokenness

When Laziness or Selfishness Reigns

Natasha would rather live without sex. It's not that it doesn't feel good—it does, actually—it's just that she'd rather watch Netflix at the end of the day than have sex. She knows her priorities are off, but frankly she just doesn't have the motivation to change.

After she and her husband come home from work, make dinner, do the dishes, and get their toddler to bed, he wants to spend time together, and she, well, doesn't. She just wants downtime. She loves her husband—that's not the problem. And he's tried everything: taking on more of the housework, giving her multiple nights a week off from childcare entirely, and booking romantic date nights out for the two of them in an effort to help her reengage in the marriage. But nothing seems to work because Natasha is, frankly, struggling with overcoming laziness when it comes to her marriage.

If your spouse has a stronger felt need for sex than you do, choosing not to give it to them because of convenience is incredibly selfish. Once we marry, our only proper way of meeting that sexual drive is with our spouse. Cutting your spouse off or only having sex infrequently despite knowing it hurts your spouse leaves him or her in a terrible situation. It is a rejection on the deepest level. Listen to this comment sent to us by a desperate woman in a sexless marriage:

> He hasn't initiated sex in over two years, and in that time we've only had sex four times, all with no participation on his part; no kissing, no touching, he can't even open his eyes unless they're glued to the Facebook feed on his cell phone. He's told me it's not me, that he's just getting older and it's just a fact of life (he's only mid-forties). I want to encourage him to see his doctor to find out if there is something wrong, but anytime I bring it up, he flies off the handle, tells me I'm being selfish, and tells me it's conversations like this that turn him off. I asked if he could simply check to see if he could switch his cholesterol medication, because I read that some of those can affect libido, and he wouldn't hear of it. He won't quit smoking or change his unhealthy eating habits, either, because he says it's his body and he'll do what he wants with it. I'm at my wit's end.

This man's selfishness is robbing his wife, and it is unacceptable. When someone doesn't have a strong felt need for sexual connection, it can be easy for laziness or selfishness to allow bad habits to squeeze sex out of our lives. But sex is a foundational piece of the marriage relationship; if you are not prioritizing sex at all in your marriage, you are not prioritizing your marriage.

If you are continuously choosing video games, Netflix, or anything else over your spouse and your marriage, your marriage will seriously suffer long-term. If you aren't making your spouse a priority, you are not fulfilling your marital vows. You married a person; your Netflix account, your console, and even your children should not come before your marriage. In fact, what your kids need more than to be in seven extracurriculars is to have a family that is stable, loving, and fun.

However, many spouses withholding sex aren't simply succumbing to laziness; instead, they may be channeling their sexual energy toward pornography. In these marriages, not only is one spouse depriving the other of sex; that spouse is also choosing to get their own needs met while simultaneously neglecting the needs of their partner. Pornography is a rot that needs to be dealt with, even aside from its effects on libido, its impact on mental health, and its implications in the sex trafficking market. Turning to pornography instead of your spouse is selfish, and your spouse has every right to stand up against that and say "enough."

> CHECK-IN: Is there something in particular that you turn to at night instead of your spouse? Why do you choose this over sex? How is this affecting your marriage?

For almost two decades, Raeleen's kids had been her world. She built a beautiful life for her family, homeschooling her six children, volunteering at church, organizing her household. She was fulfilling the call she felt God had put on her life and, overall, she was a happy woman.

But there was one thing missing. She and her husband, Bruce, were drifting further and further apart. Bruce's busy job kept him on the road. When he was home, Raeleen felt he could be more of a hindrance than a help. He was a little bit older than she was, and he didn't get along with the children as well as she did. Sometimes she'd find herself annoyed, like he was breaking up her groove. Their sex life dwindled down to next to nothing. Raeleen rarely orgasmed, and she gave up trying.

One spring weekend, at a wedding of a family friend, Raeleen had an epiphany: she wanted an awesome marriage, she was married to a great man, and there was no reason she should have to continue being bored. So she dedicated herself utterly and completely to reawakening passion in her relationship with Bruce. She encouraged him, calling him during the day and telling him how much she appreciated him. She snuggled while watching movies with him, even if there were a few dirty dishes still on the counter.

And she threw herself into fostering a fun sex life. Sex, which had never been a vital part of their relationship, became one of the defining parts. They shared inside jokes. They laughed and giggled more. They held hands more.

And they conceived a child.

Gavin was born with a serious heart defect, and their world came crashing down as their desperate prayers went up. Bruce, who had never done much of the daily care for the older children, was the perfect dad to Gavin, taking responsibility for his feeding tube and refusing to be absent for any medical treatment.

And then, after Gavin's final surgery at six months of age, Raeleen went to the crib to pick up their son one morning and found him cold.

Over the next few months of grief, Raeleen's saving grace was her marriage. "I needed sex to be able to sleep," she explained. "I'd turn to him every night, and that closeness was the only thing that quieted all the thoughts in my head and let me drift off in peace." They lost the son they loved, but they did not lose each other. Instead, it was their marriage, and even sex, that was a soothing balm for them in the weeks and months afterward.

They would not have experienced that blessing had Raeleen not made the decision years earlier to stop putting her marriage and sex life on the back burner. Sex is a blessing—do not let selfishness or laziness rob you and your spouse of a wonderful marriage.

> CHECK-IN: Are you holding your marriage back by not making it—and sex—a priority? What could your life look like if you put more energy and attention into your spouse?

When Deep-Seated Problems Aren't Being Addressed

Nevertheless, let's not be quick to assume that a spouse withholding sex is always doing so for selfish or sinful reasons. Sexual abuse and subsequent trauma are widespread, and if this is your spouse's story, they need your grace and patience. You have an opportunity to be Jesus's hands and feet in your spouse's healing journey. Do not take that role lightly.

Rachael Denhollander became a household name after her brilliant and impassioned victim impact statement at the trial of Larry Nassar, who sexually abused hundreds of young girls and women. Rachael was the first to publicly come forward, and she was the face of the fight. In her autobiography, *What Is a Girl Worth?*, she recounts the night she disclosed to her then boyfriend (now husband), Jacob, the abuse she had experienced. Here is Jacob's response:

> "You need to know this does not diminish your value. This doesn't make me think less of you. . . . All this does is give me direction for how to best serve and care for you. Honestly . . ." He laughed just a bit. "I've been wondering this whole time what I could possibly bring to the relationship. You are intelligent, kind, accomplished; there's nothing I could add to that. But walking alongside you is something I can do. If God keeps leading us together, I can walk with you through this." He paused one more time. "And that would be a privilege."[4]

If you are a spouse who is struggling with sexual trauma, please know that many have found healing. As Denhollander told us herself, "Working through the abuse together can be a long road, but it is a beautiful, redemptive road. Eventually, associations will be reshaped into the positive memories and experiences, and a safe, secure, tender spouse can bring a depth of healing that seems beyond possible."

Take advantage of the opportunities God has given us through licensed trauma counselors, pelvic floor physiotherapists, and a myriad of other mental health and medical professionals. This is a journey, and sometimes a long one, but take heart that it can be a "beautiful, redemptive road."

But what if a spouse's hesitation toward sex isn't due to trauma but sexual dysfunction issues? Not wanting sex when you're dealing with sexual dysfunction is a perfectly understandable and normal response. But whatever the sexual dysfunction, if it impedes libido and makes sex difficult or impossible, it is incumbent upon that spouse to seek and follow medical treatments. All three of us writing this book have been treated for sexual pain at one time or another, so we are not telling you to do anything we have not done ourselves. Dilators, internal massages, perineal stretches, the works—it's not fun, but it gets the job done.

Our survey also found that male sexual dysfunction, including erectile dysfunction and premature ejaculation, makes a marriage 4.94 times more likely to become sexless.[5] Refusing to treat sexual dysfunction leaves your spouse helpless, as we read in this comment:

> My husband doesn't really care that he can't get an erection. He just shrugs it off as, "Well, I tried, but it just isn't working," and that's good enough for him. His doctor gave him blood pressure medication, and said, "It shouldn't be a problem now," and pushed us out the door. But it's still a problem, and my husband doesn't care. I'm barely forty, and we've been through a lot of stress, including the death of a child. We need this connection. Despite the fact that our sex life has never been fantastic, I'm not ready to be in a sexless marriage.

If your body isn't working as it should, please seek out medical help. To ignore it hurts the both of you. And while your spouse is receiving treatment for sexual dysfunction, use this as an opportunity to show Christlike patience and love toward them. A period of sexlessness while the sexual dysfunction is being treated is not the same as your spouse imposing a sexless marriage on you; "in sickness and in health" includes sexual dysfunction too.

CHECK-IN: Is there something holding back your sex life where professional help is available? Is something stopping you from seeking help? Is something stopping your spouse?

Scenario 2: The Sexless Marriage Due to Emotional Protection

But then there are cases when sexlessness is the natural consequence of an emotionally unhealthy marriage. For instance, one man wrote in to our blog with this:

As a husband, I got more wrong than right. Mismanaged finances, anger outbursts, failure to listen to her. Ugly arguments in spades, overwhelmingly caused by me. She warned me for years this was all taking a toll on her. Several years ago she stopped having sex with me. In hindsight, I view it as the day our marriage ended.

For several years there was 100% zero sexual contact. That period was marked by vicious arguments instigated by me wanting sex. Although she had warned for some time she may do this, it still seemed to me as if she just woke up one day and declared no more sex. She has since told me it was either withdraw physically and emotionally or divorce. My moods/temperament since then have been bad. She told me how she felt like she had to walk on eggshells around me.

Two years ago, after several years of no sex, I began making a concerted effort to improve my disposition. She began allowing me to touch her again. No intercourse, but she would give me an orgasm.

At her request our sex life currently consists of me asking her for sex, and her deciding over the next few days whether she will. Believing our marriage needed something drastic, a few months ago I confessed in vivid detail my failings as her husband. I surrendered my life to her and promised to serve her for the rest of my days. I clean the kitchen after dinner, I give her massages, I bring her her favourite drinks the way she likes them. Serving her makes me feel closer to her.

Things were going well until Saturday when I randomly asked her for sex. It was awkward, and nothing happened. The next day she offered but her body language made it clear it was "let's get it over with so you leave me alone." I said I do not want it like that. I asked her if she got any mental or emotional joy out of giving me an orgasm. Her response: "No." I want to feel intimate and close with my wife again, which, for me, does include an active sex life. When I try to talk to her about it, though, she gets defensive.

Let's think about this scenario. He admits that he scared her repeatedly throughout their marriage, so much so that she felt she had to protect herself. Even though he's trying to "serve" her now, the ways he is serving are all things he should have been doing in the first place, yet he's still upset that she isn't jumping at the chance to give him a hand job.

Many sexless marriages have, at their root, not a selfish refusal on the part of one spouse but rather an attempt at emotional protection. The way sexless marriages have often been framed, though, is that she is withholding sex because she wants to. By not having sex, then, we would assume that she's getting what she wants. Logically, we would thus expect sexless marriages to be filled with unhappy husbands and more-or-less contented wives.

That is not what we found. While only 14.3% of women in sexually active marriages rated their marriages as neutral or unhappy, 63.1% of women in sexless marriages did.[6] When you divide our survey respondents into quintiles (five approximately equal-sized groups) based on happiness, women in sexless marriages are *sixty-two* times more likely to be in the unhappiest group than the happiest group.[7]

Our results suggest that many, if not most, sexless marriages may be the natural result of emotional pain that the couple has caused each other throughout the marriage. Women in sexless marriages were 9.3 times less likely to have felt close to their husbands when they used to have sex. When you have broken trust and caused emotional pain, sometimes for decades, it should not come as a surprise if your spouse doesn't want to have sex with you.

As we have shown throughout this book, our survey found that women struggle to respond sexually when things are not right relationally or situationally. When she loses her libido, maybe it's not that there's necessarily something wrong with *her* but that she's reacting to something in the marriage that's not right. Perhaps we should treat sexlessness more like the canary that stopped singing in the coal mine—it's pointing to a deeper issue.

Do you remember Jared and Melissa, who ended up in a sexless marriage a decade after saying their vows because Jared had seen sex as a way to numb his porn addiction? When sexual sin has been such an active part of a marriage, and she has been used as a "sexual methadone vial"[8] for years, the very foundation of that marriage has been damaged because of the actions of one spouse.

If you've systematically destroyed your marriage over the course of many years, and then your spouse says they're done with sex or they don't know when they'll want to have sex again, that may be a natural consequence of how you have acted. "Do not be deceived: God cannot be mocked. A man reaps what he sows" (Gal. 6:7). This does not mean that the marriage can't be fixed, but it does mean we need to realize that the responsibility for fixing it may not lie at the feet of the spouse who is refusing sex. It may instead lie at the feet of the other who has acted destructively in the marriage, even if they've done so unintentionally. Addressing why the marriage is unhappy, through open communication and often licensed counseling, may be the key to unlocking sex again.

CHECK-IN: Has your marital quality been tanking your sex life? Are there marriage issues you need to address with a counselor?

Scenario 3: The Sexless Marriage in Disguise

Stephanie's husband doesn't believe in foreplay. Sex rarely lasts more than five minutes. Yet Stephanie has a very high sex drive. She's asked her husband to help bring her to orgasm afterward or to try to help her reach orgasm beforehand, but he isn't interested in learning how. He thinks intercourse is all that's important and that Stephanie is making selfish demands. Stephanie finds herself so sexually frustrated after each encounter that she can't sleep. She ends up on the floor of the bathroom, crying, using a vibrator to try to relieve her frustration and wondering what to do. "I've only had two 'happy endings' with him in ten years of marriage," she explains. "It's so hard being left hanging every single time. I'd be so happy with just once a month . . . once a year . . . anything at this point."

Then there's Heidi. She's been married for seven years, works full-time, and has two small children. She ensures she has intercourse regularly with her husband, usually two or three times a week, because she knows she should. She's never felt more than even a little bit aroused. Each time she thinks, *Maybe this time will be different*, but it never is. Sex consists of several minutes of her husband grunting and pawing before he ejaculates, says "You're awesome, babe," rolls over, and falls asleep. She wonders how on earth this is supposed to make her feel loved. Sex is the biggest disappointment of her life.

Neither Heidi nor Stephanie meets the diagnostic criteria for sexless marriages, because at first glance it seems both of them have active sex lives. Both women, though, are experiencing sexual deprivation that is comparable to marriages in which there is no sexual contact at all.

What if we expanded the definition of sexless marriages to include a new category: sexless marriages in disguise? Currently there is no word to describe marriages in which one spouse is orgasming and the other is continuously left feeling sexually frustrated, hurt, and used. From comments, focus groups, emails, and our survey responses, though, it has become clear to us that when one person is being used for another person's pleasure while their well-being and sexual satisfaction are ignored, then they, too, are experiencing the effects of a sexless marriage. To knowingly deprive your spouse of sexual pleasure while using them to achieve your own is to treat your spouse as a masturbatory aid.

Are we saying that all marriages in which the wife doesn't orgasm 100% of the time are sexless? Of course not! Many husbands make sex a satisfying, fulfilling, and intimate experience, even if their wives find orgasm elusive. Charlotte, for example, took twenty-five years to figure out the orgasm piece but always enjoyed the emotional and physical closeness that sex brought. Her husband was so affectionate that sex was never one-sided, even if he was the only one orgasming.

The problem arises when a woman in a marriage desperately wants to experience that closeness and sexual release but is continuously deprived of these because, frankly, he doesn't care that intercourse isn't satisfying for her, or he doesn't realize it should be any different. In our survey, 6.9% of women report that they are in completely sexless marriages. However, a similar number, 5.9%, are in sexually active marriages in which they (1) almost never or never orgasm, and (2) do not feel close to their husbands during sex.[9]

Looking more deeply at the numbers, it's hardly surprising to find that these women have major communication issues around sex. These women are also

- eleven times less likely than other women in sexually active marriages to be comfortable talking to their husbands about what they want in bed[10]

- eight times more likely to have intercourse only out of obligation[11]
- almost nineteen times less likely to be satisfied with foreplay[12]
- twenty times less likely to feel their pleasure is a priority during sex[13]
- 4.7 times less likely to be comfortable having difficult conversations with their husbands[14]
- 6.3 times less likely to agree that their husbands consider their wants, opinions, and needs as much as they do their own[15]

If either Heidi or Stephanie were to say, "I would love a sex life that is about both of us, but I'm no longer willing to be part of one in which I'm not a consideration," she would not be refusing sex. She would be creating a boundary that states that the only sex she is willing to have is sex where she is treated like a human being. Hopefully, by her saying, "I am no longer willing to be treated like an object," they can begin those important conversations about what sex is supposed to be (personal, pleasurable, pure, prioritized, pressure-free, and passionate) and they can work *toward* that instead of *away* from it.

> CHECK-IN: Does your marriage match the criteria for a sexless marriage in disguise? How will you address this moving forward?

Are You Creating a Sexless Marriage?

We didn't have many surprises from our Bare Marriage survey results. We thought the every man's battle message would hurt sex; it did. We knew that there were many women who used porn and not just men; we knew that many women had higher libidos. We thought the obligation-sex message would be harmful; it was (we'll be tackling that one next). We've been hearing comments and women's stories for over a decade now, and we were prepared for what we'd find—nothing took us by surprise.

Nothing, that is, except this: *we didn't expect to find that almost no sexless marriages were caused by women giving up on sex without cause.* While in many marriages sex is certainly infrequent due to laziness or selfishness, completely sexless marriages do not tend to happen out of the blue.

After speaking at a marriage conference, my husband and I (Sheila) were approached by a middle-aged man asking what to do about his wife. After their last child was born fifteen years earlier, his wife announced suddenly that sex was over. Another man told us about how his wife, after her hysterectomy, was no longer interested in sex and told him he could take care of himself now. Over and over again, we have heard this from marriage conference attendees, emailers, and male commenters: "She just announced after menopause that she was done with sex," or "She just told me one day I was cut off."

But what our survey found was that even though these husbands felt like it was out of the blue, it very likely wasn't.

For years when I have spoken and blogged about sexless marriages, I've done what the books that we read also did. I've told people that they need to prioritize sex and that cutting your spouse off from sex when there isn't abuse or pain or porn is wrong. I framed the problem of sexless marriages as primarily being caused by women making unfair unilateral decisions because they didn't enjoy sex or had deep-seated shame about it.

But what we found is that very, very few women actually do cut their husbands off from sex when there isn't something serious going on already. In particular, we found five contributing factors to sexual dissatisfaction that correlated strongly with sexless marriages:

- porn use
- male sexual dysfunction[16]

- anorgasmia
- vaginismus
- not feeling close during sex

Of sexually active marriages, 38.0% experience none of these problems. In contrast, of sexless marriages, only 6.6% experience none of them. We found that 73.5% of sexless marriages have two or more of these problems, while only 27.1% of sexually active marriages do.

The vast majority of sexless marriages, then, don't just happen one day because women decide they don't like sex. Sexless marriages, instead, are the culmination of other factors, building up over a long period of time, that eventually wear women down until they give up entirely.

This tells us two things: many men do not realize how serious underlying marriage problems are until the marriages become sexless, and continuing to have sex when you feel degraded or used prolongs and deepens marriage problems. We're not saying that people should give up on sex whenever there's a problem or withhold sex as a way to control their spouses. Of course not—that is manipulative and cruel. But when there is a problem, you simply must address it, or you can end up creating a lonely, sexless marriage eventually anyway.

For many men, sex is their way of checking in on the health of the relationship. If everything is not okay, and a wife still has regular sex, she could be reinforcing that she is fine with the marriage, even if she continually tells him that she is not. No matter how much she says she's desperate for things to get better, he isn't believing it because she's still having sex with him. What our stats show, though, is that, in the long run, she may not be able to sustain a regular sex life if things do not improve. So, men, if you do not listen when your wife says there are serious issues in your marriage, you may find yourself, like our earlier letter writer said, with a wife who "just woke up one day and declared no more sex."

Are You at Risk of a Sexless Marriage?

Our stats showed certain markers that make it much more likely that a marriage may one day turn sexless. These two scenarios stood out:

- marriages in which the wife doesn't orgasm and doesn't feel close during sex (seven times more likely to one day become a sexless marriage)
- marriages in which the wife endures sexual pain and doesn't feel close to her husband during sex (five times more likely to one day become a sexless marriage)

Marriages with abuse, porn use, or where a wife feels used during sex are also at risk for sexlessness (we imagine that the reverse is also likely true, but we did not survey men). When people feel used and discarded, having sex intensifies these feelings of rejection. Eventually people just give up.

If your marriage matches any of these categories, seek professional counseling, medical help, or physiotherapy before the crisis hits. If the problem is simply that sex has never felt good, revisit chapters 3 and 4 or work through a couple's challenge like *31 Days to Great Sex* to discover what awakens her sexual pleasure.

Christian books on sex and marriage are adamant that sexless marriages are sinful. I used to promote this view too. What we've now realized is that we're treating a symptom rather than the cause. When there are serious problems in a marriage, telling people to just keep having sex doesn't fix them; it can actually solidify that feeling of being used and disregarded.

This is tricky to talk about. In generally good marriages, sex can smooth over small disagreements or even the occasional argument, giving the couple goodwill and energy to work on any issues they have. For these couples, the "Just have more sex" advice is often exactly right.

But for marriages that are not generally good, in which the problems are much deeper, sex isn't the answer. Addressing the problem is the answer. Sex should be life-giving in your marriage, not soul-crushing. And intercourse on its own does not suddenly turn an unhealthy relationship healthy.

We opened this chapter saying that a healthy sex life feeds into a healthy marriage, and a healthy marriage fosters a healthy sex life. The two cannot be separated. For some couples, the journey to great sex will happen mainly in the bedroom. But for others, it may primarily take place in a marriage therapist's office. Whichever it is for you, please do the work, because a marriage in which you feel truly known is bona fide "wedded bliss."

EXPLORE TOGETHER: Let's Try Preventative Medicine

Sexless marriages happen for a reason. So don't give your marriage a reason to become sexless! And the way you prevent a sexless marriage is simple: have a good, emotionally connected marriage to begin with.

For daily connection, try the "high/low" exercise. Share the best and worst parts of your day, the time you felt the most energized and the time you felt the most discouraged and frustrated. Asking your spouse, "How was your day?" is not a great conversation starter because it's so broad. Focusing on sharing two emotional moments can help you connect on a deeper level because you skip the mundane and you get right to the heart of it. This can help you learn how your spouse ticks, but it can also give you insight into your own emotional state.

To make this work well, choose the same time of day: over dinner, while you're doing dishes, while you're lying in bed before going to sleep. If one works shift work or is away from home, do this by phone every day.

To create more fun in your marriage, go to https://greatsexrescue.com/date-night-ideas/ and you'll find a smorgasbord of ideas, including

- conversation starters
- cheap date-night ideas
- hobbies to do as a couple
- personality quizzes
- visioning worksheets to make goals for your marriage and family
- and more

Choose one or two that you will try, and put them in your calendar now.

RESCUING AND REFRAMING

- Instead of saying, "You need to make sex a priority because your spouse needs it," say, "Sex is vital to a healthy marriage. Make it a priority so you don't miss out on God's blessings for both of you."
- Instead of saying, "It is a sin to withhold sex from your spouse," say all of the following:
  - "When only one person is getting any pleasure from sex, they are depriving their spouse—even if intercourse is happening."
  - "Sometimes sexlessness is the natural repercussion of long-term mistreatment or broken trust in a marriage."
  - "If you have destroyed your marriage, even unintentionally, you need to rebuild the marriage before expecting sex."

156

Sex should be *pressure-free*: Sex is a gift freely given; it's not about getting what you want through manipulation, coercion, or threat.

CHAPTER 9

"Duty Sex" Isn't Sexy

Freely you have received; freely give.

Matthew 10:8

In the movie *Bruce Almighty*, God (played by Morgan Freeman) makes Bruce (played by Jim Carrey) God of Buffalo with only two rules: he can't tell anyone he's God, and he can't mess with free will. Later in the movie, when Bruce's girlfriend, Grace, leaves him, Bruce asks God, "How do you make someone love you without affecting free will?" God replies, "Welcome to my world, son. If you come up with an answer, you let me know."

The real God (the one we like to think also sounds like Morgan Freeman) knew he could not have real intimacy with us unless we chose it ourselves. But in many marriages, sex is not being freely chosen. It becomes transactional instead of intimate or a duty instead of a joy. It can even become a weapon when a spouse is pressured to do things against their will. But love is not love if it's forced.

And that puts people like Bruce in a pickle. In any relationship, the person who is least invested holds the power. In a dating relationship, the one who loves the least determines how often they see each other or text each other, while the one who loves the most sits staring at the phone, willing the notifications to beep. In group projects at school, the kid with the 4.0 GPA ends up doing all the work because the classmates with the 2.3 GPAs don't care what grade they get. With sex and marriage, the one who wants sex the least holds the power.

You probably don't recognize actress Edie McClurg's name, even though she has 209 movie and TV credits under her belt. But I can almost guarantee you'd recognize her face and her voice. She played the school secretary in *Ferris Bueller's Day Off*—"He's one righteous dude." She was the car rental agent in *Planes, Trains and Automobiles* who caused Steve Martin's character to go ballistic. But I (Sheila) will always love her best as Herb Tarlek's wife, Lucille, in the 1970s sitcom *WKRP in Cincinnati*. One iconic line has stuck with me, even decades after hearing it: "Better mow the grass, Herbie, or no num-nums tonight. Uh-huh. Uh-huh." Herb, the socially inept advertising manager, was stuck in an elevator with the receptionist he idolized, while he complained about how demoralizing it was that his wife saw sex as a reward for good behavior.

Assigning a price for sex says, *"I don't really want to do this. I see it as a means to an end—a means to get what I really want, which is this behavior from you. So I will hold myself back from you until you give me what I want."* This feels like a rejection—I don't really want you; I only want what you can give me. It changes the nature of sex, and it ruins intimacy.

The spouse who wants sex least can either use their power, as Lucille Tarlek did, to manipulate and get what she (or he) wants, or hold it carefully, as Gary Thomas explains:

> The spiritual beauty of sexuality is seen in service, lovingly meeting the physical desires and needs of our mate. The spiritual meaning of a Christian's sexuality is found in giving. When we have power over another and use that power responsibly, appropriately, and benevolently, we grow in Christ, becoming more like God, and

159

reflect the fact that we were made to love God by serving others. But when we have power over another—particularly power in an area where someone feels so vulnerable and needy and where they can go nowhere else to be served—and then use that power irresponsibly, inappropriately, and maliciously, we become more like Satan, who loves to manipulate us in our weakness rather than like God, who serves us in our weakness.[1]

True love can't be forced, but that opens the door to manipulation. Marriages will never thrive unless we all shut that door fast!

CHECK-IN: Who in your relationship has more "power" in the bedroom? Do you feel like sex is ever used to manipulate in your marriage?

Lucille saw sex as a reward for good behavior. But what if it was her husband, Herb, who saw sex that way? Seeing sex as a tit for tat is, depressingly, also a common theme in lots of marriage advice: *"Men, if you want to get sex, just do the dishes and fold some laundry!"*

Like most things that resonate, this has a kernel of truth. Most women (though not all) find that enjoying sex is much more difficult if they are tired. When I asked on Facebook how husbands can get you in the mood, almost 50% of women said a variation of "Help get stuff done." As one woman said, "When he comes home from work and jumps in helping with the kids," she definitely feels like jumping him!

But sex is not currency that is used to pay men for doing housework. If your wife is chronically exhausted and busy, and you take the tea towel from her one night and say, "Here, honey, let me," this does not mean that she will now be in the mood. What overwhelmed wives need, more than a simple break, is for their husbands to share ownership of the household duties. That communicates "We're a team." And *that* is the gateway into sex—not

160

just doing a load of dishes to get some nookie out of it, but saying, "We're in this together."

Sex is a natural part of loving, tender, selfless relationships. That is the real reason why sex starts in the kitchen—not because if he does dishes, she owes him, but because if he is a mature, responsible, and caring husband, he grows a relationship marked by tenderness and selflessness.

> CHECK-IN: Have you as a couple ever treated sex like it's a reward for good behavior? How does that make you feel about sex? About each other?

Sex can't be pressure-free if it's transactional, because one spouse is always "owed." But let's turn the pressure up a notch: what happens when sex isn't just transactional, where they both get something out of it, but is actually an obligation where one is entitled to the use of the other?

This brings us to one of the most important insights we gleaned from our survey. When women enter marriage believing they are obligated to have sex with their husbands whenever their husbands want it, they are 37% more likely to experience sexual pain and 29% less likely to frequently orgasm.[2] So, before we move on to building a healthy sex life, we have to dismantle this last sacred cow of Christian marriage books: that women have no right to say no to their husbands—because without the ability to say no, we can never truly say yes.

Figure 9.1
Transaction, Obligation, and Coercion

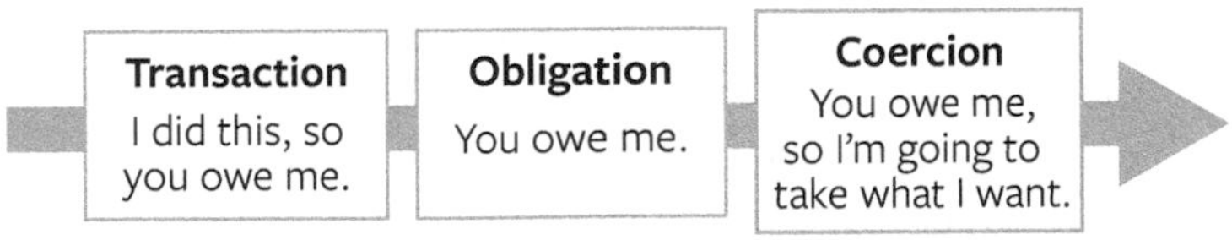

Transaction	Obligation	Coercion
I did this, so you owe me.	You owe me.	You owe me, so I'm going to take what I want.

Why Do Women Believe They Don't Have Any Right to Say No?

We conducted focus groups as a part of our research to help us delve deeper and understand why these beliefs were having the effect we found. For many of the women we talked to, the obligation-sex message wrecked their sex lives for years—for some of them, decades.

Here's what we found so fascinating in their stories:

Almost all of them said that *their husbands never gave them the obligation-sex message themselves.* Their husbands didn't see sex as something they were owed or entitled to take, but instead as a gift for them to share together. Their husbands saw the importance of honoring their wives' *no*—they just never knew she didn't feel free to say it! Each of these husbands empowered their wives by saying what they had been thinking all along: "You are allowed to say no, and in fact, I *want* you to say no if you're uncomfortable, because I don't want sex to be something you don't want to do."

Now, these women had great husbands, but some women are married to men who are not as kind as these men, and we will address that later in this chapter and the next. But how is it that women can be married to really great guys who truly want sex to be a fully mutual experience—and still believe in their hearts that they don't have the right to say no to sex?

When you look at Christian teachings, it makes sense, because that's what women have been hearing for years:

- "Both partners are forbidden to refuse the meeting of their mate's sexual needs."—*The Act of Marriage*[3]
- "Though you know you should pray for him and fulfill him sexually, sometimes you won't want to. Talk to each other openly and honestly, *then do the right thing.*"— *Every Man's Battle*[4]

- "Keep an eye on the calendar and refuse to allow much time to go by without coming together physically."— *Power of a Praying Wife*[5]

Of course we have an obligation to each other in marriage when it comes to sex. But having an obligation to make sex a vital part of your marriage does not necessitate that we say yes to every single advance. Sex is not the only need in the marriage relationship, and sometimes other needs must take precedence.

Much current teaching, though, elevates his need for intercourse above any of her needs. Even look at the subtitle of bestselling *Love & Respect: The Love She Most Desires; The Respect He Desperately Needs*. In this book, sex is included as a component of respect but not as a component of love. What he wants (sex) is a need, then, but whatever she wants is merely a desire.

The message that "whatever you are feeling doesn't matter, you need to have intercourse with your spouse" erases you as a person. It says that who you are, including your wants, desires, and feelings, doesn't matter. Then sex, which is supposed to be this deep knowing, becomes something far different. It's saying, "I don't want to know you, because your needs and desires are actually unimportant to me. I only want to use you."

When asked how they felt after sex, *used* was the word 16% of women in our follow-up survey chose. It is no surprise, considering how many Christian books, articles, and websites interpret 1 Corinthians 7:3–5 as saying that she has no right to say no:

- "God's viewpoint comes forth vigorously in 1 Corinthians 7:3–5 where the husband and wife are told they actually *defraud* (*apostereo*, the strongest New Testament Greek word meaning to cheat somebody out of something that is rightfully theirs) one another when they refuse to give physical pleasure and satisfaction to their mate. The only activity that is to break regular sexual relations is prayer

163

Figure 9.2

How Does Feeling Used after Sex Change Why You Have Sex?

Note: Results are from a follow-up survey of 1,496 women. Respondents could choose multiple answers, so percentages add to more than 100%.

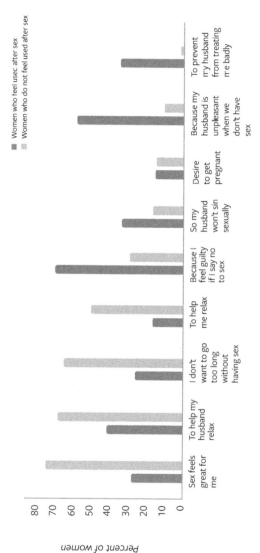

■ Women who feel used after sex
▨ Women who do not feel used after sex

Percent of women

Reasons for having sex

(x-axis categories: Sex feels great for me; To help my husband relax; I don't want to go too long without having sex; To help me relax; Because I feel guilty if I say no to sex; So my husband won't sin sexually; Desire to get pregnant; Because my husband is unpleasant when we don't have sex; To prevent my husband from treating me badly)

Women who feel used during sex are more likely to have sex to placate their husband, out of a sense of guilt, or to prevent being treated badly.

and fasting for some specific cause, and this is to be only by mutual consent for a very limited time."—*Intended for Pleasure*[6]

- After quoting the same passage, Kevin Leman writes, "If you call yourself a Christian, and if you're committed to being obedient to what the Bible teaches, then you'll have to learn to fulfill sexual obligations within marriage."— *Sheet Music*[7]

- At a Desiring God National Conference, speaker Carolyn Mahaney said, "The only exception to this rule is for the activity of prayer and then only by mutual agreement and for a limited time. We must heed this admonition and offer no excuses."[8]

When you are repeatedly told that you are not allowed to say no to sex and that what you need is less important than what your spouse needs, that is a deep rejection of you as a person. When the books, magazines, blogs, radio programs, and conferences in your Christian circle are all telling you that every time you say no to sex, you are being selfish due to the depth of his need, you may start feeling guilty about having any needs at all.

Let's look at how the obligation-sex message affects women like Jodie, a busy mom of three, a woman typical of those we interviewed and of those who write in to my blog.[9] Jodie's five-month-old baby has strep throat and an ear infection, and Tuesday night, Jodie was up four different times trying to settle him, including pacing the floor from 2:00 to 3:00 a.m, praying he wouldn't cry so hard that he'd wake Tina, Jodie's two-year-old. Thankfully, Tina stayed asleep but was up for the day at 6:00 a.m., and Jodie's been on the go ever since. She gets her oldest daughter, Chelsea, on the school bus, takes the baby to the doctor with Tina in tow, all while trying to get enough laundry done so her husband, Tyler, will have underwear for tomorrow. When Tyler gets home that night after a grueling day as a paramedic, he sits down to help with Chelsea's homework while Jodie puts the baby in a carrier and tries to get dinner ready. Tina whines at Jodie's feet, and Tyler eventually gives up on the homework since everything is so loud. "I'm going to have a shower and unwind," he says. "Call me when dinner's done."

Later that night, he reads a story to Chelsea while Jodie bathes the younger two, nurses the baby, and tries to settle them both. But the baby's still fighting the cold, and now Tina starts acting up since she's felt ignored all day. When everyone's finally quiet by 10:30 p.m., all Jodie wants is to collapse. But Tyler wants something else. Jodie heads to the bathroom to try to get herself in the right headspace for sex, but her eyes start filling with tears. She's almost at her breaking point. She knows Tyler needs it; it's been four days now. But at this point, she'd rather curl up in that cold porcelain bathtub than have sex. "It's okay, it won't take long," she thinks, as she wipes her face, heads into the bedroom, and turns off the light.

After sex, Tyler seems moody. "You weren't into it," he accuses her. Unable to hold it inside, she breaks down. "I'm just so exhausted. I need more help. In the evenings, can you please take the kids while I'm making dinner, or at least leave me with only the baby? I just can't do it all." He replies, "I'm tired, too, hon. I had three calls out today, and they were bad. You just need to get more organized during the day so you can get more rest." And he rolls over and goes to sleep.

Over the next week, things get worse. Because Jodie's spending so much time with the baby and his ear infection, Tina starts regressing, becoming even more clingy and wanting her bottle again. A few nights later, when Tyler comes home, Jodie has no idea what she's going to make for dinner. Frustrated, Tyler orders pizza and tells her things need to change. His job is extremely stressful; he needs to know she has the home under control. She feels guilty for being selfish; she knows the kids and the housework are her responsibility. So she initiates sex that night to show Tyler that she does care. But as she's drifting off to sleep later, she feels so empty. "Jesus, I'm trying to obey you," she prays. "I'm trying to fill up my husband's cup and take care of his needs. I'm trying to care for these precious little ones you've given me. But I can't do this anymore. Please change my attitude. Make me the wife Tyler needs."

Jodie and Tyler both believe what is being taught in these books: sex is the biggest need they must attend to. And because he is the one with the greater felt need for sex, then her needs are devalued. In fact, her needs are not only devalued; they're a nuisance, getting in the way of the most important need.

As we were writing this book, we were trying to figure out why the obligation message became so widespread. A "Sexual Refusal Commitment," handed out at a Solomon, Sex, and Marriage conference in 2000, went viral on Twitter as we were making our final edits. The commitment asked couples to agree to these seven principles:

1. Because God's Word forbids sexual refusal except for mutually agreed upon seasons of prayer . . . (1 Cor. 7:5a);

2. Because Satan will tempt us because our [sic] lack of self-control . . . (1 Cor. 7:5b);

3. Because I no longer have authority over my own body, but my spouse does . . . (1 Cor. 7:4);

4. Because I am commanded to fulfill my duty (what I owe) to my spouse . . . (1 Cor. 7:2);

5. Because we are now one flesh . . . (Gen. 2:24);

6. Because we are to regard one another's needs as more important than my own . . . (Phil. 2:3–4);

7. Because we are to please one another for their good and edification . . . (Rom. 15:2);

"We therefore pledge to make ourselves 100% willing and available for Biblical lovemaking and to not directly or indirectly refuse my spouse's sexual needs and desires."[10]

And then the form ends with a place for couples to sign on the dotted line.

This is very heavy-handed—"*not directly or indirectly refuse my spouse's sexual needs and desires.*" It seems to stem from a genuine fear that women don't like sex, don't want sex, and will only be motivated to have sex by threats.

> CHECK-IN: Have you heard the obligation-sex message? How does it make you feel about sex?

It begs to be asked, What would happen if instead of church leaders focusing on telling women why they have to "do it *or else,*" they taught men that they should be generous, selfless lovers? Reader, we have receipts, and they're in figure 9.3.

Many women report obligation-message motivations for having sex, whether it's to keep their husbands from sinning sexually (18.8%), because they feel guilty if they turn their husbands down (34.8%), or because when they don't have sex, their husbands become unpleasant (17.6%) or even treat them badly (6.7%).[11] But what happens when we look at women who have sex because they enjoy it? It will not surprise you that the percentage of women who have sex out of guilt or to placate their husbands goes down. And among women whose *primary* motivation for sex is because they like it? The percentages go down even more! Negative motivations for sex become less relevant the more she's having fun.

When sex is good for her, why would we feel the need for the obligation-sex message? Of course she's going to have sex—she likes it! If she says no occasionally, it's not a big deal because he can rest assured that she's going to want it again soon. But perhaps

Figure 9.3

How Women's Sexual Pleasure, or Lack of It, Affects Their Reasons for Having Sex

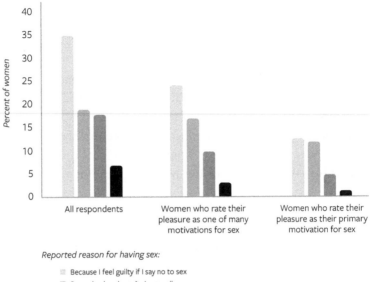

Reported reason for having sex:

- Because I feel guilty if I say no to sex
- So my husband won't sin sexually
- Because my husband is unpleasant when we don't have sex
- To prevent my husband from treating me badly

When women don't enjoy sex, they are more likely to have intercourse out of fear, guilt, or to protect themselves from mistreatment.

the fact that Christian sex and marriage advice so often ignores her pleasure has led to this phenomenon that the only reason she'd ever have sex is because she's told she has to. Give her permission to say no, and men may never get sex! And so we give very lopsided attention to one Bible verse, ignoring all the rest.

Yes, there's a specific verse that speaks about the importance of meeting each other's sexual needs, but that doesn't mean that this is the most important need. The Bible may not speak specifically about her need for sleep or about her need for emotional safety or about her need to protect her physical health. But the Bible does give us principles that we should always follow: do unto others as you would have them do unto you (Matt. 7:12); focus on serving, not on being served (Matt. 20:28); look to others' interests, not your own (Phil. 2:4). The Bible even asks men to take care of their wives as they take care of their own bodies (Eph. 5:28), which means that God wants women's physical condition to matter to their husbands as much as his own needs matter to him. The Bible may have mentioned one specific need, but it does not follow that this particular need must then supersede all others.

When I (Rebecca) was recovering from my horrible labor experience, sex was terrifying to me. A panic-attack, curl-up-in-a-little-ball-and-cry-when-I-think-about-it kind of terrifying.

Six weeks postpartum came and went, and we felt no closer to getting to a point where I would be physically or emotionally ready to have sex. Before my pregnancy, I had been a high-drive spouse, and as the weeks went by, I felt more and more guilty about not being able to give in that area of our marriage. Postpartum hormones are intense, and they heightened my panic at the thought that I wasn't doing as well as other wives—other women are able to do this after six weeks, why was I still failing months after having a baby?

Then I started initiating out of guilt. Guilt for how I was depriving Connor, guilt for not being a good enough wife, guilt for having done labor "wrong" and having a third-degree tear as a result. I lied and told him I was ready while my heart was pounding and my body was screaming, "No, no, no, don't do this yet!"

But my husband gathered me up in a big hug and said, "I know you're not ready. I'm okay. This needs to be something we do when it's good for you too. I'm not interested in anything that causes you pain. I'd rather wait for a while longer if you're okay with that."

I broke down sobbing in relief, so grateful that he could see past my efforts to convince him I was ready. I'd love to be able to tell you that entering the world of postpartum sex was easy-peasy after that, but it wasn't. I experienced sexual pain for a long time after my son was born. But Connor's Christlike sacrificial love meant that my fears that sex would never feel good again started to dissipate. He never pushed anything if I wasn't feeling up to it but went entirely at my pace. In fact, as he says, he never even viewed it as "his" sexual needs that were put on hold, but "our" sexual needs. Making my physical recovery our priority proved to me repeatedly that he was not interested in a one-sided sex life. As a result, I had the space to recover not only physically but emotionally too. Because of how my husband handled this, sex stopped being something I dreaded. He took away all the guilt, all the fear, and all the unknown and replaced it with a true *agape*, 1 Corinthians 13 kind of love.

But what might it have looked like if both Connor and I had felt that his need for sex was more important than my need to be emotionally and physically healed first? Here's a story of a marriage that is now falling apart:

My husband and I used to enjoy sexual intimacy and never had any problems—until after the birth of our first child. When we tried intercourse, it was extremely painful. We have unsuccessfully tried several times since then. The sexual dysfunction exposed underlying issues in our relationship that we have not been able to repair, and we are heading toward separation. My husband has a very fundamentalistic view of the Bible, and I think he would like me to suffer through the pain and fulfill my duty for his sake. That duty-mentality completely kills any arousal and does not help fix my problem of pain. I just can't do it. That's not to say I am not open to other ways of being sexually intimate, it is just that this hostility between us makes it seem impossible to do with a sincere heart.

It is interesting to me that when it is my body that got injured during birth (pelvic organ prolapse) and my body that now experiences pain during intercourse—he acts as if he is the only one hurting. I know he loves me, but I feel so objectified. The fact that my husband wants me to have sex with him despite intense pain disgusts me, and I really question who I chose to marry.

How did we get to a point where the husband thinks he is biblically justified to expect her to "suffer through the pain" to "fulfill my duty for his sake"? Maybe because books have intimated exactly that when they give the obligation-sex message with no caveats. Not only does this cause couples to discount her pain; it also can lead to her not prioritizing health needs—even when that relates to her and her unborn children:

> I'm pregnant with my fourth, and it's a very high-risk pregnancy. I'm supposed to be on bed rest, and my blood pressure is high and I'm not feeling well, but I still have to look after our other three as well as managing the house. My husband is really struggling with not having sex (we've been told we're not supposed to), and I'm wondering what I can do to help him out, the poor guy, because he's expressing a lot of frustration and he's really hurting.

Is there anything wrong with a pregnant woman wanting to give her husband oral sex or a hand job? No, of course not. But what sets off alarm bells for us from this email is that she is in a high-risk pregnancy and is disregarding medical advice to stay on bed rest, instead continuing to care for the kids and the house. Yet, what are they both preoccupied with? His sexual frustration. The focus of the letter is on his "hurting" and how sad it is that he can't get any release, but meanwhile, he isn't helping out enough to allow her to follow the doctor's orders to keep his child, and his wife, safe. They have both internalized this obligation-sex message so deeply that life-and-death issues are not as important as his sexual release. How on earth did we get this so wrong?

Because women are told that we can never, ever understand a man's sex drive and a man's sexual needs, when we are experiencing something horrible, we assume that men still have it worse.

CHECK-IN: In your marriage, do sexual needs have more emotional weight than other needs? If so, who do you feel is painting sex as the most important need? How does this make you feel? How do you think this makes your spouse feel?

A Closer Look at "Do Not Deprive"

Let's take a step back and ask, What is God really asking of us in 1 Corinthians 7:3–5? One woman writes:

> My husband is always reading Christian articles to help save our marriage. One in particular struck me hard. It said the partner with the lesser sex drive needs to be the one who gives in to the partner with the higher sex drive! I have three kids ages 7–17. Two kids had major surgeries this year and both are in physical therapy twice a week. I own my own business. I manage the home. I'm the parent who runs the kids everywhere. I'm exhausted! That article makes me feel like an inadequate wife and pushes me away from sex even more. If it were up to my husband, we would have sex twice a day! He likes to point out that it's the Christian thing to do!

Is it the Christian thing to do to give your spouse sex twice a day if he or she wants it, no matter what you're going through? To answer that, we need to ask two definitional questions of 1 Corinthians 7:5: what does it mean not to deprive, and what is it that we're being asked not to deprive our spouse of?[12]

Saying "Do not deprive" is not the equivalent of saying "Do not refuse." When we say "Do not deprive," we're saying, "Someone has a need that has to be fulfilled." But this is not the same thing as saying, "A person gets to have whatever they want." God made us with a need for food. If your child asks, "Can I have Cheetos?" and you refuse because lunch is in an hour, you are not depriving her of food. The child's need is for a healthy, balanced diet, not to eat anything she wants, any time she wants.

Likewise, the sexual need that God created us with is not for intercourse whenever we want or however we want. It's for a healthy, mutual, fulfilling sex life, and sometimes that means saying no for a variety of reasons. God did not say "Do not deprive" in order to allow selfishness to blossom. Can you imagine any other area of life in which God would tell a person, "You have the right to use someone else for your own gratification, even if it causes physical or emotional pain"? Or in which he would tell a woman, "It pleases me when your husband acts selfishly toward you"?

Figure 9.4

Women Report Worse Sex If They Have Sex out of Obligation

What happens to women's sex lives when they agree that "I engage in sex with my husband only because I feel I have to"? (How many times more likely are they to agree with the following statements?)

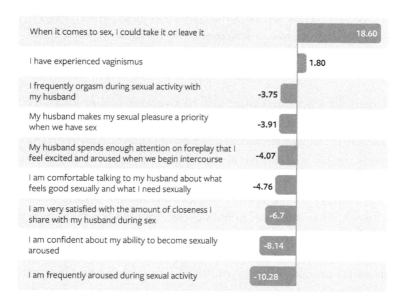

The woman on bed rest may believe she is being very pious for keeping up with housework, childcare, and sexual duties when she's supposed to be resting—but is she spurring her husband on to look more like Jesus (Rom. 8:29; Heb. 10:24)? Or would both of them be better off if he learned how to take some of that load off his wife's plate and practice self-control for the sake of his wife and unborn child?

Spouses cannot begin to challenge each other toward Christlike growth when women are constantly hearing this duty-sex message. And what makes this message especially insidious is that even when women reject it, it still hurts them if they believed it in the past. In fact, a woman's believing this message before marriage causes sexual and marital satisfaction to plummet even more than her

Figure 9.5
Women Are Less Happy in Marriage If They Have Sex out of Obligation

What happens to women's marital satisfaction when they agree that "I engage in sex with my husband only because I feel I have to"? (How many times more likely are they to agree with the following statements?)

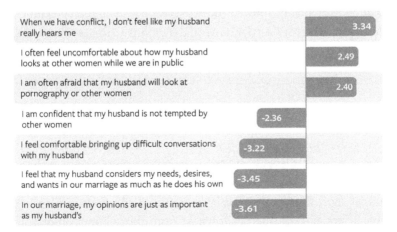

When we have conflict, I don't feel like my husband really hears me	3.34
I often feel uncomfortable about how my husband looks at other women while we are in public	2.49
I am often afraid that my husband will look at pornography or other women	2.40
I am confident that my husband is not tempted by other women	-2.36
I feel comfortable bringing up difficult conversations with my husband	-3.22
I feel that my husband considers my needs, desires, and wants in our marriage as much as he does his own	-3.45
In our marriage, my opinions are just as important as my husband's	-3.61

believing it after marriage does. It changes the very nature of sex for her, and that's very hard to untangle. Couples will continue to be robbed of the freedom and joy God designed for sex as long as they keep hearing messages like this one from *Sheet Music*:

> This means that there may be times when you have sex out of mercy, obligation, or commitment and without any real desire. Yes, it may feel forced. It might feel planned, and you may fight to stop yourself from just shoving your partner away and saying, "Enough already!" But the root issue is this: You're acting out of love. You're honoring your commitment. And that's a wonderful thing to do.[13]

Our survey definitively showed that having sex out of obligation, when you feel forced to do so, is never a wonderful thing to do. It robs her of the joy she was meant to experience, and it robs her husband of a marriage in which he is desired, not just placated.

CHECK-IN: Do any of the findings in figures 9.4 and 9.5 resonate particularly with your experience? Which ones?

Now, if the husband believes not only that he is owed sex but that he is biblically allowed to take it, we have entered even more dangerous territory. And, unfortunately, many Christian resources beat us there. That's where we'll turn next.

EXPLORE TOGETHER: No More Duty Sex!

Our survey found that when women enjoy sex, the obligation-sex message does far less harm. As a couple, take turns and each share your top three motivations for having sex. Then place yourself in one of these three categories based on (a) if you find sex pleasurable or not and (b) whether you have sex out of obligation or not.

1. Sex is pleasurable; I don't have sex out of a sense of obligation.
   - If you're both here, take time to celebrate. Talk to each other about how you can prevent the obligation-sex rut from happening if your sex life gets harder in the future (distance, pregnancies, sickness, etc.).
2. Sex is pleasurable; I have sex because I feel I have to.
   - If your spouse is here, where sex feels good but they are motivated by obligation, don't initiate for three weeks, and allow your spouse's libido to take the reins, even if that means you don't have sex in that three weeks. In the interim, show affection, talk to them, and make it clear that you are capable of loving them even without sex.
   - If you are here, talk to your spouse about what makes you feel guilted into sex. Is it something your spouse is doing, or is it something you can overcome on your own? Talk to your spouse about how you can tip the scales so that your pleasure outweighs the negative messages in your head.
3. Sex is not pleasurable; I have sex because I feel I have to.
   - If you or your spouse is here, see chapters 3 and 4.

RESCUING AND REFRAMING

- Instead of saying, "Do not deprive your husband," say, "Sex is a vital part of a healthy marriage relationship that you are both meant to enjoy."
- Instead of saying, "Do some chores to get her in the mood," say, "When both spouses pull their weight around the house, sex can flourish."

- Instead of saying, "You do not have authority over your body; your spouse does," say, "God wants sex to be a mutual, loving experience."
- Instead of saying, "The only activity that is to break regular sexual relations is prayer and fasting for some specific cause, and this is to be only by mutual consent for a very limited time," say, "Our sexual needs are very important ones, but they are not the only ones. Show love to your spouse by caring for all of their needs."

CHAPTER 10

When Duty Becomes Coercion

My command is this: Love each other as I have
loved you. Greater love has no one than this:
to lay down one's life for one's friends.

John 15:12–13

"I got really good at wrestling," Erika told us. "Curling up in a ball really tight or running and locking the door behind me."

Nothing could have prepared us for how many horrific stories of marital rape we heard in the one-on-one interviews for this book. Thankfully, most of these stories did not end there, and many of these women are living in safe and happy second marriages today. But the evangelical culture must confront what these women endured in their first marriages, because the obligation-sex message was a fundamental part of how their husbands viewed them as wives.

We hope we can all agree that forcing someone to have sex is wrong. But to our amazement, and our great dismay, far too many Christian books include incidents of marital rape or other forms of sexual assault and then dismiss these incidents as unimportant. Several books, for instance, mention spouses who feel as if a rape had occurred—but then give no commentary that rape is unacceptable:

- *Every Heart Restored* recounts a woman saying, "Without foreplay, he raped me—if that can happen when you're married,"[1] and then just leaves that hanging, not saying "Yes, rape can happen in marriage."
- Later again in *Every Heart Restored*, the authors warn, "We've heard stories about some husbands who coerced their wives into sexual intercourse one, two, and sometimes three times a day! . . . If your husband is demanding sex more than once a day, he likely has a lust problem that needs to be dealt with."[2] Coercing someone into sex apparently isn't wrong; the only problem seems to be if he exceeds his daily limit.
- *Every Man's Battle* has multiple depictions of sexual assault (one of which is the rape of a minor)[3] and simply writes them off as the natural consequence of a man's struggle with lust, without explaining the harm done to the women (or even the illegal nature of many of the acts).
- *His Needs, Her Needs* includes this: "Many men tell me they wish their sex drive weren't so strong. As one thirty-two-year-old executive put it, 'I feel like a fool—like I'm begging her or even raping her, but I can't help it. I need to make love!'"[4] We are supposed to have sympathy for the man who feels like he's raping his wife, but not for the woman enduring it.

We want to say (and we are flabbergasted that we apparently have to) that if you ever feel like you are raping someone, you probably are. Consensual, mutual, life-giving sex and *rape* feel very different from each other. If you feel something is off, trust that feeling and stop.

But one of the worst examples we found in Christian books comes from *The Act of Marriage*, which includes an anecdote about when Aunt Matilda warns a young virgin bride off of sex (warning: graphic illustrations to follow):

> Apparently her aunt, whose marriage was arranged by her parents in the old country, found herself petrified of sex on her wedding night. When her embarrassed and clumsy farmer husband, who was twenty years older, brought her to their wedding bed, he "stripped me naked and raped me in my own bed. I fought and screamed to no avail." . . . Her conclusion to her niece was, "As far as I'm concerned, marriage is just legalized rape." As much as one might feel compassion for poor Aunt Matilda and her equally unhappy spouse, we can hardly envision more unhealthy concepts to pump into the impressionable young mind of a bride-to-be.[5]

In *The Act of Marriage,* telling someone sex is bad is worse than raping someone. Matilda is the antagonist; her rapist is portrayed as "embarrassed," "clumsy," and, appallingly, *"equally unhappy"* as the woman he stripped naked and raped while she fought and screamed. There is a shocking callousness displayed toward Aunt Matilda, while the moral or legal ramifications of marital rape are never mentioned.[6]

When Christian resources fail to discuss marital rape appropriately, it leaves women without the words to describe what is happening to them. While Erika was taking a shower on her wedding night, her husband barged in and attacked her. "We hadn't had sex before we were married, and I wasn't ready yet. I remember freaking out in my mind, crying and praying, 'What is going on?' and 'What is this? I can't live with this for the rest of my life.'" The "this" that she couldn't name was repeated many times over the next few years. And it wasn't until her divorce lawyer showed concern that Erika realized that "this" was rape.

Throughout her first marriage, sex was a constant fight. It was painful, awkward, and always ended with her crying. They would argue, with him angry that she wouldn't give him sex willingly when he wanted it. She would try to reason, asking for a break from sex, to slow down, or to think for a minute first. But she quickly learned, "There was not a way to peacefully and agreeably say no. It didn't matter what I said—it was happening anyway."

Erika's reality in her first marriage is the horrible, gut-wrenching conclusion that many women have come to after reading these books: if she doesn't give her husband sex, he'll have to rape her to get it. And it's not just women married to bad men who believe this either. Listen to this comment from a survey taker:

> Deciding to mentally purge obligation/duty sex was extremely freeing and has made the quality go up! I realize now that marital rape was the thing I was so unconsciously terrified of. I completely, 200% thought that good men turned into sexual animals toward their wives. And I was willing to sacrifice for my safety, to only be victimized by one man. Now I hope I can spare my daughter and younger sister from believing that.

The way many Christian marriage and sex books handle the topic of marital rape can cause women to not trust men, even men who deserve their trust. Men are portrayed as unable to control their sexual urges: one little slipup and they might rape fifteen-year-olds or masturbate in the open.[7] Multiple books tell women that if she doesn't have sex and he has an affair, it's her fault.[8] They tell her that he can't control himself without her help.[9] They even tell her "faithfulness is a two-person job."[10]

Most men are not one slipup away from raping an underage girl. Most men do not find it difficult to refrain from masturbating in public. Most men do not have affairs. But when women are being told this lie that she must give her husband sex or he'll lose control of himself, men—even the one she is in love with—can become very frightening. And sex can feel like a threat.

Men are not more evil simply by being men.[11] Most men are

respectful people who do not harm women. But the more we unfairly portray *all* men as potential predators or potential rapists, the less we are able to notice when a man actually becomes one of those things.

Here's a heartbreaking story from one of our blog commenters experiencing this:

> My husband and I have sex every day. Every other day we have it twice a day, and often 3 times a day! When I'm on my period, tired, we still do. When I had our babies, he googled and told me it's okay after four weeks, we don't have to wait for six. When I feel like it's too much, [1 Cor. 7:3–5] is thrown at me. He also explains to me why he needs it and how he feels when I deny him (like if I'm exhausted and fall asleep before it happens). I actually feel abused. I curl up in a ball on my side and let him do it. I'm detached emotionally (not always, but almost always during my period) and this hurts him.
>
> I love my husband. He's my best friend, but sometimes I want out! I feel like I'll either lose my best friend or continue to feel abused. I tell him it hurts me when we have sex too often or when I'm on my period, but he says, then why would God say to NEVER deny each other?

How can a man force intercourse on his wife when she is curled up in a ball, stiff and in emotional turmoil, and not think this is wrong? Or, to put it more bluntly, how can this man rape his wife and think he's morally right in doing so? We believe it comes from this faulty "Christian" teaching that this behavior is actually biblical.

When he honestly believes God has ordained that her body fully belongs to him, he can feel as if he is loving toward her, *even when he is using her without her consent.* To love your spouse, after all, is to act as God wants you to act, and doesn't God say that the husband is entitled to sex whenever he wants it, since he owns her body?

Such attitudes should have no place in a sex life characterized by the kingdom principles of mutual servanthood. They represent kingdom of darkness principles, not kingdom of God principles. But this idea that women do not own their own bodies runs deep. We have even had several male commenters on the blog taking issue with the fact that women can say no to sex for the six weeks postpartum or during her period.

Referring to the 1 Corinthians 7 passage, Tony commented, "Consensual is a keyword. If he didn't consent to going six weeks [after a baby] or even one week a month [during her period], then unilaterally imposing that on him is certainly not consensual." Another man echoed him, "The period of abstinence after pregnancy and during the wife's period is not by mutual agreement so that the couple can devote themselves to prayer. It is being forced on us men because we are being told to give our wives a break." You need mutual consent to say no, these commenters feel—but apparently you don't need mutual consent to say yes.

The vast majority of the marriages represented in our survey do not align with this kind of thinking. All three of us writing this book are married to amazing men, and we're incredibly offended on their behalf when we read how bestselling Christian resources portray them. The majority of men are good people and do not act like the men in the examples above. So we are left with the strange situation in which the people who most strongly relate to the examples given in Christian marriage books are often the ones acting the least like Christ.

CHECK-IN: Have you heard the obligation-sex message in church, through Christian books, or through other Christian resources? How was it couched? How did it make you feel?

We honestly believe that the authors who have perpetuated this mentality simply did not write their books with abused women in mind. Their aim was likely to increase the frequency of marital intercourse, and they didn't consider their effect on women in abusive situations. But we suspect that the teaching that sex is something men are owed by their wives is being used as a weapon by abusive husbands.

Looking at our survey, we typically find that the effect of believing a message is greater than the effect of simply hearing it. This is exactly what we would expect to find. The one exception in our survey was this obligation-sex message. If a woman believes the obligation-sex message, she is 27% more likely to only have sex because she feels she has to. However, if she doesn't believe it personally but is being taught this message, she is 85% more likely to only have sex out of obligation. Why does teaching it lead to worse outcomes if she doesn't believe it?

We started investigating different explanations and the answers were quite sad. These women are more likely to be in sexless marriages, have vaginismus, have a spouse with sexual dysfunction,[12] and they are more likely to have a history of abuse than women who disagree with it and are not being taught it.[13] They are also 2.5 times more likely to be in the bottom quintile of marital satisfaction than in the top quintile.[14]

So what is happening? Many of these women report they are getting this message from Christian books and media, not necessarily from the pulpit.[15] Women in bad marriage situations are desperately seeking help from our evangelical resources. And apparently the best we have to offer them is "You must have more sex." Even in counseling situations, the women in our focus groups told us they were recommended evangelical books that did nothing but make matters worse.

But the other source bringing this message is the women's husbands themselves. Combine this with the fact that these women are more likely to have experienced or be currently experiencing abuse,[16] and we are left with the horrifying conclusion that abusive husbands seem to be bringing their wives Christian resources that tell women that if they won't have sex, they are in sin. As I (Joanna) was running the numbers, I felt like I could see into a living room. I could see a woman in a horrible marriage, and in her husband's brokenness and selfishness, he's lobbing the obligation-sex message at her, destroying her bit by bit.

Abusive men are using our evangelical resources as weapons. That's why Christian resources simply must do better. Not one of the books we looked at, except our secular control book, John Gottman's *The Seven Principles for Making Marriage Work*, even *mentioned* the idea of consent. This isn't acceptable. And so let's be clear: marital rape and sexual assault, whether by physical force or coercive threats, are real and are wrong. These all count as forms of sexual assault:

- If a spouse is angry and potentially violent or verbally abusive, and you feel you have to have sex in order to protect yourself or your children.
- If a spouse routinely physically abuses you, and you find this happens less often if you have sex more.
- If a spouse routinely verbally abuses you and tells you that you are worthless or tells you that you will be disobeying God if you refuse sex.
- If a spouse doesn't give you any access to money or groceries or toiletries unless you regularly have sex.
- If a spouse regularly has sex with you while you are sleeping (whether or not your spouse wakes you up in the process), *unless you have explicitly stated beforehand that you actually want this.*
- If a spouse forces a sexual act that you do not want, that is also sexual assault, even if the rest of the sexual encounter

was consensual. We received a letter from a woman saying, "I told my husband I wasn't comfortable with sex toys, but in the middle of sex, he'll use one on me suddenly, with no warning, after whipping it out from under a pillow."

• If a spouse threatens that if you do not have sex, he or she will look at porn, go on sex chat websites, go to strip clubs, or visit prostitutes.

These are all evil, even if not all are prosecutable in a court of law. And compliance does not equal consent either. Even if you did not physically fight or verbally say no, that does not mean you went along with it willingly. If any of these are happening to you, please call a domestic abuse hotline, or reach out to a licensed counselor who specializes in domestic violence.

Evangelical culture has done both men and women a great disservice in how we talk about consent in marriage. And one of the ways this teaching most affects couples is one we've touched on but want to discuss more fully: sexual pain.

How Sex under Pressure and Sexual Pain Are Linked

This teaching that sex is something women owe their husbands is the most painful, in a literal sense, when sexual pain is actually involved. And we found that sexual pain is very widespread in the Christian community. As we first discussed in chapter 3, 32.3% of women have experienced sexual pain. When we break it down,

• 26.7% of women have experienced postpartum sexual pain.

• 22.6% of women have experienced vaginismus or some other form of primary sexual dysfunction that makes penetration painful.

- Overall, 6.8% of women have had such bad sexual pain that penetration was impossible.

As we have stated before, but we must reiterate, it's long been known that sexual pain rates (unrelated to childbirth) are higher in the Christian community.[17] These are our women; this is our problem. And our messages are making it worse. Consider these women:

- Jennifer, who said her wedding night was "awkward and traumatic" but kept pushing through because she was so scared of being a bad wife.
- Piper, who was plagued with guilt over not being able to consummate her marriage for years due to excruciating pain (even though she and her husband were able to have other forms of sex).
- And me (Sheila), who gritted my teeth and forced myself to have sex despite pain, because I was afraid that my husband couldn't feel love any other way.

The cause of postpartum sexual pain is obvious, and it makes sense why the pressure to have sex too soon after delivery can exacerbate the pain and cause her to associate pain with sex, prolonging the problem. On the other hand, primary pain such as vaginismus related to muscle spasms in the pelvic floor is multifaceted. Because primary pain is so much higher in the Christian community, we know that something about what we're teaching must be contributing to the problem. So let's look at how this may play out.

Often Christian women endure sex with pain because they feel like they have to—and this makes sexual pain worse. As we discussed in chapter 4, when a woman has sex for the first time on her wedding night completely unaroused because it's what you're supposed to do, we shouldn't be surprised if many women's bodies don't cooperate, especially when combined with normal anxiety and the exhaustion from the day. Intercourse when unaroused can cause a great deal of pain. Sex then becomes associated with pain, and it becomes even harder to relax. Her body starts to tense in anticipation of the pain, creating a vicious cycle.

But the problems may also start long before the wedding night (or long before the first time she has consensual sex). When women believe before they are married the message that a wife is obligated to give her husband sex when he wants it, vaginismus/dyspareunia rates go up by 37%.[18] To understand the gravity of this, 37% is only barely statistically different from the effect we found of abuse on vaginismus/dyspareunia.[19] Our bodies interpret the obligation-sex message in similar ways to trauma, likely because obligation sex and trauma have much in common. Both say, "What you need doesn't matter." Both say, "Others can use you without your consent." Both say, "You are unimportant." What often makes this even worse for Christian women is that we feel like God condones our pain because we're told the Bible says we can't say no. When we feel unseen, unimportant, and used, not just by our husbands but also by God, that causes trauma. It feels threatening on a subconscious level, so the body freezes in order to protect itself—in a way that says "Keep out!"

Think of the implications of this for a moment: believing this obligation-sex message makes women more vulnerable to sexual pain, but if they believe this message, they're also likely to force themselves to muscle through. Forcing themselves to have frequent, painful sex makes treatment so much more difficult because it strengthens the association between sex and pain. Indeed, the group most likely to suffer from vaginismus is women who are pushing themselves to have sex despite not ever orgasming and not feeling close to their husbands. These women are twice (2.02 times) as likely to have vaginismus than other women who are married and are actively having sex.[20]

In Deborah Feldman's autobiography *Unorthodox*, she tells the story of leaving her Hasidic, Orthodox Jewish roots after an arranged marriage. On her wedding night, she discovered that sex hurt and penetration was impossible. Over the next few months, she was bombarded with pressure from her aunt, her mother-in-law, and multiple busybodies to fix her "defect" and perform anyway. Despite therapy for vaginismus, the pain endured. Her husband, who simply wanted to complete the deed with no concern for her welfare, wasn't helping. The Netflix series based on the book depicts the heartbreaking scene when they finally manage penetration. Covering her mouth with her hand, she grits her teeth and cries through the ordeal. Afterward, he rolls over and declares how amazing it felt.[21]

No one should ever take pleasure in something that causes another pain. That causes trauma, and it reinforces trauma already present.

It's not surprising that many Christian women push themselves like Feldman did since almost every Christian marriage and sex book we studied addressed women's obligation to have sex, but very few gave any caveats about pain.[22] Despite the fact that 32.3% of the women in our study have suffered significant sexual pain, most books don't even mention it. *Love & Respect* has sold two million copies, presumably to two million couples. That means that for roughly 650,000 of these couples, the wife experienced sexual pain so that penetration was painful or difficult, including 136,000 who found it impossible. Yet those couples were told, without any caveats, that wives must give their husbands unconditional sex.[23] Add the fact that so many of these books also teach that men will be tempted to lust, watch porn, or have an affair if women don't have sex, and women can feel as if they're having sex with a metaphorical gun to their marriage. All will blow up if you don't put out. Too often, the cost of his pleasure becomes her pain, either physically or emotionally.[24]

Part of the emotional turmoil caused by vaginismus is that it's easy for the couple to assume she's doing it deliberately or, if it's not consciously deliberate, that she is still somehow causing it. In *The Act of Marriage*, LaHaye intimated that this is due to fear that he wouldn't fit.[25] Then not only do women have to endure pain; they also have to endure guilt and, too often, their husband's anger or disappointment.

But vaginismus is an involuntary spasm of the muscles in the vagina that makes penetration very painful if not impossible—with *involuntary* being the operative word. A recent research project on the use of a novel treatment method for severe vaginismus allowed husbands to observe the operation (with their wife's consent, of course) and to feel the vaginal spasm with a gloved finger. "The breakthrough for many of these men . . . was often profound and allowed them to understand, often for the first time, that vaginismus is a medical condition over which the woman had no control."[26]

What makes this situation even more heartbreaking is that it can show up in marriages in which obligation sex is the last message husbands would ever want to give their wives. Husbands who want to sacrificially give to their wives, husbands who would never want to cause their wives pain, husbands who only want to experience real intimacy and not some substitute can still have wives who have internalized this message, because the message did not necessarily, or even primarily, come from husbands. It came from books, sermons, and teachings around sex that invalidated women's experiences and told women, "You don't matter."

While the go-to treatment for sexual pain is pelvic floor physiotherapy—which we highly recommend—what our survey results tell us is that it's not *only* pelvic floor physiotherapy that we need. If rates of sexual pain are higher when people believe certain things, then part of the treatment has to be challenging those beliefs.

When to See a Pelvic Floor Physiotherapist

Pelvic floor physiotherapists are trained professionals who treat muscles in the bottom of the pelvis and vagina. They use massage, dilation, exercise, and other methods to treat conditions ranging from sexual pain to incontinence. Pelvic floor physiotherapists can help with

- preparing for childbirth and recovering during the postpartum phase, including help strengthening muscles that are now too loose or dealing with scar tissue from tearing
- pain during sex that isn't mild and isn't alleviated by changing positions
- incontinence, including squirting urine or worrying about whether or not you will leak

The good news about all this for husbands, though, is that if your wife has internalized this message, you have an opportunity to prove how much you truly love your wife. By showing your wife through your words and actions that she *can* say "no" or "not right now" or "I don't want to try that" without fear, you can help to undo the years of damage these teachings have inflicted on her. By acting in a way completely counter to the obligation-sex message, you help her rediscover her agency in your marriage by giving her permission to feel safe.

Let us tell you about Sandra, one of our focus group members. When Sandra was growing up, her mom told her that "men are only after one thing" and that "one thing" was what made men stick around. Sandra's father abandoned his tumultuous marriage, and his child, when Sandra was still in elementary school. Determined not to repeat her mother's fate, Sandra married believing she would have to give her husband sex to hold on to him. But lo and behold, she was greeted early on in her marriage with a horrible case of vaginismus. She even had incontinence issues because her pelvic floor was so impacted.

Seven years into her marriage to Paul, Sandra came to Christ. Like many wives who come to faith, she pored over Christian marriage resources to see what they had to offer. "When I became a Christian, all I really heard about sex from Christian resources was that sex was the wife's duty. So when you combine those two messages: that he only really wanted one thing from me and I was duty-bound to give it to him, I started feeling I was just an object, not a person."

Turning to evangelical resources did not make her vaginismus better or make sex better. Sandra says that the majority of the time, she only had sex because she felt she had no choice. She endured it, despite the pain.

It wasn't until more than twenty years of marriage passed that Sandra and Paul finally talked about this issue. Paul, appalled to learn after all these years that his wife had been merely performing sex out of obligation and fear, reassured her that what she had heard was wrong—he was not interested in duty sex at all, and he was definitely not only in the marriage because of what she could give him sexually.

After months of talking through this and Paul proving to Sandra that she really could say no and he would be fine, it finally began to click in Sandra's mind. "My body physically changed," Sandra describes. "I had been doing pelvic floor physiotherapy for a while, but when I began to understand that I could say no, that change made a huge difference in how sex felt. It became less painful, I began to relax, and for the first time in my life, I began to experience a sense of freedom in the bedroom."

"The funny thing in all of this is that we're still doing the same things," Sandra says, "but I can see and trust his heart for me now, and I can bring my heart into the bedroom too. So it's an entirely different experience, even if the mechanics are the same."

Coming Face-to-Face with the God Who Sees Us

When the three of us think of how badly women have been hurt by the obligation-sex message, whether through manipulation, obligation, coercion, or pain, we're reminded of the Bible story of Hagar, Abraham, and Sarah. As you may remember, God had promised Abraham he would have a son and from this son God would make a great nation. The problem? Abraham and Sarah were both old, and Sarah was barren. In desperation, Sarah suggested that Abraham have a child with her slave, Hagar.

Nothing in the Bible story tells us that Hagar was a willing participant. As a servant, she would not have been able to truly consent. Her feelings and needs wouldn't matter. Nevertheless, Abraham heeded Sarah's advice and used Hagar to have a son. Some years later, miraculously Abraham does have a child with Sarah. Now Hagar and her son Ishmael were threats to Isaac, the child of the promise. Abraham sends Hagar and her son away.

While she is in the desert, God provides for her. And here's where things get interesting. Hagar is the first person in Scripture who is given the honor of bestowing a name upon God. And the name she chooses? *"The God who sees me."* After being sexually assaulted, forced to carry a baby, and then abandoned, never having her needs or wishes taken into account, being invisible and used to meet other people's needs, God sees her.

And being seen makes all the difference.

God sees women. God does not say to women, "Your experience doesn't matter compared to your husband's tremendous need." God does not tell women, "Let your husband ejaculate inside you, no matter how you feel, because otherwise you are in disobedience." No, God says, "I designed sex to be a deep knowing of two people. And that, my child, means that *both of you matter.*"

If we were to talk about sex like that, we believe there would be fewer cases of vaginismus. We believe fewer women would give up on sex because it's so emotionally damaging. We believe more

194

women would be excited about sex, enjoy sex, and feel freedom in the bedroom.

Today, Erika, who had to perfect the art of wrestling to escape her husband, is now in a safe second marriage and knows what it means to be seen. Her new marriage is reciprocal—both of their needs are valued and expressed. "We are both expected to practice self-control," Erika explained, "and that is what has allowed me to trust my husband."

At the end of our interview, Erika said that she's working on relearning who she is as a child of God, and she's grateful to be in a marriage in which her husband mirrors that image back to her.

We know some reading these "pressure-free" chapters will be uncomfortable right now. If we abandon the obligation-sex message, then what's to stop women from withholding sex altogether?

To a certain extent, this concern may be valid. Our data does show that when women believe the obligation-sex message, they are more likely to have sex at least twice a week.[27] Women who discard the message, however, are 29% more likely to reach orgasm frequently and 36% less likely to have vaginismus or other forms of dyspareunia.[28] The fear that men may not have as much sex as they want should not supersede women's need to feel safe.

So we face a choice. Do we want women to give husbands intercourse, even if sex is terrible, potentially traumatic, and coercive? Or do we want to change the way we talk about sex so women are able to freely choose to embrace and enjoy sex, even if that means the number of sexual encounters goes down? Will we decide to view sex as a life-giving mutual serving and knowing of each other, or will we continue to see it as a spirit-killing entitlement and obligation?

Hopefully, by this point in the book, we've debunked the idea that women need to accept men's sexual sin or accept the responsibility for it. We've debunked the idea that sex should be an obligation or an entitlement. Now let's change gears and look at how we can build a heathy foundation for sex, focusing on kindness and passion in a way that honors *both* people in the marriage—and leads to a fun and life-giving sex life!

EXPLORE TOGETHER:
Entering into Sex Freely and Honoring Your Spouse's No

Review the different areas of consent in your marriage, and make sure you're on the same page.

Deciding Whether to Have Sex

If your spouse doesn't want to have sex, do you do any of the following:

- Leave the bedroom or refuse to sleep in bed with them?
- Get irritable or treat them badly in the following day or two?
- Punish them in any of the ways listed earlier in the chapter?

Compare your answers with your spouse's.

Deciding What to Do in the Bedroom

If there's something you'd like to try that your spouse doesn't want to do, do you do any of the following:

- Ask repeatedly, even if they have said no?
- Try to do it anyway during a sexual encounter without asking first?
- Find resources for your spouse to read to convince them to give in?
- Withhold affection or kindness, or punish them in any way listed earlier in the chapter?

Compare your answers with your spouse's.

If your spouse is violating your boundaries, or if even having these conversations is making you feel unseen, unheard, or unsafe, please seek a licensed counselor. If you are currently in danger, please call an abuse hotline or notify the authorities.

Allowing for *No*

If you have not been honoring your spouse's *no*:

1. Apologize and seek forgiveness.
2. State what you will do differently in the future. If your spouse says no, how will you act instead?

Holding Your *No* Responsibly

While we have the freedom to say no, we hold in tension the fact that we are also the only proper sexual outlet our spouse has. Here are some ways to hold your *no* responsibly:

1. Foster a habit of watching for good opportunities to have sex and taking advantage of them so that when your spouse asks for sex at an inopportune time, they know that your *no* doesn't mean *never again*.
2. If your *no* relates to something the vast majority of people consider a healthy part of a sexual life, such as intercourse or touching various parts of the body, seek appropriate professional help so that if you're healthy and it is possible, your *no* can turn to a *not yet, but soon*.
3. If your *no* stems from a marital issue, seek professional help for your marriage. While it may be wise to take sex off the table until larger issues are dealt with, putting a moratorium on sex without seeking help is not honoring your marriage vows.
4. If your *no* is due to issues of safety or being mistreated in your marriage, approach the proper authorities or abuse help centers so you can be safe. You do not need to work toward having sex with an abusive spouse.

Freely Entering into Sex

Using a code word can help both of you know that you are staying within each other's boundaries while giving you an easy way to speak up if you're getting uncomfortable. Choose a code word that will mean "I'd like to stop now," whether it's *uncle* or something innocuous, like *pineapple* or *Appalachian*. Then, when you hear that code word, stop what you're doing. Reassure one another of your love, and decide together what you want to do next. While code words are great tools for healthy marriages, they will not stop an abusive spouse from harming you. Again, if you are in an abusive marriage, please enlist outside professional help.

RESCUING AND REFRAMING

- Instead of ignoring the reality of widespread marital rape and coercion, say repeatedly and often, "Marital rape is real, wrong, and illegal."
- Instead of talking about men's rights to sex, talk about each spouse's right to consent.
- Instead of treating sex like an entitlement within marriage, say, "Sex is a gift, not a weapon. It is always meant to be mutual and to bring couples closer together." And say, "Self-control is a fruit of the Spirit."
- Instead of telling couples, "There is no biblical reason to say no to sex except for prayer and fasting," say, "'Do not deprive' does not mean 'Do not refuse.'"
- Instead of saying, "Fulfilling your spouse's sexual needs and desires is a requirement in marriage," say, "You should not get pleasure from something that causes your spouse discomfort, embarrassment, humiliation, pain, or harm."

Sex should *put the other first:* Sex is about considering your spouse's wants and needs before you consider your own.

CHAPTER 11

Just Be Nice

Do nothing out of selfish ambition or vain conceit.
Rather, in humility value others above yourselves,
not looking to your own interests but each of you
to the interests of the others.

Philippians 2:3-4

Many well-meaning pastors, authors, and counselors have dedicated themselves to the admirable work of dispelling the myth that sex is shameful. When we graded the bestselling Christian sex books on a rubric based on mutuality, faithfulness, and pleasure, the books tended to score best in the areas related to women's sexual pleasure. Their theology around sex is aptly summarized by Genesis 2:25: "Adam and his wife were both naked, and they felt no shame." Being naked and unashamed is certainly a great place to start.

But too often our theology of sex in marriage starts and ends in the garden of Eden—and we do not live in the garden anymore. Women are given a beautiful picture of shame-free, passionate sex but then are bombarded by dangerous teachings rampant in these same books: it's her duty to give him sex when he asks, regardless of how she feels; sex is something he will take from her because he needs it so badly; all men lust, so she needs to do her part if she wants her husband to stay faithful.

Our theology of sex has to go beyond the creation story in Genesis 2:25—being naked and not ashamed—and encompass so much more. A truly Christian view must see sex through the lens of the cross.

A Cross-Centered Sex Life

Although he was the Creator of the universe, Christ decided to live among us, and he became a servant, putting others before himself, in order to restore us to intimacy with the Father. And he did so at the highest price, humbling himself to death on a cross. That selflessness, that passionate other-focused love, is what the kingdom of God looks like. What would happen if we saw sex as an opportunity to mirror Christ's servanthood to our spouse? Seeing sex through the lens of the cross encompasses so much more than being naked and unashamed; it becomes a conduit for intimate relationships and reconciliation to each other.

Sex seen through the lens of the cross has no room for taking or entitlement. That's why sex in light of kingdom principles needs to be focused not only on pleasure and freedom from shame but also on serving rather than taking. In Matthew 20:25–28, Jesus says,

> You know that the rulers of the Gentiles lord it over them, and their high officials exercise authority over them. Not so with you. Instead, whoever wants to become great among you must be your servant, and whoever wants to be first must be your slave—just as the Son of Man did not come to be served, but to serve, and to give his life as a ransom for many.

We're supposed to serve or, in Paul's words, put each other first, "not looking to your own interests but each of you to the interests of the others" (Phil. 2:4). Your needs do matter—but kindness requires we overcome our natural selfish bent by purposely considering others first so that our own needs are put in perspective. Sometimes in doing so, we realize that our needs really are the more pressing ones. But by keeping the focus on the other, we begin to serve like Christ.

As we were looking through the bestselling books on sex and marriage, we easily found the big-picture teachings we've already discussed: all men struggle with lust, women's bodies are dangerous, sex is for a husband's physical release, etc., etc.

After tackling these issues, though, we were still left with a handful of scenarios from these books that didn't fit neatly into any one harmful teaching. In trying to figure out where to slot them into the book, we realized that they shared a common denominator: following these pieces of advice meant looking less like Jesus.

As we start to wrap up this book, we want to point us back to Jesus's example of serving, not being served. And the answer is shockingly simple: please, please, people, *just be kind*.

Living Out "Putting Others First" in Sex

My (Rebecca's) agonizing twenty-two-hour labor ended when I pushed my son out in just five contractions. To absolutely no one's surprise, that speedy arrival resulted in a very bad third-degree tear—the kind where my midwives took one look down there and rang for some morphine.

I wasn't cleared to walk for four weeks postpartum, so my husband, Connor, had to do everything except feed the baby. He was cooking, folding laundry, walking the dog, bathing the baby. And don't forget the less-glamorous parts of postpartum recovery: helping me hobble to the bathroom, venturing to the store to buy me extra-absorbent menstrual pads, and getting up every two hours through the night to get me more ice packs to place you-know-where.

At my six-week follow-up appointment when my midwives told me that sex was still off the table, Connor was right there beside me. The next day I had my first appointment with a pelvic floor physiotherapist. She said I would not be cleared to have actual intercourse until I had retrained my muscles to relax enough to allow it.

The word that best describes my husband through my entire postpartum recovery is *hero*. Truly and completely—he put his all into taking care of me and our son, never complaining that I was taking too long to recover. By being selfless without having a martyr complex, he gave me the space I needed to recover—he gave me no-strings-attached kindness and sacrificial love.

Kindness is nonnegotiable. Love, as the apostle Paul said, is kind (1 Cor. 13:4). Regardless of how your spouse acts toward you, you have to be kind. But kindness doesn't always have to feel like a chore. When your marriage is characterized by just being decent people to each other, kindness naturally flows. Prior to getting pregnant, Connor and I had always been on the same page when it came to sex. We both wanted it, we both liked it, we both got pleasure from it. And both of us were in a pattern of ensuring that we set aside time for the other person, even if we were having a lower-libido week or month. Connor could wait patiently, in full confidence that this was not a moratorium on sex—he could pour himself into our little family while giving me space to recover, knowing that I prioritized intimacy as much as he did. Connor loved me sacrificially by showing me affection and waiting patiently. I loved him by going to appointments where a matronly physiotherapist with a soothing Newfoundland accent performed internal vaginal stretches on me while I lay on my back breastfeeding our newborn.

Kindness to your spouse means considering their needs as you consider your own. That's what Ephesians 5:21–33 prescribes for marriages! Whether it's about libido differences, exhaustion, or a commitment to addressing sexual dysfunction, you can be Christ to your spouse by doing what is uncomfortable in order to bless your marriage, even in the difficult times of life, like grief, infertility, and miscarriage. As Tim Keller sums it up in *The Meaning of Marriage*, "The Christian teaching does not offer a choice between fulfillment and sacrifice but rather mutual fulfillment through mutual sacrifice."[1] When we each consider the other, we build something beautiful.

> CHECK-IN: What does sex through the lens of the cross look like to you? Is that what you're experiencing in your marriage? If not, think of an example of where your sex life needs more kindness.

Let's Talk Sex and Her Period

It is human nature to be blind to our own areas of selfishness. And when our sex advice is unbalanced in who it asks to be selfless, we create unbalanced marriages. This is tricky for us to talk about, because in looking at the bestselling Christian marriage books, we found a lot of advice which, if followed, would work out great for husbands and terrible for wives. We don't want to beat up on men here, though, because most of the men we know are very selfless. But we do need to address a few of these issues, because they have repeatedly been handled poorly in evangelical resources. When you hear advice that, if you followed it, would allow you to have everything you wanted while your spouse did all the giving, it's a good practice to ask yourself, *Is this really being Christlike?*

One such topic is whether or not wives "owe" their husbands sexual release during inconvenient times, like when she's on her period or in the postpartum phase. *Sheet Music*, for instance, says, "The most difficult time for this man [who was tempted by porn] was during his wife's period, because she was unavailable to him sexually. After about ten years, she finally realized that pleasing her husband with oral sex or a simple 'hand job' did wonders to help her husband through that difficult time."[2]

Leman elaborates on this advice later with,

> There are times for whatever reason that a wife may choose to make use of what younger men affectionately refer to as "hand jobs." A woman with heavy periods that last six or seven days, or who has just gotten through a pregnancy, or perhaps is simply not feeling her best, may genuinely feel that sex is more than she can handle. But with a minimum of effort, she can help her husband who feels like he's about ready to climb the walls because it's been so long.[3]

Let's think this through. Is it kind for a man to ask for a hand job when his wife is unwell? How unwell does she have to be before it's not kind anymore? How crampy does she have to be for her physical well-being to take precedence over sexual expectations? Do we really believe that the kindness that flows from the Holy Spirit working in our lives would ask an exhausted, torn apart postpartum woman for a hand job?

Now, there is nothing wrong if she wants to give him a "gift." That can be a way to show kindness! Or even period sex—many women find that the hormones during their period actually cause a libido boost, and they enjoy sex during this time.[4] But setting this up as the expectation—that she will provide release or he will sin, even if she is sick or unwell—is just not *kind*. And the fact that it is kind if she does it does not mean it is unkind if she does not. Besides, in Old Testament law, God commanded a whole nation of men not to have sex for a minimum of a week during their wife's period.[5] Leviticus has a higher view of men's ability to maintain sexual integrity during a wife's period than many Christian marriage books published in the twenty-first century.

Some women have periods that cause cramping, fainting, pain, nausea, and more. Leman's portrayal of this as a difficult time for the husband, ignoring the far more difficult physical symptoms many wives deal with, is highly problematic. Men, if your wife is feeling unwell or just plain icky, your emphasis should not be that she needs to "help her husband through that difficult time."[6] *Just be kind.* Telling a woman who is cramping and whose genitals are engorged in a way that makes touching them feel very off-putting that she should give him a hand job shows no consideration for her experience and is very *unkind.* Rather, be Christ to your wife and recognize that this is a difficult time for *her.*

One woman, commenting on this pressure to have sex while on your period, said this:

> I honestly feel like a lot of men want only the positive aspects of our bodies (i.e., the parts that make them climax) without any of the drawbacks. Those drawbacks are everything from normal aging to menstruation to the difficulties of childbirth and the effects those have on our bodies and psyches. Being hot, young, and not on your period or not pregnant is an incredibly short time in a woman's life, and I have no idea why young men contemplating marriage are not told in the most blunt of terms that being ready for marriage and sex means accepting all of those changes.

Bodies change. Waists expand. We lose the six-pack abs. Erections may not be as hard or as reliable. Lubrication can decrease. Menopause causes hormones to tank. We get tired. We get stressed. Women can be bloody and torn and tight. But even in all of this, we are still *us.* We are still a couple. Let's prioritize sex and intimacy while being kind to our spouse.

> CHECK-IN: How do you feel about period sex? How does your spouse feel? How do you feel about abstaining from anything sexual during her period or postpartum phase? Is this something that you have talked about?

Putting Others First Means Taking Care of Yourself

There is no easy way to address what we want to tackle next, so please have grace and don't throw those tomatoes.

Let's talk health and sex.

Before we jump in, though, let's put this in the right perspective. In *His Needs, Her Needs*, Willard Harley refers to being married to a wife who had gained one hundred pounds as a "prison sentence."[7] Can you imagine Christ saying this about one of his beloved children? Harley goes on, "She should try to look the way her husband likes her to look. She should resemble the woman he married. Does that mean a woman must stay eternally young? Of course not, but getting old is not an excuse for gaining weight and dressing like a bag lady."[8] This is profoundly condescending and unkind. It's unfair to ask a woman to keep her body from the natural process of aging, especially after giving birth to children.

Now, while gaining weight is a natural part of aging and child-bearing, becoming an unhealthy weight long-term is not. But the emphasis on how she should "resemble the woman he married" and "try to look the way her husband likes her to look" takes her personhood and replaces it with a pinup poster.

When Bev first married Roger almost thirty years ago, she felt cute, spunky, and flirty. Ten years and three kids later, though, her self-confidence had taken a serious hit.

"I hated my body," Bev told us in our focus group interviews, "and it held me back sexually. My post-baby body made me mourn the loss of my youth, and I completely lost my self-confidence." Bev stopped enjoying sex, unable to feel comfortable enough with her body to allow him to pleasure her. It wasn't long until she began to experience depression and feelings of hopelessness about her marriage—she felt inadequate, ugly, and unlovable when she looked at herself in the mirror.

Her husband, though, saw something different. "Roger saved us," Bev said. "He knew how I was talking about myself in my

207

head and he decided that his words would just have to be louder than mine. About sex, about my body, about his love for me—he combatted every negative belief I had with ten positive things from him."

For fifteen years, Roger persisted. "He would tell me every day, 'I find you beautiful, I find you attractive, you are not lacking in anything, and what your body looks like is what I want and need.'" He knew what their marriage could be, and he dedicated himself to showing his wife pure Christlike love. And finally, they had a breakthrough.

"Roger rebuilt me with his words so that now I actually like my body and know not just how to have great sex but how to really make love. I felt so inadequate before, but he showed me that I had so much more to offer him than I even knew." By the time Bev finished her story, everyone in the focus group was crying. Bev's husband didn't need her to look like she did on her wedding day. He needed her just the way she was.

When these books tell women they have to maintain their spry, youthful looks so their husbands can still find them hot, they are working against the Christlike efforts of so many husbands trying to prove to their wives how they are utterly and completely adored. Now, Bev's insecurities were all a part of the natural aging process. But what about when there is a health issue that does need to be addressed?

Almost all the Christian resources we looked at talk about the importance of a wife keeping up her appearance so that her husband still finds her attractive, but very few of them talk about how a husband gaining weight isn't just unattractive to his wife; it also detracts from her ability to derive physical pleasure from sex. We are afraid that many books elevate a husband's desire to have a youthful-looking wife over a woman's ability to enjoy sex. This may be harsh, but we have heard from many women: men's excessive weight gain makes sex difficult or impossible. A husband's "beer belly" can restrict women's sexual enjoyment; it's not just an attractiveness issue. It's much harder for the clitoris to receive any attention during penetration if he has an overhanging belly, since his pelvic bone can't stimulate her in the right way. And when your spouse is very heavy, breathing becomes difficult if he's on top. In addition, when one or both spouses have more paunch, the usable length of the penis decreases. One woman explained her experience like this:

> My spouse used to blame me for lack of sex when the fact is I got sick of the hip pain trying to straddle someone three times my size. On top became the only workable position (which is boring in itself) but then as he grew it became painful. Now we have no sex life. I have explained to him that he is too big, but he tells me to get more limber! However, I'm not the one who is overeating every day. Obesity impacts everything: sex, affection, cuddling, traveling, activities together, even sitting next to each other in the movie theater (if you can even go), the furniture you can buy, the cars you can ride in together, the amount of the food bill every month.

Natalie from our previous chapters, who struggles with anorgasmia, is also married to an obese man. When he moved from the morbidly obese to the obese category after shedding fifty pounds, sex improved for both of them dramatically. He gained an inch of usable length, his erections were harder, and his stamina was better, allowing lovemaking to last longer. Natalie mused to us in our interview, "How much of women's anorgasmia is actually caused by severe obesity?"

We all want to be wildly enthusiastic about making love to our spouses, and hopefully by now we've convinced you all that sex is far more than just physical. But even though it's more than physical—*it still is physical.* When we care for our physical bodies, we care for our spouse. Eating healthy foods, exercising, getting enough sleep, and dealing with stress helps you moderate your moods. They help you live a longer life with better quality. And that's a gift!

We recognize that food-related weight issues are not just about food. Often, deep-seated emotional issues such as past trauma, mental health issues, or poor coping skills are the main contributors to why food is such an issue. If you have struggled with your weight, many people benefit from not just nutritionists or personal trainers but also licensed counselors who can work with you to set realistic goals to help you become healthier overall.

The weight-loss journey is not easy, but it is worth it, as Keisha explained on our blog:

> As we lay in bed, snuggled close one night, after a really great moment of intimacy, we both sighed deliciously and simultaneously breathed, "That was different!"
>
> For the first time in a really long time, it felt as exhilarating as it felt when we were young! We were the same two people who had slept in the same bed together for the last two and a half decades, but something was different: we both had overcome an addiction to food and had lost over 75 pounds as a result. Quietly, we savored the moment together. Then my husband smiled and said, "I didn't know you could do that anymore."

Christlike kindness includes dealing with our own health issues and being an encourager as our spouses deal with theirs. As we journey in this together, we have to ask ourselves, *How can I be kind to my spouse in this area?* Whatever the answer, we know it won't include talking about being married to your spouse as if it's a prison sentence.

> CHECK-IN: Is weight or health detracting from sexual enjoyment in your marriage? How can you address this together in a kind way?

Putting Others First Means Valuing Your Spouse's Dignity

Being a kind spouse also involves treating your spouse as precious and made in the image of God. Yes, this involves valuing what they need, but it also involves valuing who they are. This has repercussions in the bedroom that go far beyond just the question of how often couples have sex or even whether they have sex. It also impacts how we treat each other *during* sex.

Many couples don't only face libido differences. They also have to navigate sexual boundaries—what do we do in bed, and what do we steer clear from? Obviously there are some biblical commands that must be followed, such as avoiding anything involving a third party (whether with porn or an actual person), but we think it goes further than that. Putting others first also means that their preferences, fears, and self-image need to be protected.

That means if one of you feels that a certain sexual act is degrading or if it causes flashbacks to abuse, you should avoid it. Don't do anything that will cause your spouse pain, even if the pain is emotional. If intercourse itself is triggering to you or if the only acts that bring your spouse to orgasm are triggering to you, then the kind thing to do (both for yourself and for your spouse) is to see a counselor to work through your trauma. But don't push your spouse's boundaries in the bedroom, and never break their trust.

Many have grown up in the porn culture and have trained the sexual response cycle to respond to graphic things that can be degrading, dangerous, or unpleasant to the other. One spouse pressures the other to act out what they've seen or they find that "vanilla" sex just doesn't do it for them. But kind people do not force or pressure their spouses to act out their fetishes. Instead, they dedicate themselves to retraining their brains so that intimacy is what triggers desire and arousal, not only exotic (and possibly violent or degrading) sex.

Honoring your spouse's dignity also means that you view sex as a mutual experience, not something your spouse does to "service" you. Now-disgraced former megachurch pastor Mark Driscoll said this in a 2007 sermon in Edinburgh about how a wife should "repent" of the "terrible sin" of not giving oral sex:

> She [the wife] says, "I've never performed oral sex on my husband. I've refused to." I said, "You need to go home and tell your husband that you've met Jesus and you've been studying the Bible, and that you're convicted of a terrible sin in your life. And then you need to drop his trousers, and you need to serve your husband. And when he asks why, say, 'Because I'm a repentant woman. God has changed my heart and I'm supposed to be a biblical wife.'" She says, "Really?" I said, "Yeah. First Peter three says if your husband is an unbeliever to serve him with deeds of kindness."[9]

We believe oral sex can be a healthy part of couples' sex lives, provided both of you are comfortable with it. But cross-centered sex means that making love needs to be about serving and loving. To frame it as Driscoll does here, and to use Bible verses to manipulate her into giving him oral sex, strips the wife of her dignity. Driscoll has lost much of his credibility in the church, partly because of statements like this. We wonder, though, why so many authors of books can say similar things without being similarly discredited. Is it only that we do not like hearing it out loud?

But "servicing him" becomes even more sinister when his requests require her humiliation, pain, or victimization. If you only become aroused when someone else is in distress or discomfort, that is a problem. One woman wrote to us with concerning sexual dynamics in her marriage:

> There will be times when I initiate and my husband says no, which I am okay with. But then he will want to a few minutes later. Today I had to go to work and knew I would be leaving in a half an hour. I offered for us to have a quickie before I had to go. He said he was okay. Then right before I had to leave, he asked if we could go into the bedroom. I got frustrated but didn't want to deny him, which

of course killed the mood for him and he got frustrated. At night, when I initiate, he often says no. Then as soon as I fall asleep, he wakes me up and says he is horny, or I wake up and find him having sex with me.

As we explained in chapter 10, waking someone up for sex without their consent is sexual assault. But looking at the other things she described, we see even more red flags. She initiates when it is a good time for her, but if it's a good time for her, he's turned off. He only wants intercourse when it's inconvenient for her. It sounds like, for this man, power has become an aphrodisiac. When you operate under a kingdom of power, rather than under the kingdom of God (as Jesus contrasts in Matt. 20:25–28), then power over the other becomes the gateway to arousal and sexual response. When you operate instead under a kingdom where love and sacrifice reign, then love becomes the gateway into sex.

> CHECK-IN: Is your spouse taking pleasure from hurting, degrading, or humiliating you? Please know that setting up boundaries and saying, "I will not agree to be treated like this in bed" is not just okay, it is good. If you are violating your spouse's boundaries, repent and seek counseling. Repeat the exercises from chapter 2 where you learned to feel emotional closeness during sex.

Throughout this book, we hope that we have been pointing you toward a sex life that is truly about making love in every sense of the word. Sex, as part of a cross-centered marriage, isn't conceited, self-seeking, or rude. Sex is freely given, mutually pleasurable, and deeply personal. Jesus is our great rescuer, and if you want to reclaim great sex for your marriage, it all starts with acting in a Christlike way toward your spouse. And that boils down to kindness. We hope you've caught the vision of how sex like this can transform your marriage. But now we want to present the culmination of all these principles: passion.

EXPLORE TOGETHER

Have sex during which you are completely and utterly serving your spouse—not "servicing" but serving. And then reverse roles the next time you have sex.

- Run a bubble bath, start with a massage, or touch your spouse's body in a way that helps them relax.
- Tell your spouse not just that you love them, but why you love them. What you appreciate that they do for you. How they make your life better. What good qualities you see in them and how they've grown over your marriage.
- Take some time to make out in the way your spouse wants to. If your spouse is ready and rarin' to go, that's good too! But if your spouse wants a drawn-out make-out session, enjoy it.
- When you move to sex, focus entirely on bringing your spouse pleasure. You may choose to opt for nonpenetrative sex so it is easier to focus on your spouse, but even if your spouse chooses intercourse, make it about them, not you.
- Afterward, don't simply roll over and fall asleep. Hold your spouse, talk to them, pray together, whatever your spouse needs in that moment.

RESCUING AND REFRAMING

- Instead of telling only women, "Be kind by pushing your needs aside to meet your spouse's," tell both spouses, "Be kind and considerate of your spouse's needs, considering their experience as being of the same importance as your own."

- Instead of telling women, "Your husband needs you to stay attractive," tell couples, "Pursuing a healthy lifestyle is a way to show kindness to your spouse."
- Instead of presenting the ideal sex life as one where she is not menstruating, is not pregnant, is not breastfeeding, is not going through menopause, and looks the way she did when they got married, say to couples, "Women's bodies were made for more than just their husbands' pleasure. Honor your wife's body, and honor your wife."

Sex should be *passionate*: Sex was designed to allow us to enter into a state of joyful abandon, to completely surrender ourselves to the other in an ecstasy of trust and love.

CHAPTER 12

From Having Intercourse to Making Love

> The thief does not come except to steal, and to kill,
> and to destroy. I have come that they may have life,
> and that they may have it more abundantly.
>
> John 10:10 NKJV

Have you ever noticed that right before and during orgasm, you can't speak in full sentences? You're no longer being guided by thoughts; you allow your emotions to take the wheel. You're Experience, not Thought.

And that's the way God made it.

Ponder that for a moment: at the pinnacle of human emotional experience, it's not about *thinking* as much as it is about *being*. This "being" is the heart of passion.

So why is easy, carefree, passionate sex so dang elusive? Let's revisit Sandra, whom we last met when we were talking about sexual pain. Sandra's belief that sex was created for men led her to feel shameful about being a sexual person. "I had so much negative self-talk going on," Sandra explained, "and I would feel so trapped in my head while Paul was having his fun and trying so hard to please me—the poor man could never tell if I was enjoying it or not!"

Sandra often had times during sex when she would start to enjoy it, but shame didn't allow her to admit it in the moment to herself or her husband. And so for twenty years the couple just plowed ahead with bad sex.

Finally, after spending months talking to unearth the root of their problems, and months of Paul trying to prove to his wife that he didn't see sex as his entitlement, Sandra had a breakthrough: God didn't just create sex for Paul, he created sex for her too. "I realized that God made sex for two different reasons," Sandra explained, "physical reasons and oneness reasons. Sometimes sex is mainly about having fun meeting each other's physical needs, and that's okay, but the majority of the time its main purpose is to bring you closer and more united. Sex is the pinnacle of marital intimacy. Once I got that, I was finally able to allow myself to experience pleasure without feeling selfish or sinful. I'm still a work in progress, but I'm finally beginning to accept that God has given me freedom in my marriage bed, and that it is a good and holy thing."

Julie was a control freak who made sure to do everything by the book. Growing up, she always heard that sex was a wife's duty. Her mom told her, "It's a blessing," but Julie just thought, "Well, yeah, the same way that it's a blessing to cook for your spouse or take care of your kids, I guess."

So it's not surprising that when duty-focused Julie married Greg fifteen years ago, sex was never that appealing. "I saw sex as something I had to do," Julie explained. "It was my 'blessing as a wife' to be able to bring my husband so much pleasure, but I never thought it should be enjoyable for me too."

Julie felt a great deal of shame around her sexuality, which threw her into a strange cognitive dissonance. She knew it was "good" that her husband found her attractive, but she felt dirty any time she turned him on. "I was too uncomfortable to try anything more than 'vanilla' sex," Julie explained, "and I felt so shameful and timid for the first twelve years, I always kept a shirt on during sex. I couldn't even be fully naked with my husband."

Three years ago, at a women's small group, Julie's perspective shifted. "One woman led a Bible study where, for the first time, I was told that God wants me to have amazing, mind-blowing sex—and there was nothing shameful about that!" Over the next few months, Julie combed through Scripture and had an epiphany: "I finally understood that sex was a God-sanctioned way to experience a complete, ecstatic loss of control mixed with intense, overwhelming pleasure. And it completely blew my mind." She took time to process everything she learned, but when it all clicked, Julie announced to Greg, "Look, I've never fully given you my whole body. But let's do this—let's be naked, and let's have some fun."

Surprising to no one, Greg was thrilled when his wife decided to throw off shame in pursuit of passion. "Greg already knew all of this about sex well before I did," Julie said, "and he was just so happy that I was at last allowing myself to enjoy sex and allowing him to enjoy me!"

Today, Julie doesn't feel embarrassed or shameful when her husband thinks she's hot. Now she's proud to feel sexy! Unlocking passion allowed Julie to enjoy trying new things because she could finally lose herself while making love to her husband. She didn't have to be in control anymore. And Greg is so grateful they now have the sex life he always knew was possible—even if it did take twelve years.

> CHECK-IN: How do you feel about being naked in front of your spouse?

Baring It All

Nakedness can be intimidating for many of us, whether it's because of body image issues, shame, body changes after childbirth, mastectomies, the aging process, injuries, or scars. Do any of these resonate with you?

- I won't have sex with the lights on.
- We get changed in different rooms.
- I lock the door when I shower.
- We're never fully naked during sex.
- I position the sheets during sex so parts of my body stay hidden.

If this is you, here are some ways to get more comfortable sharing your body:

- Lie in bed naked together under covers (watch a show, listen to a podcast, whatever you want).
- Take a bath together where you're facing the same direction, with her lying against him.
- If she is self-conscious, buy pretty lingerie to wear to bed (not just sexy lingerie either—try introducing more feminine nightgowns and pajama pieces for regular nights too!).
- Use candles if full lights are too much.

If your spouse struggles with nakedness, here are some ways to show your spouse you love their body:

- Undress your spouse slowly and tenderly, kissing after each item of clothing. Only go to where they are comfortable.
- Use your words to build trust, not insecurity.
- Reassure your spouse every day that they are what you want and that they are what you need.

Both Sandra and Julie saw sex as a part of their marriage to-do list, a duty they owed their husbands. Now, we've already told you how dangerous the obligation-sex message is, and throughout the book we've given you many ingredients for a great sex life. But in this last piece, this passion piece, we want to make sure that we don't substitute one checklist for another:

- Are we emotionally connected? (check!)
- Did both of us orgasm? (check check!)
- Did we serve one another? (check!)

Treat sex like a checklist, and it loses its fun. And you know what? It's okay to just have fun—and passion is what unlocks fun! This final principle isn't about rescuing you from faulty teaching. We don't have any terrible quotes to share with you or shame-filled messages we want to deconstruct. We've done all that, and it's been heavy, but we hope it's been healing.

But now, to top it off, we want to give you a picture of this final piece that ties everything together. Let's figure out how to unlock passion.

Passion Isn't Tame

Describing passion is hard. We feel like we're in *The Sound of Music* trying to solve a problem like Maria: "How do you catch a cloud and pin it down?" But we're going to do our best.

Passion is what puts the "life" in sex life. It's hard to define, though, because if we reduce it to a checklist, we've lost the point of passion! Passion happens when we fully give ourselves to our spouse and we hold nothing back. But this can be difficult when, like Julie or Sandra, we have so divorced ourselves from our own sexuality that we can't let go but instead worry, *Am I still a good person? Am I doing this right?* or even, *Have I crossed the line? Is this wrong yet?* When we judge our performance, looking for mistakes, then our aim during sex is to make it *proper*.

But God designed sex so that intimacy isn't quite proper. It isn't something you can put a lid on and keep sterile and organized. It spills over. It revels. It even screams.

And you know what? God made us—both good guys and good girls—to be orgasmic. He is not afraid of extremes. He did not create relationships, even our relationship with him, to be neat and tidy. As C. S. Lewis describes Aslan, the Christ figure in *The Lion, the Witch and the Wardrobe*, "He's not a tame lion."[1]

But let's be careful to not hit another roadblock. All this talk about deep, intimate, passionate lovemaking makes sex sound super solemn. Quite frankly, we can take sex way too seriously. Passionate sex is often portrayed like it belongs in a four-hour-long foreign art film, with dark lighting and operatic music and metaphors you don't quite understand. A white stag gazes through the bedroom window. You know it has some significance, but you're not sure what it is.

But passionate sex can also happen in a Quality Inn bathroom, with fluorescent lighting and mirrors at all the wrong angles, while your kids sleep in the next room. The gift of sex in a healthy relationship is that you have nothing to prove anymore. You can just relax and be yourself, knowing you're unconditionally loved.

In contrast, being proper is emotional armor. It quells our anxieties that we won't be good enough or we might look stupid, reassuring us that we're living up to how others think we "should" be.

Passion requires taking off that armor and accepting that everything might not be perfect. It's about not having to suck in your belly when you're naked together, not having to put makeup on before he looks at you, not adjusting so the stretch marks are hidden under blankets. Passion doesn't just ignore these things—it embraces the imperfection because it's part of the picture of who we are.

Passion says I want you as you are—not who you could be, not who you should be, not who you were when we met—I want you now, and I want you in the deepest of senses.

Passion Requires Trust

That means that, at its core, passion is not about how many sex positions you know but about how much you can trust each other. Trust allows you to let go of control because it frees you from the need to protect yourself. You can let yourself feel, and you can turn your mind off just a little bit. You can stop worrying about what the other thinks about you and instead revel in the moment.

Passionate sex is like a train traveling along two railroad tracks. On one side, we have the throwing off of what is proper and embracing sexuality and its messiness. On the other, we have the steadfastness of a strong, healthy marriage that allows us to trust the other. Without both, the train runs off course. Unbridled passion is simply lust. But when passion flows from Christlike love for the other, that's when we find great sex.

Too often we think of passionate sex as sex that pushes boundaries. We focus on trying to find the new sexual high. And hey—trying new things is great! The exercises at the end of this chapter are all about trying new things! But what if the key to passionate sex lies less in forcing yourself past your comfort zone and more in embracing freedom so your comfort zone expands? Yes, we each need to work on ourselves to embrace our God-given sexuality. True passion, though, is not something you can cultivate in your sex life by yourself. Embracing freedom can only happen when your relationship is emotionally safe. That's why passionate sex starts in the less spicy parts of marriage:

- It's Roger telling Bev for fifteen years, "I find you beautiful, I find you attractive, you are not lacking in anything, and what your body looks like is what I want and need."
- It's Raeleen deciding to stop seeing her husband for who he wasn't and instead to celebrate him for who he was.
- It's Connor, waiting patiently for months on end while Rebecca's body healed from a traumatic delivery.

Sandra and Paul tried spicing things up, and for the first twenty years of marriage, Sandra couldn't look at herself in the mirror after she had sex. All the negative messages she had received made trying new things a burden, not a blessing. Often her morning prayers would start with confessing what they did in the bedroom, just in case they weren't properly sanctioned. It wasn't until Paul built Sandra's trust by freeing her from obligation sex that Sandra's lightbulb moment came. "I still sometimes have to battle those negative messages," Sandra explains, "but sex doesn't feel shameful anymore. My morning devotions aren't apologies to God for what I did last night. And now, after sex, I look in the mirror and remind myself that God loves what we just did, God made what we just did, and God loves that I love it too!"

> CHECK-IN: Have you ever felt guilty because of what you did in bed with your spouse? Was the guilt because of sin or because of unnecessary shame?

This whole book has been leading up to this point. Vulnerability, the key to passion, requires all the things we've talked about. You cannot embrace passionate vulnerability if you cannot trust your spouse. You cannot be vulnerable if you cannot be yourself (and you cannot be yourself if you're motivated by fear of your spouse having an affair or losing their love for you). You cannot be vulnerable if you're full of shame for your past. You cannot be vulnerable if trust has been broken and hasn't been rebuilt.

You cannot force passion. Passion flows from the ability to be vulnerable, which flows from the ability to trust, which flows from a safe relationship. With so much of the Christian advice telling us good marriages are built by having passionate sex, no wonder we've gone adrift—we were doing it backward.

> CHECK-IN: Are there barriers to trust or vulnerability in your marriage? How can your spouse help you?

In writing this book, we have listened to so many gut-wrenching stories. Many couples have been robbed of the joy of an easy sex life. God intended abundant life for us, and too often we have missed it because bad teachings have thrown us off track. We were given the wrong road map.

We're sorry that so many of you have had that abundance stolen. We believe God is mourning with you too. Many of us in the evangelical world have great reason to be hurt. But please know that it was never God who spread those messages. Instead of sitting in the ashes, dust yourself off and throw away these toxic messages. You've been robbed of too much already; don't lose any more time. Step into the passion and joy you were always meant to have.

EXPLORE TOGETHER: Let's Get Busy!

This has been a serious book, but now it's time to have some fun. As you embrace freedom, here are five games you can try in order to laugh, spice things up, and enhance passion.

1. Naked Couple's Yoga (Learn to laugh again!)
   - Google couple's yoga poses and try them in the bedroom—butt naked. The goal of this is to help you laugh again and get comfortable being naked in a low-pressure setting. (Look up "wide-legged boat pose for two." We dare you.)
2. Two Yays and a Nay
   - Remember the game Two Truths and a Lie that we all played at summer camp to figure out who was crushing on whom? We're switching it up a bit. Each spouse lists

225

two things they would like to try in bed and one thing
they would not. Guess which is your spouse's nay. And
then guess which is your spouse's biggest yay!

- This also helps you honor your spouse's no, as we
  talked about in chapters 9 and 10.

3. Roll the Dice

- Grab two different-colored dice. For one of them, assign an action (kiss, rub, trace, etc.) for each number,
  1–6; assign a body part (mouth, feet, chest, etc.) for
  each number of the other die. Take turns rolling the
  dice, with each of you doing the combination you roll
  to the other for one minute. Switch out the actions and
  body parts to fit your comfort levels.

4. Four Senses Sex

- Engage more than just touch and sight when you make
  love. Choose four senses to indulge while having sex—
  burn a scented candle, use feathers or ice cubes to play
  with touch, put on some music, or add in some taste
  with chocolate sauce. Be creative, and enjoy your sensual side.

5. Switch It Up

- Most sex positions really boil down to variations of
  four:
  - face-to-face, man on top
  - face-to-face, woman on top
  - man facing her back, man on top
  - man facing her back, woman on top
- Here are ways to mix up those four positions:
  - Change the angle of one spouse's legs (e.g., from on
    the bed to in the air, wrapped around the other, on
    the other's shoulders, wider or closer together).

- Rotate your hips or lean in different directions to change the angle of penetration.
- Prop yourself up. Put some pillows under your hips, kneel, sit, lean against some furniture, etc.
- Change up the motion. Try grinding or rotating instead of thrusting, or allow her to take the reins and lean backward and forward to find the right angle.
- Whatever you do, remember not to support her weight with his penis. His penis is not a supporting beam, and it can crack. (If you ever do hear a crack or if he feels pain and suddenly loses his erection, go to the emergency room immediately.)

CHAPTER 13

Where Do We Go from Here?

Forgetting what is behind and straining toward what is ahead,
I press on toward the goal to win the prize for which God
has called me heavenward in Christ Jesus.

Philippians 3:13–14

It's the end of the book, but we're not quite done with our survey findings! We have one more nugget to share.

In chapter 5, we told you that the message that "all men struggle with lust; it is every man's battle" lowers orgasm rates and rates of marital satisfaction, and increases sexual pain. But we also told you that women who believe it tend to have more frequent sex.

Well, guess what? That's not the only message that did that. The idea that the only biblical reason for divorce is an affair, the belief that frequent sex will prevent a husband from watching porn, and (as we've previously discussed) the obligation-sex message all followed this trend of hurting women's sexual and marital satisfaction while increasing frequency of sex. These beliefs make sex far worse for women while simultaneously threatening, pressuring, and cajoling them to do it more often.

We're left wondering, Is this a feature, or a bug?

228

We're worried that many pastors, authors, and Christian leaders consider any increase in frequency a success. After all, if sexual frequency is their main measure of sexual satisfaction, then these messages worked! But we hope you will agree that ignoring women's emotional, spiritual, and physical pain as long as men get pleasure is seriously messed up. Our hope is that much of this was being done in ignorance and not intentionally, because the latter is too horrible to contemplate.

In reading all of these bestselling Christian sex and marriage books, we found ourselves dumbfounded by how little is being asked of men. Of the thirteen Christian bestsellers we analyzed on our rubric, only three books asked all the following of husbands:

- stay faithful (without offering caveats)
- make sex pleasurable for her
- do not insist or expect sex of any kind when your wife is physically or emotionally unwell
- seek consent from your wife[1]

Some books asked for one or two, some gave caveats, but only three of the thirteen bestselling Christian marriage and sex books charged men to stay faithful, give their wives good sex, and not rape them. (The average book asked 1.85 of these requirements.)

However, these same books that couldn't ask the bare minimum of men asked, on average, over five of the following of women (and five books asked all of them):

- Have intercourse as frequently as the husband would like.
- Have intercourse even if he is watching porn or has a lust problem.
- Understand that without intercourse, her husband is more likely to have an affair, and if he does, it will be at least partly her fault.

- Help him reach climax in some way even when she is on her period, recovering postpartum and not sleeping, or during any other problem she may face, since her problems are not reasons to refuse sex.
- Prevent weight gain to stay attractive.
- Let her husband feel that he is a good lover (without the necessary caveat that he should actually *be* a good lover).
- Initiate intercourse and be enthusiastic.

We are not saying that all of these requirements are bad (although some clearly are). What is so stark is the contrast between how much is expected of women and how little is expected of men.

I (Sheila) have been writing and speaking about Christian marriage, and specifically sex, for over seventeen years. But until recently, I never read other Christian marriage or sex books because I was afraid I'd inadvertently plagiarize someone. I assumed, though, that because these authors knew Jesus, they must be speaking truth.

So I recommended. I trusted. I endorsed.

Then, after being prompted by a Twitter conversation, I read *Love & Respect* in the winter of 2019. My whole world fell apart.

I was horrified that the sex chapter in *Love & Respect* is aimed only at women (since, in Eggerichs's conception, sex is only a man's need). Here's my summary of what he says to women about sex:

- Men need intercourse, while women don't, and wives must have intercourse or their husbands will feel disrespected and then may cheat.[2]
- Wives must sympathize with men's lust problems.[3]
- A wife must be sympathetic if a husband wants her to lose weight, even if he's been watching porn.[4]
- It is a sin to say no to intercourse, regardless of what she is feeling, or even if he is abusive (since you must give him unconditional respect, which includes sex, even if he is

scaring you with his "withering rage" to the point that you want to "get away and hide").[5]

Yet what are men asked to do in the bedroom? *Absolutely nothing.* There was not even passing reference to making sex good for her too.

As disheartening as reading *Love & Respect* was, it also changed the course of our work and ministry. Until then, we were working with blinders on as we created helpful resources to improve people's marriages and sex lives. Once we read it, we realized that we needed to do far more. People could take our courses, read our blog and books, and listen to our podcast to their heart's content, but if they were still getting this poisonous marriage doctrine, good content alone wouldn't fully fix the problem. We needed to give people explicit permission to reject the aspects of the evangelical zeitgeist that were holding them back.

We started on a small scale. We compiled a report summarizing hundreds of women's comments from our blog, including many who found that *Love & Respect* enabled abuse, and sent it to Focus on the Family, which published the book and still heavily promotes it. I've been featured on the *Focus on the Family* broadcast three times and have been well received. I honestly thought they would listen. But after being presented with hundreds of stories of marriages made worse by this teaching, Jim Daly, the president of Focus on the Family, issued a statement declaring the book helpful: "Focus on the Family maintains that *Love & Respect* has a biblically sound, empowering message for husbands *and wives.*"[6]

We thought that if we presented them with stories of hurt from hundreds of women, there was no way they wouldn't listen. But they didn't.

So we decided to go bigger, and that's where this book got started. We decided to conduct the largest, most scientifically sound research project into Christian women's experience of sex and marriage that

231

has been done to date, and we recruited twenty thousand women to help us. Several hundred women, apparently, can be ignored. We hope the voices of twenty thousand will make people listen.

We also created a rubric to measure marriage and sex books based on twelve teachings about female sexuality. The rubric scored from 0–4 on each item. A score of 4 meant the book conveyed healthy teaching; a score of 0 meant it conveyed harmful teaching; a score of 2 meant it didn't deal with the issue. A perfectly healthy book, then, would score 48; a perfectly harmful book would score 0; and a book that didn't touch on these issues would score 24.

Sadly, most Christian marriage and sex books scored in the harmful category (see the Appendix for complete details). In fact, *Love & Respect*, which Focus on the Family called a "biblically sound, empowering message for husbands *and wives*" in response to our concerns, scored 0/48—by far the worst of any book we measured. In contrast, John Gottman's *Seven Principles for Making Marriages Work* (the bestselling secular marriage book) scored 47/48. So did Clifford and Joyce Penner's *The Gift of Sex. Boundaries in Marriage* and *Sacred Marriage* each scored 42/48. Scoring in the healthy category was certainly not out of reach. But, nevertheless, the majority of the Christian books we measured failed.

How have we gone so wrong that so few of our bestselling Christian books contain healthy teachings, and so many contain the most harmful ones? Why is it that the bestselling secular marriage book scores near perfectly, while the bestselling Christian marriage book that met our criteria fails abysmally?[7] Where is discernment in the evangelical church?

We are not saying authors and teachers can never make mistakes. Doing this survey was a humbling experience for me, as things I wrote many years ago pop up in my mind, causing me chagrin. We are all doing the best we can, and sometimes we will make mistakes. But when we put ourselves in a teaching position, we take on responsibility for those we teach. If we cause harm, we have a responsibility as teachers to amend our message to be more in line with Christ. We do not need perfection; we do need humility, compassion, and growth.

A biblical principle is that God does not hold a sin against you if you do it in ignorance. Once you have been warned, though, you are now responsible for those you could have helped. Consider this book our warning to the evangelical world. If we care about

Stories Like This Should Not Happen Again

The problems we have discussed in this book can be summarized in this woman's comment:

> In our first months of marriage I would *beg* my husband to slow down, and he never would because he was afraid sex would stop and he would be left hanging. Several years ago, in tearful post-sex frustration, I explained to him that he left me feeling that way every time we have sex. I saw a light-bulb go off, but he quickly put it out, saying, "We'll just have to work on catching you up," rolled over, and went to sleep. Nothing ever changed. My husband had multiple partners before marriage and I was a virgin. So he really thinks he's a great lover and I just don't appreciate him. I tried to explain his attitude is killing our sex life, but he thinks my lack of interest is killing it. I love my husband and sometimes I do want sex, but when I think about how he's going to jump straight to intercourse and I'm going to be left disappointed, why put myself through it? How different would my marriage be if the marriage classes we took taught him he's responsible for making sex feel good for me? Instead he has learned that I owe him sex, our sex life is bad because we don't have sex every three days, and if he chooses to have an affair, it's my fault for not giving him enough sex. Oh, and it's my job to make him believe I enjoy sex even if I don't. How can a wife even begin to combat all this bad teaching and be heard?

Our call to the evangelical church is that our resources should lead women like this commenter to feel protected, not dismissed, and should lead men like her husband to feel convicted, not validated.

healthy marriages and if we care about people, then we need to change the way we talk about sex.

This Actually Isn't Rocket Science

The overarching principles in this book are nothing new. You likely learned them when you were four years old in Sunday school. *Don't do things that harm others. Do unto others as you would have them do unto you. Care about people.* But somehow we've forgotten about them. Maybe it's because of that last bit: care about *people.*

When we were sketching out the chapters for this book, Joanna quipped, "You know, we could say it all in just four words: *women are people too.*"

Perhaps that's the fundamental issue. Sex has been taught primarily through a male lens, mostly by male authors and by male speakers at marriage conferences. Women's experiences have been largely overlooked or ignored, while women are seen as tools to help men get what they want. That's not Christian. That's not of Jesus.

Women, though, are people too.

And you know what? Men are people too, *too.* In our focus groups, over and over, we found that most men do not want their wives hearing this stuff. They don't want their wives worried and burdened by threats. They're *good guys!* They want to live like Jesus. And men have feelings. Men need emotional connection. Men are not sex zombies who masturbate in gym parking lots. Men are people too, *too.*

Frankly, we've been discouraged. How can we not be discouraged when we are faced every day with stories of marriages unnecessarily damaged by harmful teachings? How can we not be discouraged when organizations and authors with power to make a change repeatedly ignore research and choose the easier, more profitable route, even when it does great harm?

But nevertheless, there is still hope. Hearing stories through our research of so many women who were harmed by these teachings but have still recovered and thrived was more encouraging than we ever could have predicted. It shows us that even if those in power never decide to do the right thing, Jesus is our great rescuer, and he continues to rescue. The Spirit still has power. Aslan is on the move.

We know that many will write us off as weak, emotional women or maybe call us angry shrews or Jezebels (and trust us, we've heard worse). Quite frankly, we don't care. This has never been about us. This has been about Natalie and Kay and Sandra and Piper and Erika and Charlotte. It's about Bruce and Paul and Greg and all the other wonderful men who are trying to help their wives, but are fighting an uphill battle.

And so, with that, we'd like to sketch out a way forward.

A Word to Women

Your experience matters. God gave you discernment. You're allowed to use it. When you read something or hear something, you don't need to believe it just because it came from a Christian leader. Look for Jesus in what they are saying, and if he is not there, discard it.

In writing this book, we kept in mind three different groups of women. First, and most heavy on our hearts, there are the Abigails of this world who are married to Nabals (1 Sam. 25), and they need help. Some women, like Erika, are married to men who do not care about them except to use them. They are being abused, raped, and mocked. That's not of Jesus. Putting up with this is not godly submission. Abuse is not acceptable. As Leslie Vernick says, "A wife is not a body to use but a person to love."[8] If you recognize yourself in this quote, please seek help or call a domestic abuse hotline.

Then there are the Sandras and the Bevs and the Julies who have husbands who would be appalled to know what their wives have been taught in women's Bible studies and at women's conferences. Their husbands want sex to be mutual and amazing. They would never want their wives to feel used in any way. That would destroy them. If that's you, lean on your guy. Let him show you the love of Christ. Listen to what he says, not to what these books have said.

And then there are the rest of us, the messy middle. We're all a bit broken. We each came into our marriage with baggage. Don't let these toxic messages add to that baggage. Have those difficult conversations, and fight for what Jesus meant for your marriage to be all along. Work together to identify each of your harmful beliefs, and then banish them from your bedroom forever.

A Word to Men

Guys, we know that most of you are trying and truly want the best for your wife. We know that the idea of your wife forcing herself to have sex with you, despite wanting to push you away, is awful. Please, then, speak up when this stuff is being preached to your wife or when you hear other men spread this message in men's groups. Do you believe that men are not capable of remaining sexually faithful during a woman's period or postpartum phase? Do you think guys are so fragile that they can't have sexual integrity without women dressing in baggy turtlenecks or without their wives giving them frequent release? Do you think the Holy Spirit isn't enough for men? We don't think you do. Please don't allow other people to set such a low bar for you. Do you want your daughters to marry men who fit these descriptions? If not, don't put up with this. Call men to more. Call men to kindness, faithfulness, gentleness, and self-control.

And, please, don't think of porn or abuse as "women's issues" either. Think of them as kingdom issues, as justice issues. We need you.

A Word to Ministry Leaders

Our surveys had some good news for pastors and ministry leaders, but also some bad news. The good news is that many, many ministry leaders are doing marriage and sex teaching well. The majority of women who reported hearing the harmful messages about sex we've highlighted in this book did not hear them at church. Thank you, leaders!

But there's still some bad news: they were getting the messages from evangelical resources and books. To those of you in leadership, then: sometimes you can be doing everything right, working hard to build healthy relationships and marriages in your church—but the resources your parishioners are accessing are undermining your work right under your nose.

Take Janet, for instance, who recently told me that she and her husband had been attending recovery groups at church for her husband's porn addiction. She'd been through counseling that the church had recommended. They had celebrated a year porn-free, and they were slowly rebuilding and feeling like they were on an even keel again.

Then one morning Janet was driving around town doing errands when an episode of *Focus on the Family* aired. She heard the host state, "I think one of the reasons men are getting into trouble [with porn] is that that need [for sex] is not being met."[9] She told me she had to pull the minivan over as she burst into uncontrollable tears. She had fought so hard to forgive her husband and to get to a healthy place, and now the blame for his porn use was somehow back on her shoulders?

Unfortunately, too many Christian resources are sharing these negative messages. It's easy to assume that Christian resources, because they're "Christian," all say the same thing and give the same message, just with different nuance. But that's not necessarily true. The books *Love & Respect* and *Boundaries in Marriage*, for instance, are both categorized as Christian but have diametrically opposing messages. *Boundaries in Marriage* was one of the top-scoring resources on our healthy sexuality rubric; *Love & Respect* was the absolute bottom. *Boundaries* was never mentioned as a harmful resource in our open-ended survey questions but instead was overwhelmingly called helpful. *Love & Respect*, in contrast, was identified as the most harmful resource.

Part of being a ministry leader is shepherding the sheep, and that includes protecting the sheep from things that harm. If your church wants to promote healthy marriage and sexuality teachings, then watch what organizations you recommend in your sermons or whose materials you advertise in your foyer and use in your book studies. Make sure the books in your church library promote emotionally healthy marriages. And remember that some teachings—just hearing them, even if the women don't believe them—can cause trust to erode.

Sheila and Joanna once attended a church that believed marriage should be a team enterprise in which the couple follows Jesus together. The church was excellent at dealing with abuse issues. But that same church hosted a *Love & Respect* book study. Given that so many marriage books are highly problematic, please investigate before your church offers a marriage study.[10]

Finally, free people up to say no to harmful resources. Nobody can review every book, blog post, or radio program, but you can empower your congregation to exercise discernment. Say clearly and often from the pulpit, "Not all advice or 'Christian' instruction is actually Christ-centered. We're trying to point you in the right direction, but we can't monitor everything. If you ever read or hear something that doesn't sound right to you, use your discernment. It's okay to reject it. Talk to us if you want to, but know that we do not endorse everything just because it claims to be Christian, and it's okay if you don't either."

Rebecca Looks Ahead as a Mom of a Boy

I (Rebecca) am raising a son in an evangelical culture that thinks he will be incapable of respecting a woman unless she is wearing a turtleneck—and even then it's iffy. What if the turtleneck is too tight?

That is a hard pill to swallow.

When I look at my one-year-old baby boy, I do not see a predator in the making. I see purity, joy, and innocence—he even laughs at his own farts. There's no reason that any girl should ever fear him. He is not going to be the monster that so many evangelical books make men out to be. Connor and I deliberately named him Alexander, which means protector of man, in hope that he will be part of a generation of young Christian men who rise above and reclaim a definition of masculinity that is healing rather than toxic. And so I stand watch every night over his crib and pray, "May he be one who defends and protects others as he walks in the name of Christ."

I do not want my son to ever feel he has to fear or battle his maleness. I want Alex to grow up celebrating the strong women of Christ in his lineage—his great-grandmother, who dedicated her senior years to helping sex-trafficking victims in Kenya; his Mimi, who tirelessly fought to give women a voice and spearheaded this project; and all the other strong women in his family.

My son is also blessed with so many good men in his life—men like his daddy and his grandpa, who are more concerned with acting like Christ than fitting any person's distorted interpretation of "biblical manhood." May he follow in their legacy.

My prayer is that this book will make enough of a dent that by the time my son is attending youth group, it will be expected that he will simply treat women as colaborers in Christ. My prayer is that one day, if he should marry, his wife will feel as safe with him as I do with his father. But my worry is that the church's voice will be louder than mine and my husband's, and that is why I fight.

Joanna Looks Ahead as a Mom of Girls

I (Joanna) have two little girls: Mari, who is three and sports an incredible mop of blonde curls, and baby Talitha. Recently, Mari and I received a copy of Rachael Denhollander's *How Much Is a Little Girl Worth*. Being a pair of bookworms, we immediately snuggled up to read it on the floor of my bedroom. The book was a powerful statement of her value and worthiness, reminding her of who she is in Christ, that she is precious and worth fighting for.

We finished the book, and Mari asked to read it again. I happily obliged. Speaking these words over her felt so powerful. After our second reading, she hurried down the hallway to her bedroom and returned with her favorite lovey, a lion named Lyle. She clearly wanted him to hear this story too. We read it again. Over and over, we read the book and between each reading, Mari returned to her bedroom to gather yet another of her beloved stuffed animals.

We finished our seventh read-through, surrounded by animal friends, and I closed the book. Something in the book's message clearly resonated with her little toddler heart. I think, whether you're two or one hundred and two, being told how worthy and valuable you are is incredibly meaningful.

I want my daughters to grow up knowing, deep in their bones, that they are worthy, precious, and loved beyond measure, just like Rachael's book says. And I want their future spouses and churches to know that, too, and to treat them that way. I want them to be free to be who they are uniquely, and not be boxed in by shame. I hope so badly that if they need help, they can reach out and find it. And I hope they can weather whatever storms come in their lives and emerge—perhaps bedraggled—somehow more authentically themselves.

I hope they grow up seeing their bodies as powerful and precious, not dangerous or threatening. I want them to glory in the majesty of being a "daughter of Eve," to delight in their high calling to rule and reign with Christ, and to revel in their ability to uniquely show the world what God is like as his image bearers. I want them to fight back against anyone who would diminish them.

I want my precious girls to know that they are people too.

Let's Keep This Conversation Going

With this book we want to change the conversation, but we are not trying to finish it. Our book should not be the last word. Our prayer is that our survey opens up the door for more research, because we have so many unanswered questions.

- Does changing belief systems about sex, along with pelvic floor physiotherapy, hasten vaginismus recovery more than pelvic floor physiotherapy alone?
- What is the effect of a woman not being aroused the first time she has intercourse on rates of vaginismus, or on her chances of dealing with anorgasmia?
- What role does growing up in the purity culture have on men's acceptance of the "every man's battle" philosophy?
- How much are erectile dysfunction and delayed ejaculation tied in to harmful beliefs about sex?

And so many, many more. Please, church, keep asking questions. Keep listening. Let's engage. Let's refine. Let's do this well. Let's not accept that the bestselling secular resources get stuff so right, while the bestselling Christian ones get things so wrong.

Our Final Word

For years women have been told from church pulpits, "Men need sex, and you need to give it to them or you're depriving them." And what's happened? A crisis in libido and sexual satisfaction among women.

This approach doesn't work. Authors and pastors can double down on it if they'd like; they can say women need to understand men, and they can talk about how much men need sex and how men struggle with lust and how women need to help them out.

What we're saying in this book is that women *do* understand men. We know men need sex. Yelling louder about that won't help.

What we need now is for men to understand women.

If men understood women's need for intimacy and women's need to experience pleasure, and if churches started talking about mutuality, we would awaken women's libido and sexual response.

We believe that the time is ripe for that new conversation. And we believe that this new conversation is about not only how we see sex and marriage but how we see relationships in general. Let's stop talking about entitlement. Let's stop talking about rights and hierarchy and power. Let's put Jesus, who came not to be served but to serve, back at the center.

Spur one another on to love and good deeds (Heb. 10:24). And take heart, for he has overcome the world (John 16:33).

The Books We Studied for This Project

For this project, we chose the top ten Christian marriage books as rated on Amazon. We excluded three books from our study because they didn't spend significant time specifically discussing sex:

- *The 5 Love Languages* by Gary Chapman
- *How We Love* by Milan and Kay Yerkovich
- *Saving Your Marriage Before It Starts* by Les and Leslie Parrott

We also chose the six most influential books about sex, excluding any of Sheila's books, to review. We used the top-selling secular marriage book to serve as a control group, giving us fourteen books in total.

We then created a rubric of twelve elements of healthy sexuality and rated each of these fourteen books on those elements on a scale of 0–4. We divided the twelve questions into three categories—infidelity, pleasure, and mutuality—of four questions each. To receive a healthy rating, a book must not have more than two 0 scores. To receive a neutral rating, a book must pass each category.

Each of the following questions is framed with the healthy teaching first and the unhealthy teaching last. On our scoring rubric, we also delineated what messages would constitute different scores. You can find our complete scoring rubric at our website.

Infidelity and Lust

1. Does the book acknowledge that the blame for a husband's affair or porn use lies at the feet of the husband, or does it, at least in part, blame the wife?

2. Does the book acknowledge that porn use must be dealt with before a healthy sexual relationship can be built while acknowledging that very few porn habits begun in the internet age are caused by a wife's refusal to have sex, or does it suggest that the remedy to a porn habit is more frequent sexual activity?

3. Does the book acknowledge the effect of pornography on men's self-perception, sex drives, and sexual function, or does it ignore porn's harm to marriages?

4. Does the book frame lust as something both spouses may struggle with, even if men tend to struggle more, or does it state that since all men struggle with lust, it can't be defeated, and the only way to combat lust is for the woman to have sex more and dress modestly?

Pleasure and Libido

5. Does the book acknowledge women's orgasm and women's enjoyment of the physical aspects of sex, or does it imply that most or all women do not enjoy sex?

6. Does the book frame sex as something a woman will anticipate and look forward to, or does it frame sex as something she will tend to dread?

7. Does the book describe men's sexual appetite as healthy but also containable and controllable, or are men's sexual needs portrayed as ravenous, insatiable, and constant?

8. Does the book acknowledge that in a large minority of marriages, the wife has a higher libido than her husband, or does it oversimplify, implying that virtually all husbands have higher libidos than their wives?

Mutuality

9. Does the book explain that sex has many purposes, including intimacy, closeness, fun, and physical pleasure for both, or does it portray sex as being primarily about fulfilling his physical need?

10. Does the book stress personal appearance and hygiene equally for both parties, or is far more expected from wives than from husbands, and is it implied that if she does not maintain a level of attractiveness, he may have an affair?

11. Does the book discuss the importance of foreplay and a husband's role in his wife's pleasure, or does the book ignore a husband's responsibility to help his wife feel pleasure?

12. Does the book include reasons why a woman may legitimately say, "Not tonight, honey," and discuss the concept of marital rape, or does the book say that a woman refusing sex is a sin or fail to recognize rape within its anecdotes?

On each element, harmful books scored 0–1 and helpful books scored 3–4. A score of 2 meant the book didn't address a particular topic. Thus, a completely harmful book would score 0, a completely helpful book would score 48, and a neutral book would score 24. These books, in order of scoring, are as follows:

Helpful Books

1. *The Seven Principles for Making Marriage Work* by John M. Gottman (tie—scored near perfect)
1. *The Gift of Sex* by Clifford and Joyce Penner (tie—scored near perfect)
3. *Boundaries in Marriage* by Henry Cloud and John Townsend (tie)
3. *Sacred Marriage* by Gary Thomas (tie)
5. *Intimate Issues* by Linda Dillow and Lorraine Pintus

Neutral Books (minimum score 24; must pass every section)

6. *The Meaning of Marriage* by Timothy and Kathy Keller
7. *Intended for Pleasure* by Ed and Gaye Wheat

Harmful Books

8. *Sheet Music* by Kevin Leman*
9. *The Act of Marriage* by Tim and Beverly LaHaye
10. *The Power of a Praying Wife* by Stormie Omartian
11. *His Needs, Her Needs* by Willard F. Harley Jr. (tied)
11. *For Women Only* by Shaunti Feldhahn (tied)
13. *Every Man's Battle* by Stephen Arterburn and Fred Stoeker
14. *Love & Respect* by Emerson Eggerichs

Sheet Music scored in the "neutral" category, but because it failed the porn/infidelity section, it received a harmful rating.

We also read and pulled quotes from some books that accompanied others on the list, or were part of a series, including:

- *Every Heart Restored* by Fred and Brenda Stoeker (from the Every Man series)
- *Through a Man's Eyes* by Shaunti Feldhahn and Craig Gross

- *For Young Women Only* by Shaunti Feldhahn and Lisa A. Rice

We did not apply our rubric to these books but instead only used them for information or quotes. For information from our survey takers about what they reported were the most helpful and most harmful resources, visit https://greatsexrescue.com/resources.

Acknowledgments

From Sheila: There are three of us writing this book, and each of us could not have done it without the others. Joanna, thank you for having this idea in the first place. I remember FaceTiming you that March day in 2019, while doing the dishes, and you said that you wished you could go back to school so we could do an actual study of how much the messages about sex in evangelical books had hurt women. And a lightbulb went off, and we said, "We don't need a faculty to do a study! Let's do it ourselves." And we did. Through your horrible miscarriage, your eventual pregnancy, and your giving birth and moving to the Arctic, you hung in there. You even ran the last of the stats days before delivery, with a toddler in tow, during a pandemic. You're a champ.

Rebecca, way to go finishing up writing our survey questions while three days postpartum with a third-degree tear. Writing this book in the first year of Alex's life was quite the accomplishment!

From Rebecca: I found so much strength and encouragement from my church family at Sunnyside Wesleyan in Ottawa. Thank you for valuing women, championing my ministry, and offering humble corrections when necessary (thanks—and sorry—to Ken and Jill specifically on that one). But most of all, thank you to Rev. Kerry Kronberg for sitting with me in my despair at the harm being done by so many in the name of Christ. Thank you for being willing to grieve with me. It was such a gift.

From Joanna: Rebecca and Sheila, my dear friends, this project could only have been done in community. Thank you for putting words to the numbers. Sheila, you've rescued me at the hospital twice now, which means you're stuck with me for good. Thank you for everything. Rebecca, I'm so glad to have a best friend. I don't think I would have made it through the last few years without you. (Rebecca says, "Right back at you, Joanna!")

I want to say, as we each say every year at the Thanksgiving table, "I am thankful for my family." I'd write to each of you, but I'd double the manuscript length. So know that I love you.

To my mother: You're remarkable. Thank you for processing with me and for having the same conversations over and over. I need the reminders. I am grateful you are blazing the trail for women in ministry. You're my hero.

To my mother-in-law, Lynette: You have embraced into your family this weirdo American girl who often forgets to brush her hair and who writes sex books. Thank you for believing in me and in this project and for loving me so much and so well.

To Auntie Sherilyn: I am so grateful you've shared your story with me. Your courage has been a major inspiration for this book. Thank you.

To my grandmothers: Thank you for your prayers.

To Cornerstone Church in Saskatoon: You all are my hope. Thank you for being our church home. Pastor Rick and Sylvia, you're who we want to be when we grow up. Pastor Dawn, I miss coffee dates with you something fierce and can't wait to chat.

Sheila and Rebecca also want to thank Katie (Sheila's other daughter), who frequently received phone calls simultaneously from both of us when we needed to decompress, and who spent the last year and a half merging calls and calming both of us down when we read something especially horrendous. We know the emotional and spiritual toll all of this has taken on you too. You are a strong woman. Thank you for being our strength.

To Sheila's mom, who is also Rebecca's Nana, thank you for your constant prayers. To be able to translate "the look" you have into words is something we are very proud of.

Joanna and Rebecca extend a special word of thanks to our statistics and psychometrics professors who gave us our unironic love for statistics and research methodology—specifically Dr. Elizabeth Kristjansson at the University of Ottawa and Dr. Lalita Bharadwaj and Dr. Cheryl Waldner of the University of Saskatchewan.

And now a word from all of us: We all want to thank our families. To Josiah and Connor, two of the most amazing dads we know, who bounced babies and made sure their lactating wives actually ate and who kept everything together while their wives were writing and editing and running chi square tests, you guys are a credit to your generation, and your gender.

To Tammy, Emily, and Connor, who kept the blog going when we were working, thank you. Sheila has the best team in the world.

To our agent, Chip, thank you for championing this book and communicating our vision so well within hours of its conception. Thank you for always being in our corner, even when we are being difficult.

We are also indebted to Brian Thomasson from Baker, who jumped on the chance to publish this book within twenty-four hours of hearing the pitch. He believed in our vision and knew this book mattered. We are grateful for the support from you and the whole Baker team, including Kristin Adkinson, who pushed back (gently) at us many times and made this book better.

We also want to thank the over twenty thousand women who filled out our survey. We know how long it took you, and we are humbled that you sacrificed that for us. We appreciate your time, your honesty, and your stories. For those especially who partici-pated in our focus groups, we hope we captured your stories well. Thank you for trusting us with them.

To the readers of *To Love, Honor and Vacuum*, and especially to our frequent commenters who feel like friends, thank you so much for tuning in and for showing the evangelical world that women's perspectives matter. And specifically to those hundreds of readers who spoke up during our initial series on *Love & Respect*, encouraging us to keep going and stay strong in our mission, you have impacted us more than you can ever know.

Without two big groups of people, this survey, and this book, would not have been possible. First, thank you to the 156 women who shared their unique survey codes with their friends, especially to our top ten referrers—Catie L., Lindsey M., Linda M., Sandra, Sarah, Amy M., Jennifer H., Rory V., Tiffany B., and Paulette—our gratitude. Second, thank you to the forty-nine influencers who also shared our link, especially our top ten—Brittany Ann from Equipping Godly Women; Gary Thomas; Natalie Hoffman from Flying Free Now; Sarah McDugal; Lucy Rycroft from Desert-Mum; Gretchen Baskerville from The Life-Saving Divorce; Heidi St. John from The Busy Mom; Ashley Easter; Julie Anne Smith from Spiritual Sounding Board; and Erin Odom from The Hum-bled Homemaker—we are very humbled for your help. Because of these two groups, more than half of our survey respondents came from outside of my list, and our survey was representative of a wide range of theological views, church experiences, ages, marital histories, and more. We couldn't have done it without your help.

Finally, all three of us have amazing husbands. Thank you for being the picture of Christ's love, selflessness, and generosity that is too often missing from evangelical advice for husbands. We love you.

Notes

Chapter 1 What Happened to Sex?

1. Jeffrey P. Dew, Jeremy E. Uecker, and Brian J. Willoughby, "Joint Religiosity and Married Couples' Sexual Satisfaction," *Psychology of Religion and Spirituality* 12, no. 2 (2020): 201–12, https://doi.org/10.1037/rel0000243.

2. 20,738 women participated in the Bare Marriage Survey. The total number of people who started the survey was 22,009. Of those 22,009, 746 indicated that they were not female, and a further 525 left the survey without answering any of the screening questions. (Note: percentages used hereafter represent only cases for which data is complete for the questions being discussed.) Inclusion criteria for statistics regarding marital and sexual satisfaction in this book, except where noted, include being a woman, being currently married, and self-identifying as a Christian. For more information on our demographic data and our methodology, visit https://www.greatsexrescue.com/research.

3. We will be sharing confidence intervals and significance cut-offs in footnotes and endnotes when applicable for anyone who has a statistics background and wants to further understand our findings. If you want more information, go to https://greatsexrescue.com/research.

4. D. A. Frederick et al., "Differences in Orgasm Frequency among Gay, Lesbian, Bisexual, and Heterosexual Men and Women in a U.S. National Sample," *Archives of Sexual Behavior* 47 (2018): 273–88, https://doi.org/10.1007/s10508-017-0939-z.

5. See Appendix.

Chapter 2 Don't Sleep with Someone You Don't Know

1. 4.13. (95% confidence interval 3.69–4.62; 95% confidence intervals are listed after the estimate for the remainder of the book unless otherwise noted. Confidence intervals give a sense of the uncertainty around an estimate—since we can't actually measure everyone, we have to estimate the "true value" of any statistic we're looking at. Confidence intervals help us estimate the range where

that true value falls for the population of interest. The 95% confidence interval means that there is only a 5% chance that the true value lies outside of the interval's range. This 95% cutoff is considered best-practice in statistics across all fields of research.)

2. Marital satisfaction was measured using a 4 question previously validated survey instrument and categorized into quintiles.

3. 5.4 (4.96–5.88).

4. 12.35 (11.28–13.53); 14.97 (12.74–15.55).

5. Emerson Eggerichs, *Love & Respect* (Nashville: Integrity Publishers, 2004), 250. Though on page 252, Eggerichs says, "Both husband and wife need to meet each other's needs," he also states on the same page that "husbands particularly can come under satanic attack when deprived of sexual release," and only six pages later he says, "If your husband is typical, he has a need you do not have." Furthermore, sex is listed as a man's need but isn't even mentioned as a woman's need. Although Eggerichs may mention a mutual knowing through sex, he consistently teaches that men need sex in a way their wives will never understand—and it's primarily for his benefit. The benefits for her are not mentioned, while the urgency of his sexual desire is emphasized.

6. Willard F. Harley Jr., *His Needs, Her Needs* (Grand Rapids: Revell, 2001), 32.

7. Tim and Beverly LaHaye, *The Act of Marriage*, Revised Edition (Grand Rapids: Zondervan, 1998), 27. We realize that Tim and Beverly LaHaye co-authored the book, but in the book, they make it clear that Tim wrote most of it, and Beverly wrote specific parts. Tim LaHaye also uses "my" and "I" repeatedly, without clarifying, and so we are attributing these quotes to Tim LaHaye in the text of this book, rather than to both Tim and Beverly.

8. LaHaye, *The Act of Marriage*, 136.

9. Odds ratios were used to determine statistically whether there were increased odds of various marital and sexual satisfaction outcomes throughout this book at a statistical significance level of $\alpha=0.05$, meaning that the probability that our findings are due to chance is less than 5%. Christian stay-at-home moms were 1.23 (1.08–1.40) times more likely to report that their opinions matter in their marriages as much as their husbands' if they also agree that a stay-at-home mom is as good as a stay-at-home dad.

10. Eph. 5:21 shows us how we should interpret the verb *submit*. "Submit to one another out of reverence for Christ." All believers are told to submit to one another. If submission is about decision-making, this makes no sense. Here, submission is shown to be about humbling oneself and serving the other, as Jesus talks about repeatedly (see Matt. 20:25–28) and as Paul reminds us in Phil. 2:5–8. The original Greek of Eph. 5:22, "Wives, submit to your husbands as to the Lord," does not contain the word for "submit." It's inferred from v. 21, which means that it has the same meaning in v. 22 when referring to wives as in v. 21 when referring to all believers. Because Jesus said that the Christian life is not to be about power but about service, we believe that this interpretation is in line with both the immediate context and the broader context of Jesus's teaching. And, as we have found, it is in line with what our study shows and what other studies show (like studies conducted by the John Gottman Institute) about what creates

strong and enduring marriages. For further reading, see Marg Mowczko, "Mutual Submission in Ephesians 5:21 and in 1 Peter 5:5," *Marg Mowczko*, https://margmowczko.com/mutual-submission-ephesians-5_21-1-peter-5_5/. Sheila's book *9 Thoughts That Can Change Your Marriage* also shows what a "serving" interpretation of submission looks like on both sides.

11. Ed and Gaye Wheat, *Intended for Pleasure*, fourth edition (Grand Rapids: Revell, 2010), 30–31.

12. Kevin Leman, *Sheet Music* (Carol Stream, IL: Tyndale, 2003), 54.

13. LaHaye, *The Act of Marriage*, 28.

14. Eggerichs, *Love & Respect*, 221. He made this claim without reference to any studies or any external validation.

15. We compared marital decision-making behaviors between couples who are currently married and divorced couples. All were Christian and attending church at least weekly. Marriages with unilateral decision-making had much higher rates of divorce, regardless of which gender was making those decisions, showing that hierarchy is a marriage killer no matter which direction it goes.

16. John M. Gottman and Nan Silver, *The Seven Principles for Making Marriage Work* (New York: Harmony Books, 1999), 116. Our study found that many Christian couples believe husbands have decision-making authority. This belief did not cause harm to the couple until it was put into practice. This echoes Gottman's findings, and points to a need to reevaluate this theology. For more study, we recommend juniaproject.com and margmowczko.com.

17. Christian women who make decisions collaboratively are 2.52 (2.32–2.75) times less likely to agree that "when we have conflict, I don't feel my husband really hears me."

18. Christian marriages were 24.06 (20.71–27.94) times more likely to have ended in divorce if the woman indicated that her husband/ex-husband did not consider her needs as much as he did his own. They were 26.35 (23.12–30.03) times more likely to end in divorce if the woman reported that her opinions did not matter as much as her husband's during their marriage.

19. 4.36 (3.83–4.97).

20. 67% (54–82%).

Chapter 3 Bridging the Orgasm Gap

1. LaHaye, *The Act of Marriage*; Clifford and Joyce Penner, *The Gift of Sex*; Wheat, *Intended for Pleasure*; Leman, *Sheet Music*; and more (including, of course, Sheila Wray Gregoire's *The Good Girl's Guide to Great Sex*) go into detail about how a woman can reach orgasm and that a woman should reach orgasm.

2. Wheat, *Intended for Pleasure*, 90.

3. Stormie Omartian, *The Power of a Praying Wife* (Eugene, OR: Harvest House, 1997), 62.

4. Harley, *His Needs, Her Needs*, 49.

5. Eggerichs, *Love & Respect*, 245.

6. LaHaye, *The Act of Marriage*, 139.

7. Lisa D. Wade, Emily C. Kremer, and Jessica Brown, "The Incidental Orgasm: The Presence of Clitoral Knowledge and the Absence of Orgasm for Women," *Women Health* 42, no. 1 (2005): 117–38, https://www.ncbi.nlm.nih.gov/pub med/16418125. A nationally representative survey found an orgasm gap of 27%, https://nationalsexstudy.indiana.edu/. While different studies find larger or smaller gaps based on who they survey (whether they include hookups or only sex within relationships, for example, as it seems the orgasm gap is greater among the former, https://theconversation.com/the-orgasm-gap-picking-up-where-the-sexual-revolution-left-off-96178), the gap in every study we have identified is consistently large.

8. "Women's Orgasm Takes Longer During Partnered Sex," *International Society for Sexual Medicine*, October 23, 2018, https://www.issm.info/news/sex-health-headlines/womens-orgasm-takes-longer-during-partnered-sex/. See also Mary Halton, "We Need to Talk about the Orgasm Gap—and How to Fix It," Ideas.Ted.Com, June 6, 2019, https://ideas.ted.com/we-need-to-talk-about-the-orgasm-gap-and-how-to-fix-it/.

9. Thankfully, more recent books do promote women's preferred routes to orgasm. Kevin Leman in *Sheet Music* espoused oral sex, giving detailed instructions on how to do it. So did the Penners in *The Gift of Sex*.

10. Wheat, *Intended for Pleasure*, 241.

11. LaHaye, *The Act of Marriage*, 85.

12. LaHaye, *The Act of Marriage*, 225.

13. L. Y. N. Charland, I. A. N. Shrier, and E. R. A. N. Shor, "Simultaneous Penile-Vaginal Intercourse Orgasm [letter to the editor]," *The Journal of Sexual Medicine* 9, no. 1 (2012): 334.

14. Sheila Wray Gregoire, *31 Days to Great Sex* (Grand Rapids: Zondervan, 2020), 135–36.

15. (5.94–6.96).

16. Eggerichs, *Love & Respect*, 252.

17. Fred and Brenda Stoeker, *Every Heart Restored* (Colorado Springs: Waterbrook, 2004), 71.

18. Shaunti Feldhahn, *For Women Only* (Atlanta: Multnomah, 2004), 96.

19. Feldhahn, *For Women Only*, 103.

20. Feldhahn, *For Women Only*, 105.

21. This line of thinking was common at the time of publication of Feldhahn's book. I'm sure I (Sheila) said similar things in blog posts, articles, and earlier books of the same time period. Our concern is that despite new research and feedback from readers, many authors have not changed their message.

22. LaHaye, *The Act of Marriage*, 31.

23. LaHaye, *The Act of Marriage*, 39.

24. Debby Herbenick et al., "Women's Sexual Satisfaction, Communication, and Reasons for (No Longer) Faking Orgasm: Findings from a U.S. Probability Sample," *Archives of Sexual Behavior* 48, no. 8 (2019): 2461–72, https://www.ncbi.nlm.nih.gov/pubmed/31502071.

25. Timothy Keller with Kathy Keller, *The Meaning of Marriage* (New York: Penguin Books, 2011), 233.

26. Keller, *The Meaning of Marriage*, 233.

27. Very little research has been published on female sexual pain, but it is estimated that between 10% and 28% of women will experience clinical dyspareunia (painful sex) in their lifetimes: K. R. Mitchell et al., "Painful Sex (Dyspareunia) in Women: Prevalence and Associated Factors in a British Population Probability Survey," *BJOG* 124, no. 11 (2017): 1689–97, https://www.ncbi.nlm.nih.gov/pmc /articles/PMC5638059/. Even more women will experience periods of painful sex, especially after giving birth (up to 55% of women reported painful intercourse in the first three months after delivery, and 21% reported it six months after delivery): Natasha R. Alligood-Percoco, Kristen H. Kjerulff, and John T. Repke, "Risk Factors for Dyspareunia After First Childbirth," *Obstetrics & Gynocology* 128, no. 3 (2016): 512–18, https://www.ncbi.nlm.nih.gov/pmc/articles/PMC4993626/ (see also Geraldine Barrett et al., "Women's Sexual Health after Childbirth," *BJOG* 107, no. 2 (2005): 186–95, https://obgyn.onlinelibrary.wiley.com/doi/full/10.1111 /j.1471-0528.2000.tb11689.x?sid=nlm%3Apubmed).

28. Vaginismus was determined based on self-reported sexual pain that was not due to childbirth that made penetration very difficult or impossible among women who had reported on their experience of any pain during sex.

29. All searches conducted at https://www.ncbi.nlm.nih.gov/pubmed/ on April 21, 2020.

30. Özay Özdemir et al., "The Unconsummated Marriage: Its Frequency and Clinical Characteristics in a Sexual Dysfunction Clinic," *Journal of Sex & Marital Therapy* 34, no. 3 (2009): 268–79, https://www.tandfonline.com/doi/abs 10.1080/00926230701866380; P. M. Michetti et al., "Unconsummated Marriage: Can It Still Be Considered a Consequence of Vaginismus?," *International Journal of Impotence Research* 26 (2014): 28–30, https://www.nature.com/articles/ijir20 1324#Bib1; Charmaine Borg, Peter J. de Jong, and Willibrord Weijmar Schultz, "Vaginismus and Dyspareunia: Relationship with General and Sex-Related Moral Standards," *Journal of Sexual Medicine* 8, no. 1 (2011): 223–31, https://www.jsm .jsexmed.org/article/S1743-6095(15)33223-9/fulltext.

31. We searched The Gospel Coalition's website for "vaginismus," "sexual pain," "dyspareunia," and "postpartum pain" on March 27, 2020. We searched Focus on the Family for "vaginismus," "sexual pain," "vulvodynia," "dyspareunia," and "postpartum sex" on March 27, 2020.

32. Sheila Wray Gregoire, *The Good Girl's Guide to Great Sex* (Grand Rapids: Zondervan, 2012) discusses vaginismus, and we have a course for vaginismus sufferers at ToLoveHonorandVacuum.com, along with more resources. Sheila's marriage book *9 Thoughts That Can Change Your Marriage* also mentions her journey with vaginismus.

33. In the sex categories, *The Gift of Sex* by Clifford and Joyce Penner (Nashville: Thomas Nelson, 2003) did a wonderful job going over all the possible problems women may face with sex. Leman, *Sheet Music*, did mention it briefly, suggesting medical help, but failed to say to these women that sexual pain is an appropriate reason to stop intercourse so you can seek treatment.

34. LaHaye, *The Act of Marriage*, 274.

35. Wheat, *Intended for Pleasure*, 118. This advice flies in the face of peer-reviewed literature, which shows that vaginismus can, at times, be resistant to treatment.

36. So little research has been done to identify effective treatments for vaginismus that in 2012, a meta-analysis by Cochrane reviews concluded that there was insufficient evidence to show if any treatment for vaginismus was more effective than simply doing nothing and avoiding penetration (H. McGuire, K. K. Hawton, "Interventions for Vaginismus," Cochrane Database of Systematic Reviews [2001]: 2).

Chapter 4 Let Me Hear Your Body Talk

1. The Twitter and Facebook polls together had 739 responses.

2. Eric and Leslie Ludy, *When God Writes Your Love Story* (Colorado Springs: Multnomah, 2004), 223.

3. Ludy and Ludy, *When God Writes Your Love Story*, 226.

4. Shaunti Feldhahn and Lisa A. Rice, *For Young Women Only* (Colorado Springs: Multnomah, 2006), 147.

5. Feldhahn and Rice, *For Young Women Only*, 148. A note of concern is that the reported numbers here are not representative of the answers Feldhahn received. First, multiple response options are combined and treated as the most severe option, and second, the question was asked of non-Christian boys in a way that implied consent (or did not mention a lack of consent). When she replicated her survey and found differences between Christian and non-Christian respondents, she admitted that Christian boys do feel more responsibility to stop but didn't amend her 82% number.

6. Women will always have to be more vigilant because they are more vulnerable to sexual assault and bear more of the consequences of sexual activity. But vigilance should not be necessary in healthy romantic relationships characterized by trust. Being told they cannot trust romantic partners, fiancés, or husbands is what likely leads to these negative repercussions.

7. LaHaye, *The Act of Marriage*, 27.

8. The odds ratio for women believing in the gatekeeping message in high school and current ability to communicate about sexual preferences with their husbands was 1.25 (1.10–1.42).

9. LaHaye, *The Act of Marriage*, 79.

10. Leman, *Sheet Music*, 119.

11. LaHaye, *The Act of Marriage*, 139.

12. Leman, *Sheet Music*, 126.

13. Leman, *Sheet Music*, 115.

Chapter 5 Do You Only Have Eyes for Me?

1. More than 4 million copies have been sold in the Every Man series of books.

2. Stephen Arterburn and Fred Stoeker, *Every Man's Battle* (Colorado Springs: Waterbrook, 2000), 125.

3. LaHaye, *The Act of Marriage*, 298.

4. Shaunti Feldhahn and Craig Gross, *Through a Man's Eyes* (Colorado Springs: Multnomah, 2015), 8.

5. Arterburn and Stoeker, *Every Man's Battle*, 61.

6. Feldhahn, *For Women Only*, 112.

7. Paige Patterson, sermon from the January 2014 AWAKEN Conference in Las Vegas, accessed March 31, 2020, YouTube video, 1:55, https://www.youtube.com/watch?v=gDRUVmcaQ3k. See also Yonat Shimron, "Thousands of Southern Baptist women sign petition against Paige Patterson," Religion News Service, May 7, 2018, https://religionnews.com/2018/05/07/a-watershed-moment-southern-baptist-women-sign-petition-against-paige-patterson/.

8. Feldhahn and Gross, *Through a Man's Eyes*, 6–7.

9. Feldhahn and Gross, *Through a Man's Eyes*, 15.

10. When referring to books about men's struggle with lust and sexual sin, we looked at four books: Arterburn and Stoeker, *Every Man's Battle*, and Stoeker, *Every Heart Restored*, both from the Every Man series, Feldhahn, *For Women Only*, and Feldhahn and Gross, *Through a Man's Eyes*.

11. Odds ratios: obligation sex 1.79 (1.65–1.94) and arousal 1.59 (1.47–1.73).

12. Odds ratio 1.43 (1.30–1.56).

13. Along with the three incidents recounted next, *Every Man's Battle* also says this: "And my eyes? They were ravenous heat-seekers searching the horizon, locking on any target with sensual heat. Young mothers leaning over in shorts to pull children out of car seats. Soloists with silky shirts. Summer dresses with decolletage," 13. It's horrifying to normalize men enjoying sexual gratification from leering at women pulling their toddlers out of the car.

14. Arterburn and Stoeker, *Every Man's Battle*, 25.

15. Arterburn and Stoeker, *Every Man's Battle*, 68.

16. Erik Kort (@ErikMKort), Twitter reply to @sheilagregoire, March 3, 2020, 1:23 p.m., https://twitter.com/ErikMKort/status/1234907343432777728. Erik has written extensive threads on *Every Man's Battle* from the perspective of someone who has since deconstructed his faith.

17. See Appendix.

18. Arterburn and Stoeker, *Every Man's Battle*, 184.

19. Feldhahn and Gross, *Through a Man's Eyes*, 14.

20. Eggerichs, *Love & Respect*, 257–58 (emphasis ours).

21. For what it's worth, women in our survey aren't generally worried about their husbands being tempted by other women and aren't made uncomfortable by their husbands leering in public. (70.7% said they slightly to strongly disagreed that they were worried their husbands would look at porn or other women, with 8% strongly agreeing that they were worried, and 87.7% of women disagree or strongly disagree that they are uncomfortable with how their husbands looked at other women in public; 57.9% strongly disagreed, and only 2.5% strongly *agreed* that they are uncomfortable.)

22. Feldhahn and Gross, *Through a Man's Eyes*, 23.

23. Sexual abuse and assault are rampant in Amish communities, as detailed by Sarah McClure, "The Amish Keep to Themselves. And They're Hiding a Horrifying Secret," *Cosmopolitan*, January 14, 2020, https://www.cosmopolitan.com/lifestyle/a30284631/amish-sexual-abuse-incest-me-too/. Additionally, for an interesting perspective from an Iranian woman about how the modesty standards in her country make sexual harassment more common, see "How the hijab has

made sexual harassment worse in Iran," Tehran Bureau, *The Guardian*, September 15, 2015, https://www.theguardian.com/world/iran-blog/2015/sep/15/iran-hijab -backfired-sexual-harassment.

24. Dannah Gresh, "What Advertisers Know about Your Body!," *Brio and Beyond*, November 2002.

25. Shaney Irene, "Why the Rebelution's Modesty Survey Was a Bad Idea," accessed September 9, 2020, https://homeschoolersanonymous.org/2013/04/10/why -the-rebelutions-modesty-survey-was-a-bad-idea-shaney-irenes-story/.

26. Shaunti Feldhahn, "A Letter to Our Teenage Daughters about How They Dress," *Shaunti Feldhahn* blog, April 10, 2019, https://shaunti.com/2019/04/a-letter -to-our-teenage-daughters-about-how-they-dress/.

27. For more on this, see Sheila Wray Gregoire, "My 40% Modesty Rule" at https:// tolovehonorandvacuum.com/2019/03/new-look-at-christian-modesty-guidelines/.

28. S. W. Lee et al., "Sex Differences in Interactions between Nucleus Accumbens and Visual Cortex by Visual Erotic Stimuli: An fMRI Study," *International Journal of Impotence Research* 27 (2015): 161–66, https://www.nature.com /articles/ijir20158.

29. There is also debate about whether or not men actually are more visually stimulated. A recent large meta-analysis of 61 studies that looked at gender differences in brain imagery of sexual stimuli concluded, "Following a thorough statistical review of all significant neuroimaging studies, we offer strong quantitative evidence that the neuronal response to visual sexual stimuli, contrary to the widely accepted view, is independent of biological sex. Both men and women show increased activation in many cortical and subcortical brain regions thought to be involved in the response to visual sexual stimuli, while the limited sex differences that have been found and reported previously refer to subjective rating of the content": Ekaterina Mitricheva et al., "Neural Substrates of Sexual Arousal Are Not Sex Dependent," *Proceedings of the National Academy of Sciences* 116, no. 31, July 2019: 15671–76, DOI: 10.1073/pnas.1904975116.

Chapter 6 Your Spouse Is Not Your Methadone

1. Rick and Sam are composite characters created by taking themes expressed in emails received and aggregated by the To Love, Honor, and Vacuum team. Nothing has been included in the aggregates that has not been repeatedly sent to us.

2. "By The Numbers: Is The Porn Industry Connected To Sex Trafficking?," Fight the New Drug, July 30, 2020, https://fightthenewdrug.org/by-the-numbers -porn-sex-trafficking-connected/.

3. Asa Don Brown, "The Effects of Pornography," *Counselling Connect* (blog), Canadian Counselling and Psychotherapy Association, March 7, 2013, https:// www.ccpa-accp.ca/the-effects-of-pornography/.

4. Samuel L. Perry, *Addicted to Lust* (New York: Oxford University Press, 2019), 29.

5. The Christian books that addressed female porn use did not sell enough copies to be included in the bestseller list we reviewed.

6. Audrey Assad, quoted in Perry, *Addicted to Lust*, 88–89.

7. Perry, *Addicted to Lust*, 100.

8. Jessica Harris, "The False Freedom of Anonymous Confession," Beggar's Daughter, July 26, 2017, https://beggarsdaughter.com/freedom-anonymous-confession/.

9. "Building a Dream Marriage during the Parenting Years," *Focus on the Family Broadcast*, November 5, 2019, recording, 16:21, https://www.focusonthefamily.com/episodes/broadcast/building-a-dream-marriage-during-the-parenting-years/.

10. Juli Slattery, "Sex Is a Spiritual Need," Focus on the Family, January 1, 2009, https://www.focusonthefamily.com/marriage/sex-is-a-spiritual-need/.

11. Slattery, "Sex Is a Spiritual Need."

12. Leman, *Sheet Music*, 49.

13. Not to mention the harsh reality of the porn industry often means that the images and videos in pornography were created in conditions where the women actors were raped or degraded, and 88% of pornographic material depicts violence against women. See Michael Castleman, "How Much of Porn Depicts Violence against Women?," *Psychology Today*, June 15, 2016, https://www.psychologytoday.com/ca/blog/all-about-sex/201606/how-much-porn-depicts-violence-against-women.

14. Odds ratios: obligation sex 1.37 (1.26–1.49) and closeness during sex 1.38 (1.26–1.51).

15. Eggerichs, *Love & Respect*, 253.

16. Eggerichs, *Love & Respect*, 255. *Love & Respect* also includes an anecdote in which a husband is upset that his wife has gained some weight. Eggerichs then criticizes the wife for bringing up his porn use in reply, despite the fact that porn use is heavily implicated in a husband's criticism of his wife's weight. The wife's weight gain is seen as more of a problem than a husband using porn.

17. Leman, *Sheet Music*, 7.

18. Leman, *Sheet Music*, 7.

19. Arterburn and Stoeker, *Every Man's Battle*, 148 (emphasis ours).

20. Arterburn and Stoeker, *Every Man's Battle*, 118.

21. Arterburn and Stoeker, *Every Man's Battle*, 120.

22. Arterburn and Stoeker, *Every Man's Battle*, 61; Stoeker, *Every Heart Restored*, 87.

23. Brian Y. Park et al., "Is Internet Pornography Causing Sexual Dysfunctions? A Review with Clinical Reports," *Behavioral Sciences* 6, no. 3 (2016): article no. 17, https://www.ncbi.nlm.nih.gov/pmc/articles/PMC5039517/pdf/behavsci-06-00017.pdf.

24. Park et al., "Is Internet Pornography Causing Sexual Dysfunctions?"

25. Jim Sliwa, "Age of First Exposure to Pornography Shapes Men's Attitudes Toward Women," American Psychological Association, August 3, 2017, https://www.apa.org/news/press/releases/2017/08/pornography-exposure.

26. This is exactly what Kevin Leman advises in *Sheet Music*, which we further discuss in chapter 11.

27. Stoeker, *Every Heart Restored*, 84.

28. Odds ratio 1.19 (1.10–1.28).
29. Odds ratios: ability to communicate about sex 1.17 (1.08–1.28), being disinterested in sex 1.18 (1.08–1.29), having sex only out of a sense of obligation 1.37 (1.27–1.49), confidence about arousal 1.24 (1.13–1.36), and reliably orgasming 1.24 (1.13–1.36), and very frequent sex 1.42 (1.30–1.55).
30. Odds ratio 1.42 (1.30–1.55).
31. 88% (74–103%).
32. 37% (27–48%).
33. Arterburn and Stoeker, *Every Man's Battle*, 134.
34. Arterburn and Stoeker, *Every Man's Battle*, 135.
35. Stoeker, *Every Heart Restored*, 9.
36. Gabe Deem, "An Ex–Porn Addict's Message to Jennifer Lawrence," *Cosmopolitan*, October 9, 2014, https://www.cosmopolitan.com/uk/reports/news/a30287/an-ex-porn-addicts-message-to-jennifer-lawrence/.
37. Gabe Deem, "An Ex–Porn Addict's Message to Jennifer Lawrence."
38. Gary Thomas, *Sacred Marriage* (Grand Rapids: Zondervan, 2015), 193.
39. Stoeker, *Every Heart Restored*, 211 (emphasis ours).
40. Eggerichs, *Love & Respect*, 253.

Chapter 7 I Want You to Want Me

1. Karen Le Billon, *French Kids Eat Everything* (New York: William Morrow, 2012).
2. Eggerichs, *Love & Respect*, 50.
3. Stoeker, *Every Heart Restored*, 64.
4. 22.3% of women in our study report that they have approximately equal libido with their husbands and another 19.2% report that they have a higher libido than their husbands. We would, therefore, like to call into question the many Christian marriage and sex books which entirely ignore over 40% of women and instead treat libido as something that is always or almost always significantly higher in men.
5. For a great explanation of spontaneous vs. responsive desire, see Emily Nagoski's book *Come As You Are* (New York: Simon & Schuster, 2015). This was mentioned as one of the most helpful books in our survey, and many of our focus group respondents also reported this helped them discover their sexuality.
6. The differences in women's post-sex emotions based on pre-intercourse arousal levels were determined using the one sample test for proportions. Reported results are all statistically significant at $\alpha=0.05$ for comparisons between different arousal categories. Between women who are aroused pre-intercourse and women who are not aroused pre-intercourse but have confidence they will become aroused, only three of the emotions listed in fig. 7.1 showed statistically significant differences: *blissful* ($z=-10.10$), *used* ($z=9.75$), and *emotionally connected with husband* ($z=-2.48$).
7. Libido was also very dependent upon beliefs. In particular, the belief that boys will want to push girls' sexual boundaries and the belief that all men lust changed the proportion of women who indicated that their husband has a higher libido. See figs. 7.3 and 7.4 for more details.

8. When low-libido men are mentioned in evangelical resources, it is often in conjunction with conversations surrounding pornography. Certainly, porn use has been found to lower male libido, as we've discussed in previous chapters, but women can also simply have a higher libido in a healthy marriage. Sin is not required to make her libido higher than his.

9. Eggerichs, *Love & Respect*, 251.

10. LaHaye, *The Act of Marriage*, 43.

11. Harley, "The First Thing She Can't Do Without: Affection," chap. 3, and "The First Thing He Can't Do Without: Sexual Fulfillment," chap. 4 in *His Needs, Her Needs*.

12. Tony Reinke, "My Spouse Doesn't Enjoy Sex," Desiring God, February 7, 2015, https://www.desiringgod.org/articles/my-spouse-doesnt-enjoy-sex.

13. Another explanation for this couple's frustration may be that she is not experiencing sexual satisfaction during their sexual encounters and so her libido is higher due to always being "left hanging." We discussed this possible scenario in the To Love, Honor and Vacuum podcast, episode 72.

14. LaHaye, *The Act of Marriage*, 28.

15. Arterburn and Stoeker, *Every Man's Battle*, 79.

16. Arterburn and Stoeker, *Every Man's Battle*, 64. They quote from James Dobson, *What Wives Wish Their Husbands Knew About Women* (Carol Stream, IL: Tyndale, 1977).

17. Men can, and frequently do, experience testicular pain from not ejaculating after being aroused (this is called *blue-balling*) or not ejaculating for a long period of time, but there does not seem to be any evidence that simply going seventy-two hours without sex leads to pain for most men.

18. Frequency of masturbation also appears to be largely influenced in men by social norms and is dependent throughout the lifespan on the attitudes that were prevalent when they were teenagers about the frequency with which men "ought" to masturbate (O. Kontula and E. Haavio-Mannila, "Masturbation in a Generational Perspective," *Journal of Psychology & Human Sexuality* 14, no. 2–3 [2002]: 49–83). Men need to release their semen, which is why men who have passed puberty will experience a phenomenon similar to wet dreams if they go a long time without ejaculating; the time span for that need appears to be weeks and not days, based on the literature. The importance of social constructs in determining the frequency with which men masturbate indicates that Dobson's seventy-two-hour rule may in fact have the opposite of his intended effect: an increase in male masturbation in teenagers and an increase in the felt need for sexual release in married men.

19. Elizabeth A. Schoenfeld et al., "Does Sex Really Matter? Examining the Connections Between Spouses' Nonsexual Behaviors, Sexual Frequency, Sexual Satisfaction, and Marital Satisfaction," *Archives of Sexual Behavior* 46, no. 2 (2017): 489–501, https://www.ncbi.nlm.nih.gov/pubmed/26732606.

20. Marital satisfaction was scored using a previously validated four-question instrument: Fetzer Institute, *The Couples Satisfaction Index*. Differences in marital satisfaction among married, sexually active women based on orgasm rate and satisfaction with emotional closeness during sex were evaluated using the independent samples t-test and were found to be statistically significant, p<0.001.

Chapter 8 Becoming More than Roommates

1. Tolstoy's actual quote opens the book: "Happy families are all alike; every unhappy family is unhappy in its own way."

2. Unfortunately, space constraints prevented us from evaluating this question directly. We hope to conduct more research in the future on this important topic. Odds ratio for libido and sexlessness is 1.55 (1.37–1.76).

3. These numbers excluded women over the age of sixty, when health problems and the aging process are more likely to play a part in sexlessness.

4. Rachael Denhollander, *What Is a Girl Worth?* (Carol Stream, IL: Tyndale, 2019), 121.

5. (4.30–5.66).

6. For information on how we classified marital satisfaction, see our methods at greatsexrescue.com/survey-methods.

7. This statistic excludes women over 60 (95% CI: 34.98–110.22). The odds ratio for all women is 35.64 (28.8–53.2).

8. Arterburn and Stoeker, *Every Man's Battle*, 120.

9. In our survey 12.0% of women reported almost never or never orgasming. Of these women, 48.9% are dissatisfied with the amount of sexual closeness they share with their husbands during sex.

10. 10.75 (9.27–12.47).

11. 8.03 (6.94–9.29).

12. 18.5 (15.54–22.0).

13. 20.07 (17.24–23.36).

14. 4.69 (3.99–5.52).

15. 6.3 (5.46–7.21). These women are also 4.69 (3.99–5.52) times more likely to feel that their husbands don't hear them when they are having conflict, 5.39 (4.70–6.18) times less likely to feel that their opinions are as important as their husbands' in their marriages, and 2.34 (1.99–2.74) times more likely to be frequently concerned about their husbands leering at other women.

16. Only erectile dysfunction and premature ejaculation were included.

Chapter 9 "Duty Sex" Isn't Sexy

1. Thomas, *Sacred Marriage*, 179.

2. Orgasm odds ratio 1.29 (1.20–1.39) and vaginismus odds ratio 1.37 (1.26–1.48).

3. LaHaye, *The Act of Marriage*, 25.

4. Arterburn and Stoeker, *Every Man's Battle*, 35 (emphasis ours).

5. Omartian, *The Power of a Praying Wife*, 65.

6. Wheat, *Intended for Pleasure*, 21.

7. Leman, *Sheet Music*, 47.

8. Carolyn Mahaney, "Sex, Romance, and the Glory of God: What Every Christian Wife Needs to Know," Desiring God 2004 National Conference, September 25, 2004, https://www.desiringgod.org/messages/sex-romance-and-the-glory-of-god-what-every-christian-wife-needs-to-know.

9. Jodie is a composite character created by taking themes expressed in emails received and aggregated by the *To Love, Honor, and Vacuum* team. Nothing has been included in the aggregates that has not been repeatedly sent to us.

10. WelkinWings (@WelkinWings), "Here is the 'Sexual Refusal Commitment' we were asked to sign at Shane and Phyllis Womack's 'Solomon, Sex and Marriage' conference a number of years ago," Twitter, photocopy, June 9, 2019, 4:55 p.m., https://twitter.com/WelkinWings/status/1137825687715405825. It's been reposted many times, and many have made thoughtful critiques of it.

11. Women were able to choose all options that applied to them.

12. See Kenneth Bailey, *Paul Through Mediterranean Eyes* (Downers Grove, IL: IVP Academic, 2011), 201–2.

13. Leman, *Sheet Music*, 203.

Chapter 10 When Duty Becomes Coercion

1. Stoeker, *Every Heart Restored*, 15.

2. Stoeker, *Every Heart Restored*, 70.

3. Arterburn and Stoeker, *Every Man's Battle*, 156.

4. Harley, *His Needs, Her Needs*, 49.

5. LaHaye, *The Act of Marriage*, 106–7.

6. We realize that at the time *The Act of Marriage* was first written (1976), marital rape may not have been illegal in many states. However, we read the fourth edition, published in 1998, when marital rape was well known and had been made illegal in most jurisdictions. The LaHayes chose not to update this anecdote despite this.

7. Arterburn and Stoeker, *Every Man's Battle*, 25, 156.

8. Eggerichs, *Love & Respect*, 253: "The cold, hard truth is that men are often lured into affairs because they are sexually deprived at home."

LaHaye, *The Act of Marriage*, 33: "One satisfied husband summed it up rather graphically when asked if he had ever been tempted to try extramarital experiences: 'When you have a Cadillac in the garage, how can you be tempted to steal a Volkswagen off the street?'"

9. Harley, *His Needs, Her Needs*, 34: "Should my spouse fear that I might have an affair if my needs are not met? . . . Answer yes."

Leman, *Sheet Music*, 172: When talking about a couple in which the wife has a Victorian view and fear of sex, Kevin Leman tells the husband to be patient but then warns the wife, "Either you will have a love affair with your husband or somebody else will."

Eggerichs, *Love & Respect*, 253: "A man who strays is usually given total blame for his affair, but in many cases he is the victim of temptation that his wife helped bring upon him."

10. Leman, *Sheet Music*, 59. Leman says this when explaining how a wife should give her husband hand jobs more often so he will stop watching pornography. He does not tell the husband to stop watching pornography even if she doesn't give him more sex.

11. Arterburn and Stoeker, *Every Man's Battle*, 61: "Even apart from our stopping short of God's standards, we find another reason for the prevalence of sexual sin among men. We got there naturally—simply by being male."

12. We propose the obligation-sex message is damaging in a specific way for women whose husbands suffer from premature ejaculation or erectile dysfunction. If women hear that they are obligated to give their husbands sex, but those husbands can also not perform sexually in a way that gives the woman any pleasure, that obligation-sex message rubs salt in a wound, blaming her for a situation that is not in her control. We believe the dynamics for the other findings, including increased likelihood of sexless marriages, abuse, vaginismus, and low marital satisfaction, have different dynamics.

13. Odds ratios: sexless marriage 2.00 (1.70–2.36), abuse 1.91 (1.73–2.10), male factor sexual dysfunction 1.57 (1.39–1.77), and vaginismus 1.54 (1.38–1.71).

14. 2.46 (2.16–2.79).

15. Among those who agree with the idea that a wife is obligated to give her husband sex when he wants it, 13.5% report being taught it by Christian resources; in contrast, only 7.8% of those who disagree report being taught it by Christian resources.

16. Due to the nature of our survey, we could not ethically ask if women were currently experiencing abuse but only if they had ever experienced abuse in their lifetime. Thus, our population of women who have ever experienced abuse includes women currently in abusive marriages.

17. Karl O'Sullivan, "Observations on Vaginismus in Irish Women," *Archives of General Psychiatry* 36, no. 7 (1979): 824–26, https://jamanetwork.com/journals/jama psychiatry/article-abstract/492147. Notably, this paper was published in 1979.

18. Odds ratio for vaginismus 1.36 (1.26–1.48). Believing this teaching before you are married has an effect on vaginismus rates; still believing it today is not as related to sexual pain. This makes sense because the onset of primary vaginismus usually occurs when one is first sexually active. The other major time that sexual pain starts is after childbirth, but that is not primary vaginismus.

19. Odds ratios: abuse 1.60 (1.49–1.72) and obligation sex 1.37 (1.26–1.48). Abuse is one of the most well studied predictors of vaginismus. The confidence intervals for abuse (1.49–1.72) and agreement with the obligation-sex message (1.26–1.48) overlap, meaning that the values are only barely statistically different.

20. 2.02 (1.76–2.33). This increase was significantly higher than the increase in vaginismus rate observed due to abuse in married Christian women at $\alpha=0.05$, as the odds ratio for abuse was 1.60 (1.49–1.72).

21. Feldman gives this commentary: "If it's the best feeling in the world for him, why isn't it for me? Why does it get to be so great for the man and so much work for the woman?" *Unorthodox* (New York: Simon & Schuster, 2012), 186.

22. *The Gift of Sex* outlines reasons that sex may be off the table. The only book we researched that deals with consent in marriage overtly was our secular control book, John Gottman's *The Seven Principles of a Happy Marriage*.

23. Eggerichs, *Love & Respect*, 253.

24. For an excellent secular article on this, see Lili Loofbourow, "The Female Price of Male Pleasure," *The Week*, January 25, 2018, https://theweek.com/articles /749978/female-price-male-pleasure.
25. LaHaye, *The Act of Marriage*, 269–70.
26. Peter T. Pacik and Simon Geletta, "Vaginismus Treatment: Clinical Trials Follow Up 241 Patients," *Sexual Medicine* 5 (2017): 114–23, https://www.ncbi.nlm .nih.gov/pmc/articles/PMC5440634/pdf/main.pdf.
27. Pearson's standardized residuals for the cross tabulation of sexual frequency and teaching agreement are both >2.5 and thus statistically significant for sex daily and a few times a week. The global chi squared test statistic was statistically significant at α=0.05, p<0.001.
28. Odds ratios: frequent orgasm 1.26 (1.16–1.37), vaginismus 1.37 (1.26–1.48).

Chapter 11 Just Be Nice

1. Keller, *The Meaning of Marriage*, 47.
2. Leman, *Sheet Music*, 49.
3. Leman, *Sheet Music*, 206.
4. Blake Bakkila, "This Is How Many Women Actually Have Period Sex," Health.com, April 13, 2018, https://www.health.com/condition/sexual-health/how -many-woman-have-period-sex.
5. Leviticus 15:24.
6. Leman, *Sheet Music*, 49.
7. Harley, *His Needs, Her Needs*, 109.
8. Harley, *His Needs, Her Needs*, 111.
9. Christian Piatt, "Mark Driscoll's Oral Fixation," Patheos, April 30, 2013, https://www.patheos.com/blogs/christianpiatt/2013/04/mark-driscolls-oral-fix ation/.

Chapter 12 From Having Intercourse to Making Love

1. C. S. Lewis, *The Lion, the Witch and the Wardrobe* (New York: Harper-Collins, 1994), 200.

Chapter 13 Where Do We Go from Here?

1. The three books that asked all four of men were *Boundaries in Marriage*, *Sacred Marriage*, and *The Gift of Sex*. None of the three specifically used the word consent or explicitly discussed marital rape, but each gave multiple examples of how and when women can say no to sex. Only our secular control book overtly mentioned consent.
2. Eggerichs, *Love & Respect*, 249–55.
3. Eggerichs, *Love & Respect*, 256–58.
4. Eggerichs, *Love & Respect*, 233.
5. Eggerichs, *Love & Respect*, 283.
6. "Focus on the Family Statement: Sheila Gregoire and Love & Respect," Focus on the Family, January 17, 2020, https://www.focusonthefamily.com/focus

-on-the-family-love-respect/. Please see Sheila's statement replying to this here: Sheila Wray Gregoire, "Statement in Response to Focus on the Family's Statement Regarding Me," *To Love, Honor, and Vacuum*, January 22, 2020, https:// tolovehonorandvacuum.com/statement-in-response-to-focus-on-the-familys -statement-regarding-me/.

7. *The 5 Love Languages* has sold more copies than *Love & Respect*, but it does not cover sex enough to score it, and so we excluded it from our analysis.

8. Leslie Vernick, *The Emotionally Destructive Marriage* (Colorado Springs: Waterbrook, 2013). Helpful books for those in this situation would be Gary Thomas, *When to Walk Away*; Leslie Vernick, *The Emotionally Destructive Marriage*; and Natalie Hoffman, *Is It Me?*

9. "Building a Dream Marriage during the Parenting Years," *Focus on the Family Broadcast.*

10. For more information on how to identify harmful resources, see https:// greatsexrescue.com/sex-and-marriage-resources.

CONNECT WITH THE AUTHORS

Sheila Wray Gregoire

f **▶** @sheilawraygregoire

◎ @sheilagregoire

🐦 @womensspeaker

sheilawraygregoire.com

Rebecca Gregoire Lindenbach

f **🐦** @lifeasadare

lifeasadare.com

Joanna Sawatsky

🐦 @sawatskyjoanna

TAKE YOUR MARRIAGE TO
the Next Level

To Love, Honor and Vacuum

WITH AUTHOR, BLOGGER AND SPEAKER
SHEILA WRAY GREGOIRE

Down-to-earth, practical Christian help for sex
and marriage—when you're scared to Google it.
Stop making marriage a to-do list, and make it
a passionate adventure!

tolovehonorandvacuum.com

 @sheila.gregoire.books

CPSIA information can be obtained
at www.ICGtesting.com
Printed in the USA
LVHW082346100222
710839LV00002B/72

9 781540 901460